LESSONS IN LEADERSHIP
A WEEKLY READING OF THE JEWISH BIBLE

MAGGID OUPRESS

Other works by the author

Rabbi Jonathan Sacks

LESSONS IN LEADERSHIP

A Weekly Reading of the Jewish Bible

The Gluckman Family Edition

Maggid Books & The Orthodox Union

Lessons in Leadership
A Weekly Reading of the Jewish Bible

First Edition, 2015

Maggid Books
An imprint of Koren Publishers Jerusalem Ltd.

POB 8531, New Milford, CT 06776-8531, USA
& POB 4044, Jerusalem 9104001, Israel
www.korenpub.com

The publication of this book was made possible
through the generous support of *Torah Education in Israel*.

ISBN 978-1-59264-432-2, *hardcover*

A CIP catalogue record for this title is
available from the British Library

Printed and bound in the United States

This book is dedicated in honor of the 95th
birthdays of our grandparents

Frances and Robert Rub עמו״ש

who lead by example

in the way they live their life together

*in their seamless integration of
traditional Judaism with the evolving world,
to the enhancement of both*

*in their commitment to building
a vibrant home for Jews in Israel*

*in their passion for learning and educating their children,
grandchildren, and great-grandchildren*

in their engagement with their community

*in the warmth and kindness they share
with everyone they encounter*

in their unwavering devotion to their family

and, most of all, in their love for each other

With love, respect, and gratitude to our
Bubbe Frannie and Zayde Bob

Fred, Judy, JJ, and Leia Gluckman
May 2015/Iyar 5775

Contents

ix

xi

Foreword

Leadership and
Public Learning

Ronald Heifetz*

Rabbi Lord Jonathan Sacks's extraordinary commentary on the Five Books of Moses provides encyclopedic insight and wisdom into the exercise of leadership. As the former chief rabbi of Great Britain and the Commonwealth, he draws upon a unique career combining religious inquiry with leadership practice. Within the inflamed reality that divides Jews, Christians, and Muslims in our world today, his work could not be more relevant.

---

* Ronald Heifetz is the founding director of the Center for Public Leadership and the King Hussein bin Talal Senior Lecturer in Public Leadership at the Harvard Kennedy School. He advises heads of governments, businesses, and nonprofit organisations, and speaks extensively throughout the world. His first book, *Leadership Without Easy Answers* (1994), is a classic in the field and has been reprinted and translated many times. He coauthored the best-selling *Leadership on the Line: Staying Alive through the Dangers of Leading* with Marty Linsky (2002). His third book, *The Practice of Adaptive Leadership: Tools and Tactics for Changing Your Organization and the World* (2009), was coauthored with Linsky and Alexander Grashow.

In an earlier volume, *The Great Partnership*, Sacks distinguishes the domains, and explains the synergy, of scientific and religious exploration.[1] Science explores causal relationships and seeks explanations. Religion explores interpretations and seeks meaning. In the pursuit of meaning, the three Abrahamic faith traditions draw on the stories and laws of the Five Books of Moses for interpretations that orient our lives. Indeed, in our interdependent world, these five books touch religious and philosophical communities everywhere.

It thus becomes particularly important to understand how these books can inform and correct the widespread cultural assumptions about leadership and authority that determine the way our societies tackle our toughest problems and seize opportunities to develop and grow. As I have argued elsewhere, some of these cultural assumptions work against us. Rather than achieve collective success, they too often lead us to corruption of our values, destruction in our lives, and finally, the extinction of our communities. As we see from the Bible, this is true not only in contemporary societies, but in ancient civilisations as well.

The Bible itself is a product of a people who, more than three thousand years ago, struggled to generate better forms of social organisation in the wake of the first agricultural revolution. For several million years up until that time, our ancestors were very well-adapted to nomadic life in communities of less than forty people. But the land available to sustain the low-density needs of a foraging economy in that region became scarce; the population had grown too large for hunting and gathering. With the advent of agriculture, density became feasible and humanity challenged itself to develop new capacities to coordinate village, city, and national life with four hundred, four thousand, 400,000, and more people. We therefore had to develop new forms of governance, authority, and social architecture.

In the Five Books of Moses, we see small communities of herdsmen – Abraham, Isaac, and Jacob – encounter Egypt, already an empire; we then see Moses and his colleagues establish, with God's guidance, the norms and governance of a society that would learn the

---

1. Jonathan Sacks, *The Great Partnership: Science, Religion, and the Search for Meaning* (New York: Schocken, 2012).

lessons of Pharaoh's Egypt – and depart from its vices – to build something new and adaptive for all time.

We continue to face this struggle of governance and organisation today. There is a compelling logic to imperial thinking, to a social contract of habitual deference and authoritative command as a means of governing large organisational systems or populations of people. At the same time, this kind of thinking often gets it wrong. Empires usually go extinct. When does this approach fail?

My colleagues and I have found that the most common source of failure in leadership is diagnostic. People treat adaptive challenges as if they were technical problems. Technical problems are those that are largely known, and therefore the systems, processes, and cultural norms of a community are already in place to solve them. They are much more readily amenable to authoritative expertise and command. To use a medical analogy, these are the problems that doctors and nurses can fix by performing surgery or prescribing medication. In contrast, adaptive challenges demand a change of people's attitudes, values, and behaviour. One has to sift through what to keep, what to discard, and which innovations will enable one to survive and, hopefully, thrive. In medicine, these challenges might be compared to the fundamental changes in lifestyle often required of patients and their families.

Thus, the authoritative problem-solving response that would be appropriate in the case of a technical matter becomes inadequate when the challenge is adaptive and demands the more complex response of social learning, innovation, and change. These are the times that call for leadership and not just authoritative decision, coordination, and command – when our organisations and communities must develop new capacities. Yet it seems nearly universal that in these times of distress, people yearn for technical solutions that require a minimum of personal or collective responsibility and disruption. Too often,

> we look for the wrong kind of leadership. We call for someone with answers, decision, strength, and a map of the future, someone who knows where we ought to be going – in short, someone who can make hard problems simple.... Instead of looking for saviours, we should be calling for leadership that will challenge

us to face the problems for which there are no simple, painless solutions – the problems that require us to learn new ways.

Making progress on these problems demands not just someone who provides answers from on high, but changes in our attitudes, behaviour, and values. To meet challenges such as these, we need a different idea of leadership and a new social contract that promote our adaptive capacities rather than inappropriate expectations of authority. We need to reconceive and revitalise our civic life and the meaning of citizenship.[2]

This is the challenge that Rabbi Sacks explores between these pages. By analysing the practices of leadership and structures of authority in the Bible, Sacks shows us how the struggle we face today, every day, can be guided by the stories of our ancestors. Our struggle is neither entirely new, nor are we alone in having to discover solutions.

Every generation faces a variation of this challenge, because every generation faces the natural inclination to invest its authorities with more answers than they have. We are born into the world looking to authority (our parents, originally) to know the way to go. We have a strong natural tendency to retreat back to dependency on authority when times get tough and problems seem to be beyond our capacity to resolve. We create a market for charlatans and demagogues, and many are only too happy to volunteer. As I've advised several CEOs, directors, and presidents and prime ministers of countries, *leadership should generate capacity, not dependency*.

Sacks provides us with profound insight into this fundamental question of leadership: how can an individual with a grant of authority, human or divine, maintain the self-discipline to focus on the very hard work of developing collective capacity, rather than succumb to the temptation of generating perpetual dependency?

In biblical terms, we might ask how a culture of dependency can transform into a culture of widely distributed leadership, how a people enslaved for generations can become a society in which all members are called upon to take responsibility whenever they see fit, whoever they

---

2. Ronald Heifetz, *Leadership Without Easy Answers* (Cambridge, Mass.: Belknap/ Harvard University Press, 1994), 2.

are. As Sacks puts it, how do we become God's partners in the ongoing work of creation?

Central to meeting this challenge, both in ancient and modern times, is the need to comprehend the difference between leadership as a practice and a calling for all of us, and the structures of authority and governance that specify which roles we are to play in an organisation or community. Leadership and authority are not the same. Many lead from a position of authority, but many others lead without it, going beyond the call of duty.

We have to create authority structures, as Yitro counsels Moses, in order to organise our large communities. We need chains of command to coordinate complex living. And we need checks and balances of authority to prevent the corruption of power, as Sacks explains: between kings, prophets, and priests in biblical times and between executive, legislative, and judicial branches of government in our day. Indeed, we quite desperately need authorities who are worthy of our trust. At the same time, we cannot rely solely on authorities, even when they are trustworthy. As I've suggested, adaptive challenges – challenges such as climate change, poverty, population growth, gender equality, terrorism – are located within us, are distributed among us, and can only be solved by all of us.

To survive and thrive in a changing world, we need an evolution in our cultures that will allow for the generation of wisdom, critical thinking, and innovation from the bottom up. Leadership cannot be reserved as the province of the few in high positions of authority. Authorities must serve as the backbone of a trusting society, but the leadership of that society cannot come from there only. We need the people to transform from followers to citizens, to see that citizenship is a call for leadership, mobilising others within one's reach to take responsibility for the problems and opportunities we share. As Sacks suggests, we need passion, initiative, and genius to emerge from anywhere it can.

Sacks's commentary shows us how the lessons of our ancestors, because they are embedded in our collective memory, can help us meet the challenges of leadership and authority in our time. They are profoundly useful both for personal guidance and for public engagement. These stories provide practical leadership tools to explain to people the move from dependency to capacity, from responsibility lodged in authority to responsibility shared by a community, from technical problems to adaptive change. They can help us refashion the historic narrative of our peoples so that, rather than live in the past, we can build from it towards a better future.

The Five Books of Moses can begin to answer the central questions of authority and leadership: How can authority figures remain honest and trustworthy? How can we check the corrupting tendencies of centralised governance? How can a people scarred by abusive authorities renew its ability to authorise and trust others? How did Moses, "the nursing father," succeed in transforming a slave-minded people – both deeply dependent on and deeply skeptical of authority – into a self-governing society? What principles of adaptability have enabled the Jewish community to survive and flourish over time?

Finally, this volume hints at a question close to my heart. Does God learn? Sacks suggests that, since the partnership between God and humankind is real, perspectives flow both ways. Deliberation takes place – top down, bottom up. God changes the plan based on dialogue. We must learn to listen; God listens, too. And if God, the ultimate authority, listens and learns, then why shouldn't people in positions of authority be able to publicly learn, too?

This volume contributes profoundly to our understanding of authority, both human and divine, and of leadership as the building of the adaptive capacity of a people. I hope it inspires us to grant our authorities and ourselves as we practise leadership greater permission to learn in public, together. Moses and Aaron fell on their faces before the people. The need of leadership today is less that we know, and more that collectively we have the courage to learn.

Introduction

Daring Greatly

Throughout the twenty-two years that I served as chief rabbi of the United Hebrew Congregations of the Commonwealth, my team and I faced many challenges. Early on, whenever this happened, we developed the habit of sitting down and studying Torah together. We would search for the most appropriate text, and let it speak to us. It was astonishing how often it did so. That was when we discovered that there are three types of Torah. Two we were familiar with: the Torah you learn from books, and the Torah you learn from teachers. The leadership challenges taught us a third kind: the Torah you learn from life. That is how this book was born, as a series of insights we learned from a life in active dialogue with Torah, the central text of our tradition.

It was fascinating to discover how much of the Torah is, in fact, about leadership, not in the narrow sense of holding formal office, but rather as a general approach to life. The heroes and heroines of the Torah, the patriarchs and matriarchs and their children, and the Israelites as they left Egypt and journeyed to the Promised Land, were all faced with the *responsibilities of freedom*. That, it seems to me, is the central drama of Judaism. The ancient Greeks produced a monumental literature about character and fate, with larger-than-life heroes and often tragic outcomes. Ancient Israel produced a quite different literature about will and choice, with figures with whom we can identify, often battling with their own emotions against defeat and despair.

The Torah offers us some dramatic and unexpected scenarios. It was not Noah, the "righteous man, perfect in his generations," who became the role model for the religious life but rather Abraham, who confronted God with some of the most audacious words in the history of faith: "Shall the Judge of all the earth not do justice?" Moses, the hero of four of the Torah's five books, is surely one of the most unexpected leaders of all time, inarticulate and tongue-tied at first, and utterly unconvinced of his capacity to fulfil the task to which God has summoned him.

It is a pattern that continued throughout Jewish history. Saul, Israel's first king, looked every inch the part, "heads and shoulders above" his contemporaries, yet he turned out to lack both courage and confidence, earning the stinging rebuke of the prophet Samuel, "You may be small in your own eyes, yet you are head of the tribes of Israel" (1 Sam. 15:17). David, his successor, was so unlikely a candidate that when Samuel was told to anoint one of Jesse's sons as king, no one even thought of including him among the candidates. The battles the Greek heroes had to fight were against their enemies. The battles their Jewish counterparts had to fight were against themselves: their fears, their hesitations, their sense of unworthiness. In that sense, it seems to me, the Torah speaks to all of us, whether we see ourselves as leaders or not.

During those twenty-two years, I came to know many leaders in many fields: politicians, business people, other faith leaders, and so on. I soon discovered the difference between the public face that leaders must always show, bold, confident and unshakable, and the private face, when a leader is no longer on display and can share his or her feelings with friends. That is when you realise that even the great leaders have their doubts and hesitations. They have their moments of depression and near despair, and they are all the more human for it.

Don't ever think that leaders are different from the rest of us. They aren't. We all need the courage to live with the challenges, the mistakes and mishaps, and to keep going. One of the truest as well as most amusing remarks is the one attributed to Winston Churchill: "Success is going from failure to failure without loss of enthusiasm." It is not their victories that make people leaders; it is the way they cope with their defeats – their ability to learn, to recover, and to grow.

Most of all, I began to understand that we are all called on to be leaders within our sphere of influence, be it the family, the community, at work among colleagues, or in play among teammates. What distinguishes a leader from a non-leader is not position or office or role but rather, a basic attitude to life. Others wait for something to happen; leaders help *make* something happen. While others curse the darkness, a leader lights a light. The sages said that whenever we see the word *vayehi*, "And it came to pass," it is always a prelude to tragedy. Leaders don't wait for things to come to pass. They say not *vayehi* but *yehi*, "Let there be." That was the word with which God created the universe. It is also the word with which we create a meaningful life, one that leaves the world a little better for our presence.

It was during one of the worst crises of my life that I first discovered the work of Ronald Heifetz and Marty Linsky at the John F. Kennedy School of Government at Harvard. One sleepless night, I was surfing the pages of a well-known internet bookshop when I came across a book entitled *Leadership on the Line*.[1] It was the subtitle that caught my eye: "Staying alive through the dangers of leading." This sounded radically unlike any book on the subject I had encountered before. The others seemed to say that leadership means seeing the path ahead and inspiring others to follow. None had used words like "danger." None had hinted that you might need help staying alive.

I ordered the book, read it, and realised immediately that I was reading the insights of people who understood the problems and pressures of leadership better than anyone else I had encountered. Not only did they make sense of what I was feeling at the time, they also helped me understand Torah, and the Hebrew Bible as a whole.

---

1. Ronald Heifetz and Marty Linsky, *Leadership on the Line: Staying Alive through the Dangers of Leading* (Boston: Harvard Business School Press, 2002).

For instance, there is an extraordinary passage in which, after the people complain about the food, Moses says to God, "If this is how You are going to treat me, please kill me now, if I have found favour in Your eyes, and let me not see my own ruin" (Num. 11:15). What puzzled me is that the people had complained to Moses about the food before (Ex. 16), and on that earlier occasion he had not given way to despair.

What I now realised through Ronald and Marty's book was that on the first occasion, Moses was faced with a *technical* challenge: the people needed food. On the second occasion he was faced with an *adaptive* challenge. The problem was no longer the food but the people. They had begun the second half of their journey, from Sinai to the Promised Land. They had escaped from slavery; they now needed to develop the strength and self-confidence necessary to fight battles and create a free society. They were the problem. They had to change. That, I now learned, was what made adaptive leadership so difficult. People resist change, and can become angry and hostile when faced with the need for it. "Receiving anger with grace," I read, can be "a sacred task."[2] This was a breathtaking insight, and it helped me through some difficult moments.

I felt moved to write to Ronald Heifetz and thank him for the truthfulness of his book. He wrote back, said he would be in London in a fortnight's time, and suggested we meet. We did, and became friends. Elaine and I have cherished his wisdom ever since.

I say this because the essays in this book were not intended as a technical study of leadership, but simply as the way we – the members of our team – learned to study the Torah in a way that spoke to us, wrestling as we were with the challenges of a religious community in the twenty-first century. In them I did not strive for terminological exactitude. So it is worth making two distinctions at the outset that I learned from Ronald Heifetz's work.

The first is the distinction between *leadership* and *authority*. Authority is something you have in virtue of office or the position you hold in a family, community, or society. Presidents and prime ministers, chief

2. Ibid., 146.

executives and team captains all have authority. But they do not necessarily lead. They can be unimaginative or defensive; they can resist
change even when it is clear that change is needed. The classic example
is Pharaoh in the book of Exodus. Long after it has become clear that
his refusal to let the Israelites leave is bringing disaster on his people, he
continues obstinately to refuse.

Conversely, one can lead without authority. Here the classic
example is Nahshon son of Aminadav who, according to tradition, was
the first to wade into the Red Sea, after which the waters parted so that
the Israelites could cross over on dry land.[3] The fact that tradition has
preserved this detail despite the fact that it is not mentioned in the Torah
tells us how deeply the sages knew that we cannot leave everything to
divine intervention. God needs us to act so that He can act through us.
Hence the profound wisdom of the Jewish tradition, that faith does not
mean leaving everything to God. It is not what God does for us that
changes the human situation. It is what we do for God.

One of the most moving traditions of the sages concerns Miriam,
the sister of Moses. A midrash says that after Pharaoh issued his decree
that every male Jewish child be thrown into the river, the men resolved
that they would have no more children. It goes on to say that Amram, the
father of Miriam, was head of the Sanhedrin, the court that took this decision, and it was Miriam who persuaded him to rescind it. Only because
of this was Moses born. Implicit in this tradition is the judgement that a
young girl had more faith than the man who was in effect the religious
head of the community. He had authority, but it was Miriam who had
the gift of leadership.

The way I have put the point in these essays has been to contrast
influence and power. Judaism has tended to be critical of power. Kings
had it and often abused it. Prophets had none, but their influence has
lasted to this day. The Talmud tells us that one *nasi* (head of the Jewish
community), Rabban Gamliel, asserted the authority of his office in such
a way as to humiliate his deputy, R. Yehoshua, and was deposed for so
doing (Berakhot 27b). The *gedolei hador*, the great sages of the generation whose interpretation of Jewish law is usually followed, rarely – if

3. Mekhilta, *Beshallaḥ*; Sota 37a.

ever – had formal authority. They simply emerged through common consent as the leading voices of their time. To a remarkable degree, Judaism is about leadership by influence, not about authority in virtue of formal office.

The second distinction worth making is between leadership as a gift – a talent, a set of characteristics – and leadership as a process through which we acquire the skills and experience it takes to influence others, and the qualities of character needed to be able to make space for others. Often in the Torah we see people grow into leadership rather than being singled out for it from birth. Genesis traces this out in different ways in relation to both Joseph and Judah. We see both grow. Only in Egypt, after many shifts of fortune, does Joseph become a leader, and only after several trials do we see Judah do likewise. Moses undergoes a series of personal crises in the book of Numbers before he emerges, in Deuteronomy, as the figure through which he is best known to tradition: *Moshe Rabbenu*, the leader as teacher. Leadership is not a gift with which we are endowed at birth. It is something we acquire in the course of time, often after many setbacks, failures, and disappointments.

There is a story I have told elsewhere, but it is worth retelling in the present context. It happened in the summer of 1968, when I was an undergraduate student at Cambridge. Like most of the Jews of my generation I was deeply affected by the anxious weeks leading up to the Six Day War in June 1967, when it seemed as if Israel was facing a massive onslaught by its neighbours. We, the generation born after the Holocaust, felt as if we were about to witness, God forbid, a second Holocaust.

The little synagogue in Thompsons Lane was thronged with students, many of whom had shown little engagement with Jewish life until then. The sudden, extraordinary victory of Israel released a wave of relief and exhilaration. Unbeknown to us, something similar was happening throughout the Jewish world, and it led to some dramatic consequences: the awakening of Soviet Jewry, the birth of a new type of yeshiva for *baalei teshuva*, people returning to tradition, and a new sense of confidence in Jewish identity. It was, for instance, the first time Jewish students felt able, or moved, to wear a yarmulke in public.

I decided to spend the next summer travelling around the United States and Canada, meeting as many rabbis and Jewish thinkers as possible, to get some sense of where they were spiritually and intellectually. I was studying secular philosophy at the time, and it was almost taken for granted, in Britain at least, that being a philosopher meant that you were an atheist, or at the very least an agnostic. I wanted to know how Jewish thinkers in America were responding to these challenges. In 1966, *Commentary*, an American Jewish magazine, had published an issue titled *The Condition of Jewish Belief*, in which thirty-eight leading rabbis and theologians gave their answers to a series of questions about faith. There was no equivalent in British Jewry. So I booked a flight and a Greyhound bus ticket, and in the spirit of Simon and Garfunkel counting the cars on the New Jersey Turnpike, I came to look for America.

I met many impressive thinkers, but two names kept coming up in conversation: Rabbi Joseph Soloveitchik at Yeshiva University, and the Lubavitcher Rebbe, Rabbi Menachem Mendel Schneersohn. Rabbi Soloveitchik was the outstanding Jewish mind of the age, an intellectual giant who combined, as few have done, Talmudic mastery with philosophical depth, exegetical genius, and poetic insight into the human condition.

The Lubavitcher Rebbe, meanwhile, had emerged as a unique leader in Jewish life. He had done something very unusual: he had turned his hasidic group outwards, sending them to campuses and small communities, places that had never encountered that kind of Orthodoxy before. It is hard now, half a century later, to realise that almost no one had engaged in Jewish "outreach" before. He was a genuine pioneer, the rarest of phenomena in an ultra-traditionalist segment of Jewish life better known for its segregation from the rest of the Jewish world. Wherever I went, people spoke of him with awe.

I was determined to meet them both. The story of my encounter with Rabbi Soloveitchik belongs elsewhere. It was the meeting with the Rebbe that has to do with leadership, in a way that was completely unexpected. Full of chutzpah, I had gone to his headquarters at 770 Eastern Parkway in Brooklyn, asking the first Hasid I met how to arrange a meeting. He collapsed laughing. "Do you realise how many thousands of people want to see the Rebbe?" he said. He told me to forget about it. It was simply not possible. Undaunted, I told him I would be travelling around the United States and Canada for the next few weeks, but that in a few weeks' time I would be staying with my aunt in Los Angeles, and if by any chance there was a possibility of a meeting, I could be contacted there. I gave him my aunt's phone number.

To my surprise, four weeks later, on a Sunday night, the phone rang. The Rebbe, I was told, could see me for a few minutes on Thursday evening. I packed my case, said goodbye to my aunt, and travelled by Greyhound bus from Los Angeles to New York, not a journey I would necessarily recommend to anyone wanting to travel coast to coast. That Thursday night I met the Rebbe. It was a meeting that changed my life.

He was quite unlike what I expected. There was no charisma, no overflowing personality. To the contrary, he was so self-effacing that there seemed to be only one person in the room: the person to whom he was speaking. This in itself was surprising. I later discovered that this was one of the fundamental principles of Jewish mysticism, *bittul hayesh*, the nullification of the self, the better to be open to the Divine, and also the human, Other.

More surprising still was what happened halfway into our conversation. Having patiently answered my questions, he performed a role reversal and started asking questions of his own. How many Jewish students were there at Cambridge University? How many of them were engaged with Jewish life? How many came to the synagogue? And when he heard the answers – at the time, only about ten per cent of the Jewish students were in any way actively engaged with Jewish life – he asked me what I was personally doing about this.

This was not what I was expecting. I had not the slightest intention of taking on any leadership role. I began a tortuous statement explaining why this had nothing to do with me: "In the situation in which I find myself...," I began. The Rebbe let the sentence go no further. "You do not *find* yourself in a situation," he said. "You put yourself in one. And if you put yourself in one situation you can put yourself in another." Quite soon it became clear what he was doing. He was challenging me to act. Something was evidently wrong with Jewish student life in Cambridge, and he was encouraging me to get involved, to do something to change the situation.

What happened over the next few decades is a story for another time and place. Suffice it to say that this encounter was the beginning of a long journey that led, in time, to a young man who had plans of becoming a lawyer, an economist, or an academic, becoming instead a rabbi, a teacher of rabbis, and eventually a chief rabbi. In retrospect I said that people misjudged the Rebbe. They saw him as a man with thousands of followers. It was true, but it was the least interesting thing about him. What I learned from him was that a good leader creates followers. A great leader creates leaders. That is what the Rebbe did.

It is as a way of saying a belated thank you to him that I wrote this book. One of the most important tasks of a leader is to encourage leadership in others. That is what I hope these essays do in some small way for you. We each have a role to play in strengthening Jewish life, and the scale in which we do so does not matter. If we make a positive difference to one other person, that is enough. One life, said the sages, is like a universe. Therefore, if you change a life you begin to change the universe in the only way we can: one person at a time, one day at a time, one act at a time.

To offer help to those in need, hospitality to the lonely, or encouragement to those wrestling with difficulties, is to do a mitzva, a holy deed. It is to do what God does: He "supports the fallen, heals the sick, and releases those who are bound." We can heal some of the wounds of this world. We can do something; and we should never be discouraged that we can't do everything. As R. Tarfon said, "It is not for you to complete the task but neither are you free to stand aside from it."

We are all called on to be leaders. But we are also called on to be followers. In Judaism the two concepts are not opposites as they are in many cultures. They are part of the same process. Leaders and followers sit around the same table, engaged in the same task, asking the same question: how, together, can we lift one another? A leader is one who challenges a follower. A follower is one who challenges a leader. A Talmudic sage once said, "I learned much from my teachers, more from my colleagues, but most of all from my students." That is one of the great insights of Jewish leadership. We are all part of the team and only as a team can we change the world.

Perhaps the most profound and unexpected lesson I learned in the course of those twenty-two years was that leadership is not only about what you achieve by it. It is what you become because of it. Leading forces you to develop muscles you did not know you had. It changes you. It gives you strength and courage and the willingness to take risks. It teaches you emotional intelligence and the ability to see the good – often the great – in other people. Moses began his career as a leader unable to speak in public; he ended it as one of the most eloquent visionaries the world has ever known. Leading makes you grow. It is the most powerful thing that does.

The Jewish people right now needs leaders, people unafraid to face the challenges of today and build for tomorrow instead of, as so often happens, fighting the battles of yesterday. At the dawn of time, said the rabbis, God showed Adam each generation and its searchers, each generation and its leaders – meaning, no two generations are alike. The world changes and leaders help us to adapt to the new without breaking faith with the old. I hope something in these essays moves you to take on one leadership challenge, however small, that you may not have done before.

Happiness is a life lived in the active mode. It comes not to those who complain, but to those who do. The greatest word uttered by the Jewish people at the holiest moment of their history, when they met God at the mountain and became His people, was *Naaseh*, "We will do." Judaism is a religion of doing, and what we do together is greater than any of us could do alone. That is the challenge of leadership. Jews dared believe that together, and with heaven's help, we can change the world. Daring greatly makes us great. There is no other way.

My deepest thanks for the ideas in this book go to the people with whom I worked most closely in the Chief Rabbinate. The first director of my office, Jonathan (now Lord) Kestenbaum, framed the questions that led to the study sessions out of which this book was born. His successor, Syma Weinberg, taught me about the personal dimensions of leadership and the importance of emotional intelligence. Joanna Benarroch and Dan Sacker helped me think through ways of communicating these ideas in new ways to a new generation, and in a new role. Working with each of them has been a privilege.

So too was serving British and Commonwealth Jewry. My colleagues in the London Beth Din and the rabbinate were always good friends, and it was a blessing to see Jewish life in Britain, under their leadership, grow more spiritual over the years.

The presidents and honorary officers of the United Synagogue were the most loyal friends any leader could wish for. The British Jewish community was and is blessed by the time, energy, and commitment its members give to enrich every facet of Jewish life. Ours is a community of leaders, doers, and givers out of all proportion to its numbers, and it was inspiring to be a part of it.

My thanks as always to my publisher, Matthew Miller, my editor, Gila Fine, and the team at Maggid Books for their enthusiasm and professionalism far beyond the line of duty. I am indebted to Professor Ronald Heifetz not only for his lovely preface to this book, but for all he has taught me over the years about leadership, its challenges, and possibilities. It is a privilege to call him and his wife, Kathryn, friends.

I always save my deepest thanks for my wife Elaine, never more so than in the case of this book. Throughout the years she has been my lifeline, and her humour, her groundedness, her deep calm, simplicity, and constancy of faith made every day a blessing. I thank God for the gift of her love, and if I achieved anything as a leader, the credit is hers.

Jonathan Sacks
London
Iyar 5775

Genesis
בראשית

Bereshit

Taking Responsibility

If leadership is the solution, what is the problem? On this, the Torah could not be more specific. It is a failure of responsibility.

The early chapters of Genesis focus on two stories: the first is Adam and Eve; the second, Cain and Abel. Both are about a specific kind of failure.

First, Adam and Eve. As we know, they sin. Embarrassed and ashamed, they hide, only to discover that one cannot hide from God:

> The Lord God called to the man, "Where are you?" He answered, "I heard You in the garden, and I was afraid because I was naked, so I hid." And He said, "Who told you that you were naked? Have you eaten from the tree that I commanded you not to eat from?" The man said, "The woman You put here with me – she gave me some fruit from the tree, and I ate it." Then the Lord God said to the woman, "What is this you have done?" The woman said, "The serpent deceived me, and I ate." (Gen. 3:9–12)

Both insist that it was not their fault. Adam blames the woman. The woman blames the serpent. The result is that they are both punished and exiled from Eden. Adam and Eve deny *personal responsibility*. They say, in effect, "It wasn't me."

The second story is more tragic. The first instance of sibling rivalry in the Torah leads to the first murder:

> Cain said to his brother Abel. And it came to pass while they were in the field, Cain attacked his brother Abel and killed him. Then the Lord said to Cain, "Where is your brother Abel?" "I don't know," he replied. "Am I my brother's keeper?" The Lord said, "What have you done? Listen! Your brother's blood cries out to Me from the ground." (Gen. 4:8–10)

Cain does not deny personal responsibility. He does not say, "It wasn't me" or "It wasn't my fault." He denies *moral responsibility*. In effect, he asks why he should be concerned with the welfare of anyone but himself. Why should we not do what we want if we have the power to do it? In Plato's *Republic*, Glaucon argues that justice is whatever is in the interest of the stronger party. Might makes right. If life is a Darwinian struggle to survive, why should we restrain ourselves for the sake of others if we are more powerful than they are? If there is no morality in nature, then I am responsible only to myself. That is the voice of Cain throughout the ages.

These two stories are not *just* stories. They are an account, at the beginning of the Torah's narrative history of humankind, of a failure, first personal and then moral, to *take responsibility* – and it is this for which leadership is the answer.

There is a fascinating phrase in the story of Moses' early years. He grows up, goes out to his people, the Israelites, and sees them labouring as slaves. He witnesses an Egyptian officer beating one of them. The text then says: "He looked this way and that and saw no one [*vayar ki ein ish*; literally, 'he saw that there was no man']" (Ex. 2:12). It is difficult to read this literally. A building site is not a closed location. There must have been many people present. A mere two verses later we discover that there were Israelites who knew exactly what he had done. Therefore, the phrase almost certainly means, "He looked this way and that and saw that there was no one else willing to intervene."

If this is so, then we have here the first instance of what came to be known as the "Genovese syndrome" or "the bystander effect,"[1] so called after a case in which a woman was attacked in New York in the presence of a large number of people who knew that she was being assaulted but failed to come to her rescue.

Social scientists have undertaken many experiments to try to determine what happens in situations like this. Some argue that the presence of other bystanders affects an individual's interpretation of what is happening. Since no one else is coming to the rescue, they conclude that what is happening is not an emergency. Others, though, argue that the key factor is *diffusion of responsibility*. People assume that since there are many people present someone else will step forwards and act. That seems to be the correct interpretation of what was happening in the case of Moses. No one else was prepared to come to the rescue. Who, in any case, was likely to do so? The Egyptians were slave-masters. Why should they bother to take a risk to save an Israelite? And the Israelites were slaves. Why should they come to the aid of one of their fellows if, by doing so, they would put their own lives at risk?

It took a Moses to act. But that is what makes a leader. A leader is one who takes responsibility. Leadership is born when we become active rather than passive, when we do not wait for someone else to act because perhaps there is no one else – at least not here, not now. When bad things happen, some avert their eyes. Some wait for others to act. Some blame others for failing to act. Some simply complain. But there are people who say, "If something is wrong, let me be among the first to put it right." They are the leaders. They are the ones who make a difference in their lifetimes. They are the ones who make ours a better world.

Many of the great religions and civilisations are based on acceptance. If there is violence, suffering, poverty, and pain in the world, then that is the way the world is. Or that is the will of God. Or that is the nature of nature itself. All will be well in the World to Come.

1. Martin Gansberg, "Thirty-Eight Who Saw Murder Didn't Call the Police," *New York Times*, March 27, 1964.

Judaism was and remains the world's great religion of protest. The heroes of faith did not accept; they protested. They were willing to confront God Himself. Abraham said, "Shall the Judge of all the earth not do justice?" (Gen. 18:25). Moses said, "Why have You done evil to this people?" (Ex. 5:22). Jeremiah said, "Why are the wicked at ease?" (Jer. 12:1). That is how God wants us to respond. *Judaism is God's call to human responsibility.* The highest achievement is to become God's partner in the work of creation.

When Adam and Eve sinned, God called out, "Where are you?" As Rabbi Shneur Zalman of Liadi, the first Lubavitcher Rebbe, pointed out, this call was not directed only to the first humans.[2] It echoes in every generation. God gave us freedom, but with freedom comes responsibility. God teaches us what we ought to do but He does not do it for us. With rare exceptions, God does not intervene in history. He acts *through* us, not *to* us. His is the voice that tells us, as He told Cain before he committed his crime, that we can resist the evil within us as well as the evil that surrounds us.

The responsible life is a life that responds. The Hebrew for responsibility, *aḥrayut*, comes from the word *aḥer*, meaning "other." Our great Other is God Himself, calling us to use the freedom He gave us, to make the world more like the world that ought to be. The great question, the question that the life we lead answers, is: which voice will we listen to? Will we heed the voice of desire, as in the case of Adam and Eve? Will we listen to the voice of anger, as in the case of Cain? Or will we follow the voice of God calling on us to make this a more just and gracious world?

2. Noted in Nissan Mindel, *Rabbi Schneur Zalman of Liadi, A Biography* (New York: Kehot Publication Society, 1969).

Righteousness Is Not Leadership

The praise accorded to Noah is unparallelled anywhere in Tanakh. He was, says the Torah, "a righteous man, perfect in his generations; Noah walked with God" (Gen. 6:9). No such praise is given to Abraham or Moses or any of the prophets. The only person in the Bible who comes close is Job, described as "blameless and upright [*tam veyashar*]; he feared God and shunned evil" (Job 1:1). Noah is in fact the only individual in Tanakh described as righteous (*tzaddik*).

Yet the man we see at the end of his life is not the person we saw at the beginning. After the Flood,

> Noah, a man of the soil, proceeded to plant a vineyard. When he drank some of its wine, he became drunk and lay uncovered inside his tent. Ham, the father of Canaan, saw his father naked and told his two brothers outside. But Shem and Yaphet took a garment and laid it across their shoulders; then they walked in backwards and covered their father's naked body. Their faces

were turned the other way so that they would not see their father naked. (Gen. 9:20–23)

The man of God has become a man of the soil. The upright man has become a drunkard. The man clothed in virtue now lies naked and unashamed. The man who saved his family from the Flood is now so undignified that two of his sons are ashamed to look at him. This is a tale of decline. Why?

Noah is the classic case of someone who is righteous but not a leader. In a disastrous age, when all has been corrupted, when the world is filled with violence, when even God Himself – in the most poignant line in the whole Torah – "regretted that He had made man on earth, and He was pained to His very core" (Gen. 6:6), Noah alone justifies God's faith in humanity, the faith that led Him to create mankind in the first place. That is an immense achievement, and nothing should detract from it. Noah is, after all, the man through whom God makes a covenant with all humanity. Noah is to humanity what Abraham is to the Jewish people.

Noah was a good man in a bad age. But his influence on the life of his contemporaries was, apparently, non-existent. That is implicit in God's statement, *"You alone* have I found righteous in this whole generation" (Gen. 7:1). It is implicit also in the fact that only Noah and his family, together with the animals, were saved. It is reasonable to assume that these two facts – Noah's righteousness and his lack of influence on his contemporaries – are intimately related. Noah preserved his virtue by separating himself from his environment. That is how, in a world gone mad, he stayed sane.

The famous debate among the sages as to whether the phrase "perfect in his generations" (Gen. 6:9) is praise or criticism may well be related to this. Some say that "perfect in his generations" means that he was perfect only relative to the low standard then prevailing. Had he lived in the generation of Abraham, they claim, he would have been insignificant. Others say the opposite: if in a wicked generation Noah was righteous, how much greater he would have been in a generation with role models like Abraham.

The argument, it seems to me, turns on whether Noah's isolation was part of his character – he was a loner – or merely a necessary tactic in that time and place. If he were naturally a loner he would not have gained by the presence of heroes like Abraham. He would have been impervious to influence, whether for good or bad. If he was not a loner by nature but merely by circumstance, then in another age he would have sought out kindred spirits and become greater still.

Yet what exactly was Noah supposed to do? How could he have been an influence for good in a society bent on evil? Was he really meant to speak in an age when no one would listen? Sometimes people do not listen even to the voice of God Himself. We had an example of this just two chapters earlier, when God warned Cain of the danger of his violent feelings towards Abel – "Why are you so furious? Why are you depressed? ... sin is crouching at the door. It lusts after you, but you can dominate it" (Gen. 4:6–7). Yet Cain did not listen, and instead went on to murder his brother. If God speaks and men do not listen, how can we criticise Noah for not speaking when all the evidence suggests that they would not have listened anyway?

The Talmud raises this very question in a different context, in another lawless age: the years leading up to the Babylonian conquest and the destruction of the First Temple.

> R. Aḥa b. R. Ḥanina said: Never did a favourable word go forth from the mouth of the Holy One, Blessed Be He, of which He retracted for evil, except the following, where it is written, "And the Lord said unto him: Go through the midst of the city, through the midst of Jerusalem, and set a mark upon the fore-heads of the men that sigh and that cry for all the abominations that be done in the midst thereof" [Ezek. 9:4]. The Holy One, Blessed Be He, said to Gabriel, "Go and set a mark of ink on the foreheads of the righteous, that the destroying angels may have no power over them; and a mark of blood upon the foreheads of the wicked, that the destroying angels may have power over them." Said the Attribute of Justice before the Holy One, Blessed Be He, "Sovereign of the Universe! How are these

different from those?" "Those are completely righteous men, while these are completely wicked," He replied. "Sovereign of the Universe!" said Justice, "They had the power to protest but did not." Said God, "It was fully known to them that had they protested they would not have heeded them." "Sovereign of the Universe!" said Justice, "If it was revealed to You, was it revealed to them?" Hence it is written, "[Slay] the old man, the young and the maiden, and little children and women, but do not come near any man on whom is the mark, and begin at My Sanctuary [*Mikdashi*]. Then they began at the elders which were before the house" [9:6]. R. Yosef said, "Read not *Mikdashi* but *mekuddashai* [My sanctified ones]: this refers to the people who fulfilled the Torah from *aleph* to *tav*." (Shabbat 55a)

According to this passage, even the righteous in Jerusalem were punished at the time of the destruction of the Temple because they did not protest the actions of their contemporaries. God objects to Justice's claim: why punish them for their failure to protest when it was clear that had they done so, no one would have listened? Justice replies: this may be clear to angels – translate this to mean, this may be clear in hindsight – but at the time, no human could have been sure that his words would have no impact. Justice asks: how can you be sure you will fail if you never try?

According to the Talmud, God reluctantly agreed. Hence the vital principle: when bad things are happening in society, when corruption, violence, and injustice prevail, it is our duty to register a protest, even if it seems likely that it will have no effect. Why? Because that is what moral integrity demands. Silence may be taken as consent. And besides, we can never be sure that no one will listen. Morality demands that we ignore probability and focus on possibility. Perhaps someone will take notice and change his or her ways – and that "perhaps" is enough.

This idea did not suddenly appear for the first time in the Talmud. It is stated explicitly in the book of Ezekiel. This is what God says to the prophet:

Son of man, I am sending you to the Israelites, to a rebellious nation that has rebelled against Me; they and their ancestors have been in revolt against Me to this very day. The people to whom I am sending you are obstinate and stubborn. Say to them, "This is what the Sovereign Lord says." And whether they listen or fail to listen – for they are a rebellious people – they will know that a prophet has been among them. (Ezek. 2:3–5)

God tells the prophet to speak, regardless of whether people will listen.

So, one way of reading the story of Noah is as a failure of leadership. Noah was righteous but not a leader. He was a good man who had no influence on his environment. There are, to be sure, other ways of reading the story, but this seems to me the most straightforward. If so, then Noah was the third case in a series of failures of responsibility. As we saw earlier, Adam and Eve failed to take personal responsibility for their actions ("It wasn't me"). Cain refused to take moral responsibility ("Am I my brother's keeper?"). Noah failed the test of collective responsibility.

This way of interpreting the story, if correct, entails a significant conclusion. We know that Judaism involves collective responsibility (*kol Yisrael arevim ze bazeh*, "All Israelites are responsible for one another," Shevuot 39a). But it may be that being human also involves collective responsibility. Not only are Jews responsible for one another – so are we all, regardless of our faith or lack of it. So, at any rate, the Rambam argued, though Ramban disagreed.[1]

Hasidim had a simple way of making this point. They called Noah a *tzaddik im peltz*, "a righteous man in a fur coat." There are two ways of keeping warm on a cold night. You can wear a fur coat or light a fire. Wear a fur coat and you warm only yourself. Light a fire and you warm others. We are supposed to light a fire.

Noah was a good man who was not a leader. Was he, after the Flood, haunted by guilt? Did he think of the lives he might have saved

---

1. *Mishneh Torah, Hilkhot Melakhim* 9:14; Ramban to Genesis 34:13, s.v. *verabbim*.

if only he had spoken out, whether to his contemporaries or to God? We cannot be sure. The text is suggestive but not conclusive.

It seems, though, that the Torah sets a high standard for the moral life. It is not enough to be righteous if that means turning our backs on a society that is guilty of wrongdoing. We must take a stand. We must protest. We must register dissent even if the probability of changing minds is small. That is because the moral life is a life we share with others. We are, in some sense, responsible for the society of which we are a part. It is not enough to be good. We must encourage others to be good. There are times when each of us must lead.

Lekh Lekha

The Courage Not to Conform

Leaders lead. That does not mean to say that they do not follow. But what they follow is different from what most people follow. They do not conform for the sake of conforming. They do not do what others do merely because others are doing it. They follow an inner voice, a call. They have a vision, not of what is, but of what might be. They think outside the box. They march to a different tune.

Never was this more dramatically signalled than in the first words of God to Abraham, the words that set Jewish history in motion: "Leave your land, your birthplace, and your father's house and go to the land that I will show you" (Gen. 12:1). Why? Because people *do* conform. They adopt the standards and absorb the culture of the time and place in which they live – "your land." At a deeper level, they are influenced by friends and neighbours – "your birthplace." More deeply still, they are shaped by their parents and the family in which they grew up – "your father's house."

I want you, says God to Abraham, to be different. Not for the sake of being different, but for the sake of starting something new: a religion that will not worship power and the symbols of power – for that is what idols really were and are. I want you, says God, to "teach your children and your household afterwards to follow the way of the Lord by doing what is right and just" (Gen. 18:19).

To be a Jew is to be willing to challenge the prevailing consensus when, as so often happens, nations slip into worshipping the old gods. They did so in Europe throughout the nineteenth and early twentieth century. That was the age of nationalism, the pursuit of power in the name of the nation-state that led to two world wars and tens of millions of deaths. It is the age we are living in now as North Korea acquires and Iran pursues nuclear weapons so that they can impose their ambitions by force. It is what is happening today throughout much of the Middle East and Africa as nations descend into violence and what Hobbes called "the war of every man against every man."[1]

We make a mistake when we think of idols in terms of their physical appearance – statues, figurines, icons. In that sense they belong to ancient times we have long outgrown. Instead, the right way to think of idols is in terms of what they represent. They symbolise power. That is what Ra was for the Egyptians, what Baal was for the Canaanites, what Chemosh was for the Moabites, what Zeus was for the Greeks, and what missiles and bombs are for terrorists and rogue states today.

Power allows us to rule over others without their consent. As the Greek historian Thucydides put it: "The strong do what they wish and the weak suffer what they must."[2] Judaism is a sustained critique of power. That is the conclusion I have reached after a lifetime of studying our sacred texts. It is about how a nation can be formed on the basis of shared commitment and collective responsibility. It is about how to construct a society that honours the human person as the image and likeness of God. It is about a vision, never fully realised but never abandoned, of a world based on justice and compassion, in

---

1. Thomas Hobbes, *The Leviathan*, ed. Richard Tuck (Cambridge, England: Cambridge University Press, 1991), part 1, ch. 13.
2. Thucydides, 5.89.

which "They will neither harm nor destroy on all My holy mountain, for the earth will be filled with the knowledge of the Lord as the waters cover the sea" (Is. 11:9).

Abraham is without doubt the most influential person who ever lived. Today he is claimed as the spiritual ancestor of 2.4 billion Christians, 1.6 billion Muslims, and 13 million Jews, more than half the people alive today. Yet he ruled no empire, commanded no great army, performed no miracles, and proclaimed no prophecy. He is the supreme example in all of history of *influence without power* (a concept we will study more closely in our discussion of *Parashat Behaalotekha*).

Why? Because he was prepared to be different. As the sages say, he was called *ha'ivri*, "the Hebrew," because "all the world was on one side [*be'ever eḥad*] and he was on the other."[3] Leadership, as every leader knows, can be lonely. Yet you continue to do what you have to do because you know that the majority is not always right and conventional wisdom is not always wise. Dead fish go with the flow. Live fish swim against the current. So it is with conscience and courage. So it is with the children of Abraham. They are prepared to challenge the idols of the age.

After the Holocaust, some social scientists were haunted by the question of why so many people were prepared, whether by active participation or silent consent, to go along with a regime that they knew was committing one of the great crimes against humanity. One key experiment was conducted by Solomon Asch. He assembled a group of people, asking them to perform a series of simple cognitive tasks. They were shown two cards – one with one line on it, the other with three lines of different lengths – and asked which of the lines on the second card was the same length as the line on the first card. Unbeknown to one participant, all the others had been briefed by Asch to give the right answer for the first few cards, then the wrong one for most of the rest. On a significant number of occasions the subject gave an answer he could see was wrong because everyone else had done so. Such is the power of the pressure to conform: it can lead us to say what we know is untrue.

3. Genesis Rabba, 42:8.

More frightening still was the Stanford experiment carried out in the early 1970s by Philip Zimbardo. The student participants were randomly assigned roles as guards or prisoners in a mock prison. Within days the students cast as guards were behaving abusively, some of them subjecting the "prisoners" to psychological torture. The students cast as prisoners put up with this passively, even siding with the guards against those who resisted. The experiment was called off after six days, during which time even Zimbardo found himself drawn into the artificial reality he had created. The pressure to conform to assigned roles is strong enough to lead people into doing what they know is wrong.

That is why Abraham, at the start of his mission, was told to leave "his land, his birthplace, and his father's house," to free himself from the pressure to conform. Leaders must be prepared not to follow the consensus. One of the great writers on leadership, Warren Bennis, writes: "By the time we reach puberty, the world has shaped us to a greater extent than we realise. Our family, friends, and society in general have told us – by word and example – how to be. But people begin to become leaders at that moment when they decide for themselves how to be."[4]

One reason that Jews have become, out of all proportion to their numbers, leaders in almost every sphere of human endeavour is precisely this willingness to be different. Throughout the centuries Jews have been the most striking example of a group that refused to assimilate to the dominant culture or to convert to the dominant faith.

One other finding of Solomon Asch is worth noting. If just one other person was willing to support the individual who could see that the others were giving the wrong answer, it gave him the strength to stand out against the consensus. That is why, however small their numbers, Jews created communities. It is hard to lead alone, far less hard to lead in the company of others, even if you are a minority.

Judaism is the counter-voice in the conversation of humankind. As Jews, we do not follow the majority merely because it is the majority.

4. Warren Bennis, *On Becoming a Leader* (New York: Basic Books, 1989), 49.

In age after age, century after century, Jews were prepared to do what the poet Robert Frost immortalised:

> Two roads diverged in a wood, and I,
> I took the one less traveled by,
> And that has made all the difference.[5]

It is what makes a nation of leaders.

---

5. Robert Frost, *The Road Not Taken, Birches, and Other Poems* (New York: H. Holt and Co., 1916), 10.

Vayera

Answering the Call

The early history of humanity as told in the Torah is a series of disappointments. God gave human beings freedom, which they then misused. Adam and Eve ate the forbidden fruit. Cain murdered Abel. Within a relatively short time the world before the Flood became dominated by violence. All flesh perverted its way on the earth. God created order; man created chaos. Even after the Flood, humanity, in the form of the builders of Babel, was guilty of hubris, thinking that people could build a tower whose top "reaches heaven" (Gen. 11:4).

Humans failed to respond to God, which is where Abraham enters the picture. We are not quite sure, at the beginning, what it is that Abraham is summoned to do. We know he is commanded to leave his land, birthplace, and father's house and travel "to the land I will show you" (Gen. 12:1), but what he is to do there we do not know. On this the Torah is silent. What is Abraham's mission? What makes him special? What makes him not simply a good man in a bad age, as was Noah, but a leader and the father of a nation of leaders?

To decode the mystery we have to recall what the Torah has been signalling prior to this point. I suggested earlier that a – perhaps *the* – key theme of Genesis is a failure of responsibility. Adam and Eve lack *personal* responsibility. Adam says, "It wasn't me; it was the woman." Eve says, "It wasn't me, it was the serpent." It is as if they deny being the authors of their own acts – as if they do not understand either freedom or the responsibility it entails. Cain does not deny personal responsibility. He does not say, "It wasn't me. It was Abel's fault for provoking me." Instead he denies *moral* responsibility: "Am I my brother's keeper?" Noah fails the test of *collective* responsibility. He is a man of virtue in an age of vice, but he makes no impact on his contemporaries. He saves his family (and the animals) but no one else. According to the plain reading of the text, he does not even try.

If we understand this, we understand Abraham. He exercises *personal* responsibility. A quarrel breaks out between his herdsmen and those of his nephew Lot. Seeing that this was no random occurrence but the result of their having too many cattle to be able to graze together, Abraham immediately proposes a solution:

> Abram said to Lot, "Let there not be a quarrel between you and me, or between your herders and mine, for we are brothers. Is not the whole land before you? Let us part company. If you go to the left, I will go to the right; if you go to the right, I will go to the left." (Gen. 13:8–9)

Note that Abraham passes no judgement. He does not ask whose fault the argument was. He does not ask who will gain from any particular outcome. He gives Lot the choice. He sees the problem and acts.

In the next chapter of Genesis we are told about a local war, as a result of which Lot is among the people taken captive. Immediately Abraham gathers a force, pursues the invaders, and rescues Lot, and with him, all the other captives. He returns these captives safely to their homes, refusing to take any of the spoils of victory that he is offered by the grateful king of Sodom.

This is a strange passage – the image of Abraham it depicts is not the one of the nomadic shepherd we see elsewhere. The passage is best understood in the context of the story of Cain. Abraham shows he *is* his brother's (or brother's son's) keeper. He immediately understands the nature of *moral* responsibility. Despite the fact that Lot chose to live where he did with its attendant risks, Abraham does not say, "His safety is his responsibility, not mine."

Then, in *Parashat Vayera*, comes the great moment: for the first time a human being challenges God Himself. God is about to pass judgement on Sodom. Abraham, fearing that this will mean that the city will be destroyed, says:

> Will You sweep away the righteous with the wicked? What if there are fifty righteous people in the city? Will You really sweep it away and not spare the place for the sake of the fifty righteous people in it? Far be it from You to do such a thing – to kill the righteous with the wicked, treating the righteous and the wicked alike. Far be it from You! Shall the Judge of all the earth not do justice? (Gen. 18:23–25)

This is a remarkable speech. By what right does a mere mortal challenge God Himself?

The short answer is that God Himself signalled that he should. Listen carefully to the text:

> Then the Lord said, "Shall I hide from Abraham what I am about to do? Abraham will surely become a great and powerful nation, and all nations on earth will be blessed through him …." Then the Lord said, "The outcry against Sodom and Gomorrah is so great and their sin so grievous that I will go down and see if what they have done is as bad as the outcry that has reached Me. If not, I will know." (Gen. 18:17–21)

Those words – "Shall I hide from Abraham what I am about to do?" – are a clear hint that God wants Abraham to respond; otherwise, why would He have said them?

The story of Abraham can only be understood against the backdrop of the story of Noah. There too, God told Noah in advance that He was about to bring punishment to the world. "So God said to Noah, 'I am going to put an end to all people, for the earth is filled with violence because of them. I am surely going to destroy both them and the earth'" (Gen. 6:13). Noah did not protest. To the contrary, we are told three times that Noah "did as God commanded him" (Gen. 6:22; 7:5; 7:9). Noah accepted the verdict. Abraham challenges it. Abraham understands the third principle: *collective* responsibility.

The people of Sodom are not his brothers and sisters, so he is going beyond what he did in rescuing Lot. He prays on their behalf because he understands the idea of human solidarity, immortally expressed by John Donne:

> No man is an island,
> Entire of itself...
> Any man's death diminishes me,
> For I am involved in mankind.[1]

But a question remains. *Why* did God call on Abraham to challenge Him? Was there anything Abraham knew that God did not know? The idea is absurd. The answer is surely this: Abraham was to become the role model and initiator of a new faith, one that would not defend the human status quo but challenge it.

Abraham had to have the courage to challenge God if his descendants were to challenge human rulers, as Moses and the prophets did. Jews do not accept the world that is. They challenge it in the name of the world that ought to be. This is a critical turning point in human history: the birth of the world's first religion of protest – a faith that challenges the world instead of accepting it.

Abraham was not a conventional leader. He did not rule a nation. There was as yet no nation for him to lead. But he was the role model of leadership as Judaism understands it. He took responsibility. He acted; he did not wait for others to act. Of Noah, the Torah says, "he walked *with* God" (Gen. 6:9). But to Abraham, God Himself says, "Walk *before* Me" (17:1), meaning: be a leader. Walk ahead. Take personal responsibility. Take moral responsibility. Take collective responsibility.

Judaism is God's call to responsibility.

---

1. John Donne, *Devotions Upon Emergent Occasions*, Meditation XVII.

Ḥayei Sara

Beginning the Journey

Awhile back, a British newspaper, *The Times*, interviewed a prominent member of the Jewish community and a member of the House of Lords – let's call him Lord X – on his ninety-second birthday. The interviewer said, "Most people, when they reach their ninety-second birthday, start thinking about slowing down. You seem to be speeding up. Why is that?" Lord X's reply was this: "When you get to ninety-two, you start seeing the door begin to close, and I have so much to do before the door closes that the older I get, the harder I have to work."

Something like that is the impression we get of Abraham in *Parashat Ḥayei Sara*. Sarah, his constant companion throughout their journeys, has died. He is 137 years old. We see him mourn Sarah's death, and then he moves into action. He engages in an elaborate negotiation to buy a plot of land in which to bury her. As the narrative makes clear, this is not a simple task. He confesses to the local people, the Hittites, that he is "an immigrant and a resident among you" (Gen. 23:4), meaning that he knows he has no right to buy land. It will take a special concession on their part for him to do so. The Hittites politely but firmly try to discourage him. He has no need to buy a burial plot: "No one among us will deny you his burial site to bury your dead" (23:6). He can bury Sarah in someone else's graveyard. Equally politely but no less insistently, Abraham makes it clear that he is determined to buy land. In the end, he pays a highly inflated price (four hundred silver shekels) to do so.

The purchase of the cave of Makhpela is evidently a highly significant event, because it is recorded in great detail and highly legal terminology, not just here, but three times subsequently in Genesis (here in 23:17 and subsequently in 25:9; 49:30; and 50:13), each time with the same formality. Here, for instance, is Jacob on his deathbed, speaking to his sons:

> Bury me with my fathers in the cave in the field of Ephron the Hittite, the cave in the field of Makhpela, near Mamre in Canaan, which Abraham bought along with the field as a burial place from Ephron the Hittite. There Abraham and his wife Sarah were buried, there Isaac and his wife Rebecca were buried, and there I buried Leah. The field and the cave in it were bought from the Hittites. (Gen. 49:29–32)

Something significant is being hinted here; otherwise why mention, each time, exactly where the field is and whom Abraham bought it from?

Immediately after the story of the land purchase, we read, "Abraham was old, well-advanced in years, and God had blessed Abraham with everything" (Gen. 24:1). Again this sounds like the end of a life, not a preface to a new course of action, and again our expectation is confounded. Abraham launches into a new initiative, this time to find a suitable wife for his son Isaac, who by now is at least thirty-seven years old. Abraham leaves nothing to chance. He does not speak to Isaac himself but to his most trusted servant, whom he instructs to go "to my native land, to my birthplace" (24:2), and find the appropriate woman. He wants Isaac to have a wife who will share his faith and way of life. Abraham does not specify that she should come from his own family, but this seems to be an assumption hovering in the background.

As with the purchase of the field, this course of events is described in more detail than almost anything else in the Torah. Every conversational exchange is recorded. The contrast with the story of the Binding of Isaac could not be greater. There, almost everything – Abraham's thoughts, Isaac's feelings – is left unsaid. Here, everything is said. Again, the literary style calls our attention to the significance of what is happening, without telling us precisely what it is.

The explanation is simple and unexpected. Throughout the story of Abraham and Sarah, God promises them two things: children and a land. The promise of the land ("Rise, walk in the land throughout its length and breadth, for I will give it to you," Gen. 13:17) is repeated no less than seven times. The promise of children occurs four times. Abraham's descendants will be "a great nation" (12:2) as many as "the dust of the earth" (13:16) and "the stars in the sky" (15:5); he will be the father not of one nation but of many (17:5).

Despite this, when Sarah dies, Abraham has not a single inch of the land that he can call his own, and has only one child who will continue the covenant – Isaac, currently unmarried. Neither promise has been fulfilled. Hence the extraordinary detail of the two main stories in *Ḥayei Sara*: the purchase of land and the finding of a wife for Isaac. There is a moral here, and the Torah slows down the speed of the narrative so that we will not miss the point.

God promises, but we have to act. God promised Abraham the land, but he had to buy the first field. God promised Abraham many descendants, but Abraham had to ensure that his son was married, and to a woman who would share the life of the covenant, so that Abraham would have, as we say today, "Jewish grandchildren."

Despite all the promises, God does not and will not do it alone. By the very act of self-limitation (*tzimtzum*) through which He creates the space for human freedom, He gives us responsibility, and only by exercising it do we reach our full stature as human beings. God saved Noah from the Flood, but Noah had to make the ark. He gave the land of Israel to the people of Israel, but they had to fight the battles. God gives us the strength to act, but we have to do the deed. What changes the world, what fulfils our destiny, is *not what God does for us but what we do for God.*

That is what leaders understand, and it is what made Abraham the first Jewish leader. Leaders take responsibility for creating the conditions through which God's purposes can be fulfilled. They are not passive but active – even in old age, like Abraham in *Parashat Ḥayei Sara*. Indeed in the chapter immediately following the story of finding a wife for Isaac, to our surprise, we read that after Sarah's death, Abraham takes another wife and has eight more children. Whatever else this tells us – and there are many interpretations (the most likely is that it explains how Abraham became "the father of many nations") – it certainly conveys the point that Abraham stayed young the way Moses stayed young: "His eyes were undimmed and his natural energy unabated" (Deut. 34:7). Though action takes energy, it gives us energy. The contrast between Noah in old age and Abraham in old age could not be greater.

Perhaps, though, the most important point of this *parasha* is that large promises – a land, countless children – become real through small beginnings. Leaders begin with an envisioned future, but they also know that there is a long journey between here and there; we can only reach it one act at a time, one day at a time. There is no miraculous shortcut – and if there were, it would not help. The use of a shortcut would culminate in an achievement like Jonah's gourd, which grew overnight – and then died overnight. Abraham acquired only a single field and had just one son who would continue the covenant. Yet he did not complain, and he died serene and satisfied. Because he had begun. Because he had left future generations something on which to build. All great change is the work of more than one generation, and none of us will live to see the full fruit of our endeavours.

Leaders see the destination, begin the journey, and leave behind them those who will continue it. That is enough to endow a life with immortality.

Toledot

The Price of Silence

The Netziv (Naftali Zvi Yehuda Berlin, 1816–1893, dean of the yeshiva in Volozhin) made the sharp observation that Isaac and Rebecca seem not to have communicated closely. Rebecca's "relationship with Isaac was not the same as that between Sarah and Abraham or Rachel and Jacob. When they had a problem they were not afraid to speak about it. Not so with Rebecca" (*Haamek Davar* to Gen. 24:65).

The Netziv senses this distance from the very first moment when Rebecca sees Isaac "meditating in the field" (Gen. 24:63), at which point she "covered herself with a veil" (24:65). He comments, "She covered herself out of awe and a sense of inadequacy, as if she felt she was unworthy to be his wife, and from then on this trepidation was fixed in her mind."

Their relationship, suggests the Netziv, was never casual, candid, and communicative. The result was, at a series of critical moments, a failure of communication. It seems likely that Rebecca never informed Isaac of the oracle she had before the twins, Esau and Jacob, were born, in which God told her "the elder will serve the younger" (Gen. 25:23). That apparently is one reason she loved Jacob rather than Esau, knowing that he was the one chosen by God. If Isaac knew this, why did he favour Esau? He probably did not know, because Rebecca had not told him. That is why, many years later, when she hears that Isaac is about to bless Esau, she is forced into a plan of deception: she tells Jacob to pretend he is Esau. Why did she not simply tell Isaac that it was Jacob who was to be blessed? Because that would force her to admit that she had kept her husband in ignorance about the prophecy all the years the children were growing up.

Had she spoken to Isaac on the day of the blessing, Isaac might have said something that would have changed the entire course of their, and their children's, lives. I imagine Isaac saying this: "Of course I know that it will be Jacob and not Esau who will continue the covenant. But I have two quite different blessings in mind, one for each of our sons. I will give Esau a blessing of *wealth* and *power*: 'May God give you the dew of heaven and the richness of the earth …. May nations serve you and peoples bow down to you' (Gen. 27:28–29). I will give Jacob the blessing God gave to Abraham and to me, the blessing of *children* and the *promised land*: 'May God Almighty bless you and make you fruitful and increase your numbers until you become a community of peoples. May He give you and your descendants the blessing given to Abraham, so that you may take possession of the land where you now reside as a foreigner, the land God gave to Abraham' (Gen. 28:3–4)."

Isaac never did intend to give the blessing of the covenant to Esau. He intended to give each child the blessing that suited him. The entire deceit planned by Rebecca and carried out by Jacob was never necessary in the first place. Why did Rebecca not understand this? Because she and her husband did not communicate.

Now let us count the consequences. Isaac, old and blind, feels betrayed by Jacob. He "trembled violently" (Gen. 27:33) when he realised what had happened, saying to Esau, "Your brother came deceitfully" (27:35). Esau likewise feels betrayed and feels such violent hatred towards Jacob that he vows to kill him. Rebecca is forced to send Jacob into exile, thus depriving herself for more than two decades of the company of the son she loves. As for Jacob, the consequences of the deceit last a lifetime, resulting in strife between his wives and between his children. "Few and evil have been the days of my life" (47:9), he says to Pharaoh as an old man. Four lives are scarred by one act which was not even necessary in the first place – Isaac did in fact give Jacob "the blessing of Abraham" without any deception, knowing him to be Jacob and not Esau.

Such is the human price we pay for a failure to communicate. The Torah is exceptionally candid about such matters, which is what makes it so powerful a guide to life: real life, among real people with real problems. Communication matters. In the beginning God created the natural world with words: "And God said: 'Let there be…'" We create the social world with words. The *Targum* translates the phrase "And man became a *living* soul" (Gen 2:7) as "And man became a *speaking* soul." For us, speech is life. Life is relationship. And human relationships only exist because we can speak. We can tell other people our hopes, our fears, our feelings and thoughts.

That is why any leader – from a parent to a CEO – must set as his or her task good, strong, honest, open communication. That is what makes families, teams, and corporate cultures healthy. People must know what their overall aims are as a team, what their specific roles are, what responsibilities they carry, and what values and behaviours they are expected to exemplify. There must be praise for those who do well, as well as constructive criticism when people do badly. Criticism must be of the act, not the person; the person must feel respected whatever his or her failures. This last feature is one of the fundamental differences between a "guilt morality" of which Judaism is the supreme example, and a "shame morality" like that of ancient Greece (guilt makes a clear distinction between the act and the person; shame does not).

There are times when much depends on clear communication. It is not too much to say that there was a moment at which the fate of the world depended on it. It happened during the Cuban missile crisis of 1962 when the United States and the Soviet Union were on the brink of nuclear war. At the height of the crisis, as described by Robert McNamara in his film, *The Fog of War*, John F. Kennedy received two messages from the Soviet leader Nikita Khrushchev. One was conciliatory, the other far more hawkish. Most of Kennedy's advisers believed that the second represented Khrushchev's real views and should be taken seriously.

However, one man, Llewellyn Thompson Jr., had been American ambassador to the Soviet Union from 1957 to 1962 and had come to know the Russian president well. He had even spent a period of time living with Khrushchev and his wife. He told Kennedy that the conciliatory message sounded like Khrushchev's own personal view while the hawkish letter, which did not sound like him, had probably been written to appease the Russian generals. Kennedy listened to Thompson and gave Khrushchev a way of backing down without losing face – and the result was that war was averted. It is terrifying to imagine what might have happened had Thompson not been there to establish which was and which was not the real act of communication.

Parents and leaders must establish a culture in which honest, open, respectful communication takes place, one that involves not just speaking but also listening. Without it, tragedy is waiting in the wings.

Vayetzeh

Light in Dark Times

What is it that made Jacob – not Abraham or Isaac or Moses – the true father of the Jewish people? We are the "congregation of Jacob," "the Children of Israel." Jacob/Israel is the man whose name we bear. Yet Jacob did not begin the Jewish journey; Abraham did. Jacob faced no trial like that of Isaac at the binding. He did not lead the people out of Egypt or bring them the Torah. To be sure, all his children stayed within the faith, unlike Abraham or Isaac. But that simply pushes the question back one level. Why did he succeed where Abraham and Isaac failed?

It seems that the answer lies in *Parashat Vayetzeh* and *Parashat Vayishlaḥ*. Jacob was the man whose greatest visions came to him when he was alone at night, far from home, fleeing from one danger to the next. In *Parashat Vayetzeh*, escaping from Esau, he stops and rests for the night with only stones to lie on and has an epiphany:

> He had a dream in which he saw a stairway resting on the earth, with its top reaching to heaven, and the angels of God were ascending and descending on it.... When Jacob awoke from

his sleep, he thought, "Surely the Lord is in this place, and I was not aware of it." He was afraid and said, "How awesome is this place! This is none other than the house of God; this is the gate of heaven." (Gen. 28:12–17)

In *Parashat Vayishlaḥ*, fleeing from Laban and terrified at the prospect of meeting Esau again, he wrestles alone at night with an unnamed stranger.

Then the man said, "Your name will no longer be Jacob, but Israel, because you have struggled with God and with humans and have overcome."... So Jacob called the place Peniel, saying, "It is because I saw God face to face, and yet my life was spared." (Gen. 32:29–31)

These are the decisive spiritual encounters of Jacob's life, yet they happen in liminal space (the space between, neither a starting point nor a destination), at a time when Jacob is at risk in both directions – where he comes from and where he is going to. Yet it is at these points of maximal vulnerability that he encounters God and finds the courage to continue despite all the hazards of the journey.

That is the strength Jacob bequeathed to the Jewish people. What is remarkable is not merely that this one tiny people survived tragedies that would have spelled the end of any other people: the destruction of two temples; the Babylonian and Roman conquests; the expulsions, persecutions, and pogroms of the Middle Ages; the rise of anti-Semitism in nineteenth-century Europe; and the Holocaust. What is remarkable is that after each cataclysm, Judaism renewed itself, scaling new heights of achievement.

During the Babylonian exile Judaism deepened its engagement with the Torah. After the Roman destruction of Jerusalem it produced the great literary monuments of the Oral Torah: Midrash, Mishna, and Gemara. During the Middle Ages it produced masterpieces of law and Torah commentary, poetry, and philosophy. A mere three years after the Holocaust it proclaimed the State of Israel, the Jewish return to history after the darkest night of exile.

When I became Chief Rabbi I had to undergo a medical examination. The doctor put me on a treadmill, walking at a very brisk pace. "What are you testing?" I asked him. "How fast I can go, or how long?" "Neither," he replied. "What I am testing is how long it takes, when you come off the treadmill, for your pulse to return to normal." That is when I discovered that health is measured by the power of recovery. That is true for everyone, but doubly so for leaders and for the Jewish people, a nation of leaders (that, I believe, is what the phrase "a kingdom of priests" [Ex. 19:6] means).

Leaders suffer crises. That is a given of leadership. When Harold Macmillan, prime minister of Britain between 1957 and 1963, was asked what the most difficult aspect of his time in office was, he famously replied, "Events, dear boy, events." Bad things happen, and when they do, the leader must take the strain so that others can sleep easily in their beds.

Leadership, especially in matters of the spirit, is deeply stressful. Four figures in Tanakh – Moses, Elijah, Jeremiah, and Jonah – actually prayed to die rather than continue. This was not only true in the distant past. Abraham Lincoln suffered deep bouts of depression. So did Churchill, who called it his "black dog." Gandhi and Martin Luther King Jr. both attempted suicide in adolescence and experienced depressive illness in adult life. The same was true of many great creative artists, among them Michelangelo, Beethoven, and Van Gogh.

Is it greatness that leads to moments of despair, or moments of despair that lead to greatness? Is it that those who lead internalise the stresses and tensions of their time? Or is it that those who are used to stress in their emotional lives find release in leading exceptional lives? There is no convincing answer to this in the literature thus far. But Jacob was a more emotionally volatile individual than either Abraham, who was often serene even in the face of great trials, or Isaac, who was particularly withdrawn. Jacob feared; Jacob loved; Jacob spent more of his time in exile than the other patriarchs. But Jacob endured and persisted. Of all the figures in Genesis, he was the great survivor.

The ability to survive and to recover is part of what it takes to be a leader. It is the willingness to live a life of risks that makes such individuals different from others. So said Theodore Roosevelt in one of the greatest speeches ever made on the subject:

It is not the critic who counts; not the man who points out how the strong man stumbles, or where the doer of deeds could have done them better. The credit belongs to the man who is actually in the arena, whose face is marred by dust and sweat and blood; who strives valiantly; who errs, who comes short again and again, because there is no effort without error and shortcoming; but who does actually strive to do the deeds; who knows great enthusiasms, great devotions; who spends himself in a worthy cause; who at the best knows in the end the triumph of high achievement, and who at the worst, if he fails, at least fails while daring greatly, so that his place shall never be with those cold and timid souls who neither know victory nor defeat.[1]

Jacob endured the rivalry of Esau, the resentment of Laban, the tension between his wives and children, the early death of his beloved Rachel, and the loss – for twenty-two years – of his favourite son, Joseph. He said to Pharaoh, "Few and evil have been the days of my life" (Gen. 47:9). Yet, on the way he "encountered" angels, and whether they were wrestling with him or climbing the ladder to heaven, they lit the night with the aura of transcendence.

To try, to fall, to fear, and yet to keep going: that is what it takes to be a leader. That was Jacob, the man who at the lowest ebbs of his life had his greatest visions of heaven.

1. Theodore Roosevelt, "Citizenship in a Republic," speech given at the Sorbonne, Paris, April 23, 1910.

Vayishlaḥ

Be Thyself

I have often argued that the episode in which the Jewish people acquired its name – when Jacob wrestled with an unnamed adversary at night and received the name Israel, as we saw earlier – is essential to an understanding of what it is to be a Jew. I argue here that it is equally critical to understanding what it is to lead.

There are several theories as to the identity of "the man" who wrestled with the patriarch that night. The Torah calls him a man. The prophet Hosea calls him an angel (Hos. 12:4–5). The sages say it was Samael, guardian angel of Esau and a force for evil.[1] Jacob himself was convinced it was God. "Jacob called the place Peniel, saying, 'It is because I saw God face to face, and yet my life was spared'" (Gen. 32:31).

My argument is that we can only understand the passage against the entire background of Jacob's life. Jacob was born holding onto Esau's heel. He bought Esau's birthright. He stole Esau's blessing. When his blind father asked him who he was, he replied, "I am Esau your firstborn" (Gen. 27:19). Jacob was the child who wanted to be Esau.

1. Genesis Rabba, 77; Rashi to Genesis 32:35; Zohar I, *Vayishlaḥ*, 170a.

Why? Because Esau was the elder. Because Esau was strong, physically mature, a hunter. Above all, because Esau was his father's favourite: "Isaac, who had a taste for wild game, loved Esau, but Rebecca loved Jacob" (Gen. 25:28). Jacob is the paradigm of what the French literary theorist and anthropologist Rene Girard called *mimetic desire*, meaning, we want what someone else wants, because we want to *be* that someone else.[2] The result is tension between Jacob and Esau. This tension rises to an unbearable intensity when Esau discovers that Jacob has taken the blessing Isaac had reserved for him, and vows to kill Jacob when Isaac is no longer alive.

Jacob flees to Laban where he encounters more conflict; he is on his way home when he hears that Esau is coming to meet him with a force of four hundred men. In an unusually strong description of emotion the Torah tells us that Jacob was "very frightened and distressed" (Gen. 32:7) – frightened, no doubt, that Esau would try to kill him, and perhaps distressed that his brother's animosity was not without cause.

Jacob had indeed wronged his brother, as we saw earlier. Isaac says to Esau, "Your brother came deceitfully and took your blessing" (Gen. 27:35). Centuries later, the prophet Hosea says, "The Lord has a charge to bring against Judah; he will punish Jacob according to his ways and repay him according to his deeds. In the womb he grasped his brother's heel; as a man he struggled with God" (Hos. 12:3–4). Jeremiah uses the name Jacob to mean someone who practises deception: "Beware of your friends; do not trust anyone in your clan; for every one of them is a deceiver [*akov Yaakov*], and every friend a slanderer" (Jer. 9:3).

As long as Jacob sought to be Esau there was tension, conflict, rivalry. Esau felt cheated; Jacob felt fear. That night, about to meet Esau again after an absence of twenty-two years, Jacob wrestles with himself; finally, he throws off the image of Esau, the person he wants to be, which he has carried with him all these years. This is the critical moment in Jacob's life. From now on, he is content to be himself. And it is only when we stop wanting to be someone else (in Shakespeare's words, "desiring this man's art, and that man's scope, With what I most enjoy contented least"[3]) that we can be at peace with ourselves and with the world.

---

2.   Rene Girard, *Violence and the Sacred* (London: Athlone Press, 1988).
3.   Shakespeare, "Sonnet 29."

This is one of the great challenges of leadership. It is all too easy for a leader to pursue popularity by being what people want him or her to be – a liberal to liberals, a conservative to conservatives, taking decisions that win temporary acclaim rather than flowing from principle and conviction. Presidential adviser David Gergen wrote about Bill Clinton that he "isn't exactly sure who he is yet and tries to define himself by how well others like him. That leads him into all sorts of contradictions, and the view by others that he seems a constant mixture of strengths and weaknesses."[4]

Leaders sometimes try to "hold the team together" by saying different things to different people, but eventually these contradictions become clear – especially in the total transparency that modern media imposes – and the result is that the leader appears to lack integrity. People no longer trust his or her remarks. There is a loss of confidence and authority that may take a long time to restore. The leader may find that his or her position has become untenable and may even be forced to resign. Few things make a leader more unpopular than the pursuit of popularity.

Great leaders have the courage to live with unpopularity. Lincoln was reviled and ridiculed during his lifetime. In 1864 the *New York Times* wrote of him: "He has been denounced without end as a perjurer, a usurper, a tyrant, a subverter of the Constitution, a destroyer of the liberties of his country, a reckless desperado, a heartless trifler over the last agonies of an expiring nation."[5] Churchill, until he became prime minister during the Second World War, had been written off as a failure. After the war he was defeated in the 1945 general election. John F. Kennedy and Martin Luther King Jr. were assassinated. When Margaret Thatcher died, some people celebrated in the streets.

Jacob was not a leader; there was as yet no nation for him to lead. Yet the Torah goes to great lengths to give us an insight into his struggle for identity, because it was not his alone. It happens to most of us (the word *avot* used to describe Abraham, Isaac, and Jacob means not only

---

4. David Gergen, *Eyewitness to Power* (New York: Simon & Schuster, 2001), 328.
5. Quoted in John Kane, *The Politics of Moral Capital* (Cambridge, England: Cambridge University Press, 2001), 71.

"fathers" or "patriarchs" but also "archetypes"). It is not easy to overcome the desire to be someone else, to want what they have, to be what they are. Most of us have such feelings from time to time. Girard argues that this has been the main source of conflict throughout history. It can take a lifetime of wrestling before we know who we are and relinquish the desire to be who we are not.

More than anyone else in Genesis, Jacob is surrounded by conflict: not just between himself and Esau, but between himself and Laban, between Rachel and Leah, and between his children, Joseph and his brothers. It is as if the Torah were telling us that so long as there is a conflict *within* us, there will be a conflict *around* us. We have to resolve the tension in ourselves before we can do so for others. We have to be at peace with ourselves before we can be at peace with the world.

That is what happens in this *parasha*. After his wrestling match with the stranger, Jacob undergoes a change of personality. He gives back to Esau the blessing he took from him. The previous day he had given him back the material blessing by sending him hundreds of goats, ewes, rams, camels, cows, bulls, and donkeys. Now he gives him back the blessing that said, "Be lord over your brothers, and may the sons of your mother bow down to you" (Gen. 27:29). Jacob bows down seven times to Esau. He calls Esau "My lord" (33:8), and himself "your servant" (33:5). He actually uses the word "blessing," though this fact is often obscured in translation. He says "Please take my blessing that has been brought to you" (33:11). The result is that the two brothers meet and part in peace.

People conflict. They have different interests, passions, desires, temperaments. Even if they did not, they would still conflict, as every parent knows. Children – and not just children – seek attention, and one cannot attend to everyone equally all the time. Managing the conflicts that affect every human group is the work of the leader – and if the leader is not sure of and confident in his or her identity, the conflicts will persist. Even if the leader sees himself as a peacemaker, the conflicts will still endure.

The only answer is to "know thyself." People must wrestle with themselves as Jacob did on that fateful night, throwing off the person they might like to be but are not; they must accept that some people will like them and what they stand for while others will not; they must understand that it is better to seek the respect of some than the popularity of all. This may involve a lifetime of struggle, but the outcome is an immense strength. No one is stronger than the person who knows who and what he is.

Vayeshev

The Power of Praise

Reuben is the leader who might have been but never was. He was Jacob's firstborn. Jacob said of him on his deathbed, "Reuben, you are my firstborn, my might, the first sign of my strength, excelling in honour, excelling in power" (Gen. 49:3). This is an impressive tribute, suggesting physical presence and commanding demeanour.

More significantly, in his early years Reuben consistently appeared to be the most morally sensitive of Jacob's children. He was Leah's son, and keenly felt his mother's disappointment that she was not Jacob's favourite. Here is the first description of him as a child: "During wheat harvest, Reuben went out into the fields and found some mandrake plants, which he brought to his mother Leah" (Gen. 30:14). Mandrakes were thought to be an aphrodisiac. Reuben knew this and immediately thought of his mother. It was a touching gesture but it misfired because he presented them to Leah in the presence of Rachel and unintentionally caused an argument between them.

The next episode in which we see Reuben is far more tragic: "Rachel died and was buried on the way to Ephrat, that is, Bethlehem.... While Israel was living in that region, Reuben went in and slept

41

[*vayishkav*] with his father's concubine Bilhah" (Gen. 35:19–22). If understood literally this would amount to a major sin. Sleeping with your father's concubine was not only a sexual crime; it was an unforgivable act of treason and betrayal, as we discover later in Tanakh. Absalom decides to rebel against his father David and replace him as king. Ahitophel gives him the following advice: "Sleep with your father's concubines whom he left to take care of the palace. Then all Israel will hear that you have made yourself obnoxious to your father, and the hands of everyone with you will be more resolute" (II Sam. 16:21).

According to the sages, the text about Reuben is not to be understood literally. After Rachel died, Jacob had moved his bed to the tent of Bilhah, Rachel's handmaid. This, felt Reuben, was an intolerable humiliation for his mother. It was hard for Leah to tolerate the fact that Jacob loved her sister more. It would have been altogether unbearable for her to discover that he even preferred Rachel's handmaid. So Reuben moved Jacob's bed from Bilhah's tent to Leah's. The verb *vayishkav* should therefore be translated not as "slept with" but "changed the sleeping arrangement" (Shabbat 55a–b).

At this point, however, the text does a strange thing. It says, "Reuben went in and slept with [or changed the sleeping arrangement of] his father's concubine Bilhah, and Israel heard of it" and then signals *a paragraph break in the middle of the sentence*. The sentence ends: "Jacob had twelve sons." This is very rare indeed. What it suggests is *an audible silence*. Communication had completely broken down between Jacob and Reuben. If the sages are correct in their interpretation, then this is one of the greatest tragedies in the whole of Genesis. Jacob clearly believed that Reuben had slept with his concubine Bilhah. He cursed him for it on his deathbed: "Unstable as water, you will not excel, for you went up onto your father's bed, onto my couch and defiled it" (Gen. 49:4).

Yet according to the sages this did not happen. Had Jacob been willing to speak to Reuben he would have discovered the truth, but Jacob grew up in a family that lacked open, candid communication (as we saw earlier in our discussion of *Parashat Toledot*). Thus for years Reuben was suspected by his father of a sin he had not committed – all because he cared about the feelings of his mother.

This brings us to the third episode in Reuben's life, the most tragic of all. Jacob favoured Joseph, son of his beloved Rachel, and the other brothers knew it. When he gave Joseph a visible sign of favouritism, the richly embroidered cloak, the brothers resented it yet more. When Joseph began to have dreams of the rest of the family bowing down to him, the brothers' animosity reached its boiling point. When they were far from home, tending the flocks, and Joseph appeared in the distance, their hatred made them decide, there and then, to kill him. Reuben alone resisted:

> When Reuben heard this, he tried to rescue him from their hands. "Let us not take his life," he said. "Do not shed any blood. Throw him into this cistern here in the wilderness, but do not lay a hand on him." Reuben said this to rescue him from them and take him back to his father. (Gen. 37:21–22)

Reuben's plan was simple. He persuaded the brothers not to kill Joseph but rather to let him die by leaving him in a pit to starve. He intended to return later, when the brothers had moved on, to rescue him. When he returned, however, Joseph was no longer there. He had been sold as a slave. Reuben was devastated.

Three times Reuben tried to help, but despite his best intentions, his efforts failed. He was responsible for the one recorded quarrel between Leah and Rachel. His father wrongly suspected him of a major sin and cursed him on his deathbed. He failed to save Joseph. *Reuben knew what would be the right thing to do, but somehow lacked the confidence or courage to carry it through to completion.* He should have waited to give Leah the mandrakes when she was alone. He should have remonstrated with his father about his sleeping arrangements. He should have physically taken Joseph safely back home.

What happened to Reuben to make him lack confidence? The Torah gives a poignant and unmistakable hint. Listen to these verses describing the birth of Leah's (and Jacob's) first two children:

> When the Lord saw that Leah was not loved, He enabled her to conceive, but Rachel remained childless. Leah became pregnant

and gave birth to a son. She named him Reuben, for she said, "*It is because the Lord has seen my misery. Surely my husband will love me now.*"

She conceived again, and when she gave birth to a son she said, "*Because the Lord heard that I am not loved, He gave me this one too.*" So she named him Simeon. (Gen. 29:32–33)

Both times, it was Leah, not Jacob, who named the child – and both names were a cry to Jacob to notice her and love her – if not for herself then at least because she had given him children. Jacob evidently did not notice.

Reuben became what he became because – so the text seems to imply – his father's attention was elsewhere; he did not care for either Leah or her sons (the text itself says, "the Lord saw that Leah was not loved"). Reuben knew this and felt his mother's shame and his father's apparent indifference intensely.

People need encouragement if they are to lead. It is fascinating to contrast the hesitant Reuben with the confident – even overconfident – Joseph, loved and favoured by his father. If we want our children to have the confidence to act when action is needed, then we have to empower, encourage, and praise them.

There is a fascinating mishna in Avot:

R. Yoḥanan b. Zakkai had five [pre-eminent] disciples, namely R. Eliezer b. Hyrcanus, R. Yehoshua b. Ḥanania, R. Yose the priest, R. Shimon b. Netanel, and R. Elazar b. Arakh. He used to recount their praise: Eliezer b. Hyrcanus – a plastered well that never loses a drop. Yehoshua b. Ḥanania – happy is the one who gave him birth. Yose the priest – a pious man. Shimon b. Netanel – a man who fears sin. Elazar b. Arakh – an ever-flowing spring. (Mishna Avot 2:10–11)

Why does the Mishna, whose aim is to teach us lasting truths, give us this apparently trivial account of R. Yoḥanan b. Zakkai's pupils and what he used to call them? The answer, I believe, is that the Mishna is telling us how to raise disciples, how to be a coach, mentor, and guide: using *focused praise*.

The Mishna does not simply say that R. Yoḥanan b. Zakkai said good things about his students. It uses an unusual locution: "He used to count [*moneh*] their praise," meaning, his positive remarks were precise and accurately targeted. He told each of his disciples what their specific strength was.

Eliezer b. Hyrcanus had an outstanding memory. At a time when the Oral Law was not yet written down, he could recall the teachings of the tradition better than anyone else. Elazar b. Arakh was creative, able to come up with an endless stream of fresh interpretations. When we follow our particular passions and gifts, we contribute to the world what only we can give.

However, the fact that we may have an exceptional gift may also mean that we have conspicuous deficiencies. No one has all the strengths. Suffice it if we have one. But we must also know what we lack. Eliezer b. Hyrcanus became so fixated on the past that he resisted change even when it was agreed upon by the majority of his colleagues. Eventually he was excommunicated for failing to accept his colleagues' ruling (Bava Metzia 59b).

Elazar b. Arakh's fate was even sadder. After the death of R. Yoḥanan b. Zakkai, he separated from his colleagues. They went to Yavneh; he went to Hamat (Emmaus). It was a pleasant place to live and it was where his wife's family lived. Apparently he was so confident in his intellectual gifts that he believed he could maintain his scholarship by himself. Eventually he forgot everything he had ever learned (*Avot DeRabbi Natan* 14:6). The man more gifted than his contemporaries eventually died while making almost no lasting contribution to the tradition.

There is a delicate balance between the neglect that leads someone to lack the confidence to do the necessary deed and the excessive praise or favouritism that creates overconfidence and the belief that you are better than others. That balance is necessary if we are to be the sunlight that helps others grow.

Miketz

The Power of Dreams

I n one of the greatest transformations in all literature, Joseph moves in one bound from prisoner to prime minister. What was it about Joseph – a complete outsider to Egyptian culture, a "Hebrew," a man who had for years been languishing in jail on a false charge of attempted rape – that marked him out as a leader of the greatest empire of the ancient world?

Joseph had three gifts that many people have in isolation but few have in combination. The first is that he dreamed dreams. Initially we do not know whether his two adolescent dreams – of his brothers' sheaves bowing down to his and of the sun, moon, and eleven stars bowing down to him – are a genuine presentiment of future greatness or merely the overactive imagination of a spoiled child with delusions of grandeur.

Only in *Parashat Miketz* do we discover a vital piece of information that has been withheld from us until now. Joseph says to Pharaoh, who has also had two dreams: "The reason the dream was given to Pharaoh in two forms is that the matter has been firmly decided by God, and God will do it soon" (Gen. 41:32). Only in retrospect do we realise that Joseph's double dream was a sign that this too was no mere imagining. Joseph really was destined to be a leader to whom his family would bow.

Second, like Sigmund Freud many centuries later, Joseph could interpret the dreams of others. He did so for the butler and baker in prison and, in this *parasha*, for Pharaoh. His interpretations were neither magical nor miraculous. In the case of the butler and baker he remembered that in three days' time it would be Pharaoh's birthday (Gen. 40:20). It was the custom of rulers to make a feast on their birthday and decide the fate of certain individuals (in Britain, the Queen's birthday honours continue this tradition). It was reasonable therefore to assume that the butler's and baker's dreams related to this event and their unconscious hopes and fears (Ibn Ezra 40:12 and *Bekhor Shor* 40:12 both make this suggestion).

In the case of Pharaoh's dreams, Joseph may have known ancient Egyptian traditions about seven-year famines. Nahum Sarna quotes an Egyptian text from the reign of King Djoser (ca. twenty-eighth century BCE):

> I was in distress on the Great Throne, and those who are in the palace were in heart's affliction from a very great evil, since the Nile had not come in my time for a space of seven years. Grain was scant, fruits were dried up, and everything which they eat was short.[1]

Joseph's most impressive achievement, though, was his third gift, the ability to implement dreams, solving the problem for which they were an early warning. No sooner had he told of a seven-year famine than he continued, without pause, to provide a solution:

> Now let Pharaoh look for a discerning and wise man and put him in charge of the land of Egypt. Let Pharaoh appoint commissioners over the land to take a fifth of the harvest of Egypt during the seven years of abundance. They should collect all the food of these good years that are coming and store up the grain

1.   Nahum Sarna, *Understanding Genesis* (Tel Aviv: Schocken, 1966), 219.

under the authority of Pharaoh, to be kept in the cities for food. This food should be held in reserve for the country, to be used during the seven years of famine that will come upon Egypt, so that the country may not be ruined by the famine. (Gen. 41:33–36)

We have seen Joseph the brilliant administrator before, both in Potiphar's house and in the prison. It was this gift, demonstrated at precisely the right time, that led to his appointment as viceroy of Egypt.

From Joseph, therefore, we learn three principles. The first principle is: dream dreams. Never be afraid to let your imagination soar. When people come to me for advice about leadership I tell them to give themselves the time and space and imagination to dream. In dreams we discover our passion, and following our passion is the best way to live a rewarding life.[2]

Dreaming is often thought to be impractical. Not so; it is one of the most practical things we can do. There are people who spend months planning a holiday but not even a day planning a life. They let themselves be carried by the winds of chance and circumstance. That is a mistake. The sages said, "Wherever [in the Torah] we find the word *vayehi* ['And it came to pass'], it is always the prelude to tragedy" (Megilla 10b). A *vayehi* life is one in which we passively let things happen. A *yehi* ("Let there be") life is one in which we make things happen, and it is our dreams that give us direction.

Theodor Herzl, to whom more than any other person we owe the existence of the State of Israel, used to say, "If you will it, it is no dream." I once heard a wonderful story from Elie Wiesel. There was a time when Sigmund Freud and Theodor Herzl lived in the same district of Vienna. "Fortunately," Wiesel said, "they never met. Can you imagine what would have happened had they met? Theodor Herzl would have said: 'I have a dream of a Jewish state.' Freud would have replied: 'Tell me, Herr Herzl, how long have you been having this dream? Lie down on my couch, and I will psychoanalyse you.' Herzl would have been cured

---

2. One of the classic texts on this subject is Ken Robinson, *The Element: How Finding Your Passion Changes Everything* (New York: Penguin Books, 2009).

of his dreams and today there would be no Jewish state." Fortunately, the Jewish people have never been cured of their dreams.

The second principle is that leaders interpret other people's dreams. They articulate the inchoate. They find a way of expressing the hopes and fears of a generation. Martin Luther King Jr.'s "I have a dream" speech was about taking the hopes of African-Americans and giving them wings. It was not Joseph's dreams that made him a leader; it was Pharaoh's. Our own dreams give us direction; it is other people's dreams that give us opportunity.

The third principle is: find a way to implement dreams. First see the problem, then find a way of solving it. The Kotzker Rebbe once drew attention to a difficulty in Rashi's writing. Rashi (Ex. 18:1) says that Yitro was given the name Yeter ("he added") because "he added a passage to the Torah beginning [with the words], 'Choose from among the people...'" (18:21). This was when Yitro saw Moses leading alone and told him that what he was doing was not good; he would wear himself and the people to exhaustion. Therefore he should choose good people and delegate much of the burden of leadership to them.

The Kotzker pointed out that the passage that Yitro added to the Torah did not begin, "Choose from among the people." It began several verses earlier when he said, "What you are doing is not good" (Ex. 18:17). The answer the Kotzker gave was simple. Saying "What you are doing is not good" is not an addition to the Torah – it is merely stating a problem. The addition consisted of the solution: delegate.

Good leaders either are, or surround themselves with, problem-solvers. It is easy to see what is going wrong. What makes someone a leader is the ability to find a way of putting it right. Joseph's genius lay not in predicting seven years of plenty followed by seven years of famine, but in devising a system of storage that would ensure food supplies in the lean and hungry years.

Dream dreams, understand and articulate the dreams of others, and find ways of turning a dream into a reality – these three gifts are leadership, the Joseph way.

Vayigash

The Unexpected Leader

I was once present when the great historian of Islam, Bernard Lewis, was asked to predict the course of events in the Middle East. He replied, "I'm a historian, so I only make predictions about the past. What is more, I am a *retired* historian, so even my past is passé." Predictions are impossible in the affairs of living, breathing human beings because we are free and there is no way of knowing in advance how an individual will react to the great challenges of his or her life.

If one thing seems clear throughout the last third of Genesis, it is that Joseph will emerge as the archetypal leader. He is the central character of the story, and his dreams and the shifting circumstances of his fate all point in that direction. Least likely as a candidate for leadership is Judah, the man who proposed selling Joseph as a slave (Gen. 37:26–27), whom we next see separated from his brothers, living among the Canaanites, intermarried with them, losing two of his sons because of sin, and having sexual relations with a woman he takes to be a prostitute. The chapter in which this is described begins with the phrase, "At that time Judah *went down* from among his brothers" (38:1). The commentators take this to mean moral decline.

Yet history turned out otherwise. Joseph's descendants, the tribes of Ephraim and Menashe, disappeared from the pages of history after the Assyrian conquest in 722 BCE, while Judah's descendants, starting with David, became kings. The tribe of Judah survived the Babylonian conquest, and it is Judah whose name we bear as a people. We are *Yehudim,* "Jews." *Parashat Vayigash* explains why.

Already in the previous *parasha* we began to see Judah's leadership qualities. The family had reached deadlock. They desperately needed food, but they knew that the Egyptian viceroy had insisted that they bring their brother Benjamin with them, and Jacob refused to let this happen. He had lost one child of his beloved wife Rachel (Joseph) and he was not about to let the other, Benjamin, be taken on a hazardous journey. Reuben, in keeping with his unstable character, made an absurd suggestion: "Kill my two sons if I do not bring Benjamin back safely" (Gen. 42:37). It was Judah, with his quiet authority – "I myself will guarantee his safety; you can hold me personally responsible for him" (43:9) – who persuaded Jacob to let Benjamin go with them.

Now in Egypt, the nightmare scenario has unfolded. Benjamin has been found with the viceroy's silver cup in his possession. The official delivers his verdict. Benjamin is to be held as a slave. The other brothers can go free. At this point Judah steps forward and makes a speech that changes history. He speaks eloquently about their father's grief at the loss of one of Rachel's sons. If Jacob loses the other, Judah states, he will die of grief. I, says Judah, personally guaranteed his safe return. He concludes: "Now then, please let your servant remain here as my lord's slave in place of the boy, and let the boy return with his brothers. How can I go back to my father if the boy is not with me? No! Do not let me see the misery that would come on my father" (Gen. 44:33–34).

No sooner has he said these words than Joseph, overcome with emotion, reveals his identity and the whole elaborate drama reaches closure. What is happening here and how does it have a bearing on leadership?

The sages articulated a principle: "Where penitents stand even the perfectly righteous cannot stand" (Berakhot 34b). The Talmud brings a prooftext from Isaiah, "Peace, peace, to those far and near" (Is. 57:19), placing the far (the penitent sinner) before the near (the perfectly righteous). However, almost certainly the real source is here in the story of Joseph and Judah. Joseph is known to tradition as *hatzaddik*, the righteous.[1] Judah, as we will see, is a penitent. Joseph became "second to the king." Judah, however, became the ancestor of kings. Hence, where penitents stand even the perfectly righteous cannot stand.

Judah is the first person in the Torah to achieve perfect repentance (*teshuva gemura*), defined by the sages as one who finds himself in a situation to repeat an earlier sin but who does not do so because he is now a changed person.[2] Many years before, Judah was responsible for Joseph being sold as a slave: "Judah said to his brothers, 'What will we gain if we kill our brother and cover up his blood? Come, let us sell him to the Ishmaelites and not lay our hands on him; after all, he is our brother, our own flesh and blood.' His brothers agreed" (Gen. 37:26–27). Now, faced with the prospect of leaving Benjamin as a slave, he says, "Let me stay as a slave and let my brother go free" (44:33). That is perfect repentance, and it is what allows Joseph to reveal his identity and forgive his brothers.

The Torah had already hinted at the change in Judah's character. Having accused his daughter-in-law Tamar of becoming pregnant by a forbidden sexual relationship, he is confronted by her with evidence that he himself is the father of the child and immediately admits: "She is more righteous than I" (Gen. 38:26). This is the first time in the Torah that we see a character admit that he is wrong. If Judah was the first penitent, it was Tamar – mother of Peretz from whom King David was descended – who was ultimately responsible.

Perhaps Judah's future was already implicit in his name, for though the verb *lehodot* from which it is derived means "to thank" (Leah called her fourth son Judah saying, "This time I will thank the Lord," Gen. 29:35), it is also related to the verb *lehitvadot*, which means "to admit," "to confess" – and confession is, according to the Rambam, the core of the command to repent.

Leaders make mistakes. That is an occupational hazard of the role. Managers follow the rules, but leaders find themselves in situations for

---

1. See Tanḥuma (Buber), *Noaḥ*, 4, s.v. *eleh*, on the basis of Amos 2:6, "They sold the righteous for silver."
2. *Mishneh Torah, Hilkhot Teshuva* 2:1.

which there are no rules. Do you declare a war in which people will die, or do you refrain from doing so at the risk of letting your enemy grow stronger with the result that more will die later? That was the dilemma faced by Chamberlain in 1939, and it was only some time later that it became clear that he was wrong and Churchill right.

But leaders are also human and they make mistakes that have nothing to do with leadership and everything to do with human weakness and temptation. The sexual conduct of John F. Kennedy and Bill Clinton was less than perfect. Does this affect our judgement of them as leaders or not? Judaism suggests it should. The prophet Nathan was unsparing of King David when he sinned with another man's wife.

What matters, suggests the Torah, is that you repent – you recognise and admit your wrongs, and you change as a result. As Rabbi Soloveitchik points out, both Saul and David, Israel's first two kings, sinned. Both were reprimanded by a prophet. Both said "ḥatati," "I have sinned" (i Sam. 15:24, ii Sam. 12:13). But their fates were radically different. Saul lost his throne; David did not. The reason, says the Rav, was that David confessed immediately. Saul prevaricated and made excuses before admitting his sin.[3]

The stories of Judah and his descendant David tell us that what marks a leader is not necessarily perfect righteousness. It is the ability to admit mistakes, to learn from them and grow from them. The Judah we see at the beginning of the story is not the man we see at the end, just as the Moses we see at the burning bush – stammering, hesitant – is not the mighty hero we see at the end, "his eyes…undimmed and his natural energy unabated" (Deut. 34:7). A leader is one who, though he may stumble and fall, arises more honest, humble, and courageous than he was before.

3. Joseph Soloveitchik, *Kol Dodi Dofek: Listen – My Beloved Knocks* (Jersey City, N.J.: Ktav, 2006), 26.

54

Vayeḥi

Surviving Failure

The book of Genesis ends on a sublime note of reconciliation between Joseph and his brothers. His brothers were afraid that he had not really forgiven them for selling him into slavery. They suspected that he was merely delaying his revenge until their father died. After Jacob's death, they express their fear. But Joseph insists:

> "Do not be afraid. Am I in the place of God? You intended to harm me, but God intended it for good to accomplish what is now being done, the saving of many lives. So then, do not be afraid. I will provide for you and your children." And he reassured them and spoke kindly to them. (Gen. 50:19–21)

This is the second time he has said something like this to them. Earlier he spoke similarly when he first disclosed that he – the man they thought was an Egyptian viceroy called *Tzofnat Paane'aḥ* – was in fact their brother Joseph:

I am your brother Joseph, the one you sold into Egypt! And now, do not be distressed and do not be angry with yourselves for selling me here, because it was to save lives that God sent me ahead of you. For two years now there has been famine in the land, and for the next five years there will be no ploughing and reaping. But God sent me ahead of you to preserve for you a remnant on earth and to save your lives by a great deliverance. So then, it was not you who sent me here, but God. (Gen. 45:3–8)

This is a crucial moment in the history of faith. It marks the birth of forgiveness, the first recorded moment at which one person forgives another for a wrong they have done. But it also establishes another important principle: the idea of divine providence. History is not, as Joseph Heller called it, "a trash bag of random coincidences blown open in the wind."[1] It has a purpose, a point, a plot. God is at work behind the scenes. "There's a divinity that shapes our ends," says Hamlet, "rough-hew them how we will."[2]

Joseph's greatness was that he sensed this. Nothing in his life, he now knew, had happened by accident. The plot to kill him, his sale as a slave, the false accusations of Potiphar's wife, his time in prison, and his disappointed hope that the chief butler would remember him and secure his release – all these events that might have cast him into ever-deeper depths of despair turned out in retrospect to be necessary steps in the journey that eventuated in his becoming second-in-command in Egypt and the one person capable of saving the whole country – as well as his own family – from starving in the years of famine.

Joseph had in double measure one of the necessary gifts of a leader: the ability to keep going despite opposition, envy, false accusation, and repeated setbacks. Every leader who stands for anything will face opposition. This may be a genuine conflict of interests. A leader elected to make society more equitable will almost certainly win the support of the poor and the antagonism of the rich. One elected to reduce the tax burden will do the opposite. It cannot be avoided. Politics without conflict is a contradiction in terms.

---

1. Joseph Heller, *Good as Gold* (New York: Simon & Schuster, 1979), 74.
2. *Hamlet*, act 5, scene 2.

Any leader elected to anything, any leader more loved or gifted than others, will face envy. Rivals will say, "Why wasn't it me?" That is what Korah thought about Moses and Aaron. It is what the brothers thought about Joseph when they saw that their father loved him more than he did them. It is what Antonio Salieri thought about the more gifted Mozart, according to Peter Shaffer's play *Amadeus*.

As for false accusations, they have occurred often enough in history. Joan of Arc was accused of heresy and burned at the stake. A quarter century later, she was posthumously declared innocent by an official court of inquiry. More than twenty people were put to death as a result of the Salem witch trials in 1692–1693. Years later, as their innocence began to be perceived, a priest present at the trials, John Hale, admitted, "Such was the darkness of that day...that we walked in the clouds, and could not see our way."[3] The most famous false accusation of modern times was the trial of Alfred Dreyfus, a French officer of Jewish descent accused of being a German spy. The affair rocked France between the years 1894 and 1906 before Dreyfus was finally acquitted.

Setbacks too are part of the life story of the most successful. J. K. Rowling's initial Harry Potter novel was rejected by the first twelve publishers she sent it to. Another writer of a book about children suffered twenty-one rejections. That book was called *Lord of the Flies*, and its author, William Golding, was eventually awarded the Nobel Prize for Literature. In his famous commencement address at Stanford University, the late Steve Jobs told the story of the three blows of fate that shaped his life: dropping out of university; being fired from Apple, the company he founded; and being diagnosed with pancreatic cancer. Rather than being defeated by them, he turned them all to creative use. For twenty-two years, I lived close to Abbey Road, North London, where a famous pop group recorded all their hits. At their first audition, they performed for a record company who told them that guitar bands were "on their way out." The verdict on their performance (in January 1962) was: "The Beatles have no future in show business."

All this explains Winston Churchill's great remark that "success is going from failure to failure without loss of enthusiasm."

3.   Quoted in Robert A. Divine et al., *America Past and Present*, vol. 1 (Pearson, 2001), 94.

It may be that what sustains people through repeated setbacks is belief in themselves, or sheer tenacity, or lack of alternatives. What sustained Joseph, though, was his insight into divine providence. A plan was unfolding whose end he could only dimly discern, but at some stage he seems to have realised that he was one of the characters in a far larger drama and that all the bad things that had happened to him were necessary if the intended outcome was to occur. As he said to his brothers, "It was not you who sent me here, but God."

This willingness to let events work themselves out in accordance with providence, this understanding that we are at best no more than co-authors of our lives, allowed Joseph to survive without resentment about the past or despair in the face of the future. Trust in God gave him immense strength, which is what a leader needs if he is to dare greatly. Whatever malice other people harbour against leaders – and the more successful they are, the more malice there is – if they can say, "You intended to harm me, but God intended it for good," they will survive, their strength intact, their energy undiminished.

Exodus
שמות

Women as Leaders

P*arashat Shemot* could be entitled "The Birth of a Leader." We see Moses, adopted by Pharaoh's daughter, growing up as a prince of Egypt. We see him as a young man, for the first time realising the implications of his true identity. He is, and knows he is, a member of an enslaved and suffering people: "Growing up, he went out to where his own people were and watched them at their hard labour. He saw an Egyptian beating a Hebrew, one of his own people" (Ex. 2:10).

He intervenes. He acts – the mark of a true leader. We see him intervene three times – twice in Egypt, once in Midian – to rescue victims of violence. We then witness the great scene at the burning bush where God summons him to lead his people to freedom. Moses hesitates four times until God becomes angry and Moses knows he has no other choice. This is a classic account of the childhood of a hero.

But this is only the surface. The Torah is a deep and subtle book, and it does not always deliver its message on the surface. Just beneath is another – and far more remarkable – story, not about a hero but about six heroines, six courageous women without whom there would not have been a Moses.

First is Yokheved, wife of Amram and mother of the three people who were to become the great leaders of the Israelites: Miriam, Aaron, and Moses himself. It was Yokheved who, at the height of Egyptian persecution, had the courage to have a child, hide him for three months, and then devise a plan to give him a chance of being rescued. We know all too little of Yokheved. In her first appearance in the Torah she is unnamed. Yet, reading the narrative, we are left in no doubt about her bravery and resourcefulness. Not by accident did her children all become leaders.

The second is Miriam, Yokheved's daughter and Moses' elder sister. It was she who kept watch over the child as the ark floated down the river, she who approached Pharaoh's daughter with the suggestion that he be nursed among his own people. The biblical text paints a portrait of the young Miriam as a figure of unusual fearlessness and presence of mind. Rabbinic tradition goes further. In a remarkable midrash, we read of how the young Miriam confronted her father Amram and persuaded him to change his mind. Hearing of the decree that every male Israelite baby would be drowned in the river, Amram led the Israelites in divorcing their wives so that there would be no more children. He had logic on his side. Could it be right to bring children into the world if there was a fifty per cent chance that they would be killed at birth? Yet Miriam, so the tradition goes, remonstrated with him. "Your decree," she said, "is worse than Pharaoh's. His affects only the boys; yours affects all. His deprives children of life in this world; yours will deprive them of life even in the World to Come." Amram relented, and as a result, Moses was born.[1] The implication is clear: Miriam had more faith than her father.

Third and fourth were the two midwives, Shifra and Puah, who frustrated Pharaoh's first attempt at genocide. Told to kill the male Israelite children at birth, they "feared God and did not do what the king of Egypt had told them to do; they let the boys live" (Ex. 1:17). Summoned and accused of disobedience, they outwitted Pharaoh by constructing an ingenious cover story: the Hebrew women, they said, are vigorous and give birth before we arrive. They escaped punishment and saved lives.

The significance of this story is that it is the first recorded instance of one of Judaism's greatest contributions to civilisation: the idea that

1.   Exodus Rabba, 1:13.

there are moral limits to power. There are instructions that should not be obeyed. There are crimes against humanity that cannot be excused by the claim that "I was only obeying orders." This concept, generally known as "civil disobedience," is usually attributed to the nineteenth-century American writer Henry David Thoreau, and entered international consciousness after the Holocaust and the Nuremberg trials. Its true origin, though, lies thousands of years earlier in the actions of two women, Shifra and Puah. Through their understated courage they earned a high place among the moral heroes of history, teaching us the primacy of conscience over conformity, the law of justice over the law of the land.[2]

The fifth is Tzippora, Moses' wife. The daughter of a Midianite priest, she was nonetheless determined to accompany Moses on his mission to Egypt, despite the fact that she had no reason to risk her life on such a hazardous venture. In a deeply enigmatic passage, we see that it was she who saved Moses' life by performing a circumcision on their son (Ex. 4:24–26). The impression we have of her is as a figure of monumental determination who, at a crucial moment, has a better sense than Moses himself of what God requires.

I have saved until last the most intriguing of them all: Pharaoh's daughter. It was she who had the courage to rescue an Israelite child and bring him up as her own in the very palace where her father was plotting the destruction of the Israelite people. Could we imagine a daughter of Hitler, or Eichmann, or Stalin, doing the same? There is something at once heroic and gracious about this lightly sketched figure, the woman who gave Moses his name.

Who was she? The Torah does not give her a name. However, the first book of Chronicles (4:18) mentions a daughter of Pharaoh, named Bitya, and it was she whom the sages identified as the woman who saved Moses. The name Bitya (sometimes rendered as Batya) means "the daughter of God." From this, the sages drew one of their most striking lessons: "The Holy One, Blessed Be He, said to her: 'Moses was not your son, yet you called him your son. You are not My daughter, but I

2. There is, of course, a midrashic tradition that Shifra and Puah were other names for Yokheved and Miriam (Sota 11b). In the text I am following the interpretation given by Abrabanel and Rabbi Moshe Chaim Luzzatto.

shall call you My daughter.'"[3] They added that she was one of the few (tradition enumerates nine) who were so righteous that they entered paradise in their lifetime.[4]

So, on the surface, the *parasha* is about the initiation into leadership of one remarkable man, but just beneath the surface is a counternarrative of six extraordinary women without whom there would not have been a Moses. They belong to a long tradition of strong women throughout Jewish history, from Deborah, Hannah, Ruth, and Esther in the Bible to more modern religious figures, like Sarah Schenirer and Nehama Leibowitz, to more secular figures like Anne Frank, Hannah Senesh, and Golda Meir.

How then, if women emerge so powerfully as leaders, were they excluded in Jewish law from certain leadership roles? If we look carefully we will see that women were historically excluded from two areas. One was the "crown of priesthood," which went to Aaron and his sons. The other was the "crown of kingship," which went to David and his sons. These were two roles built on the principle of dynastic succession. From the third crown – the "crown of Torah" – however, women were not excluded. There were prophetesses, not just prophets. The sages enumerate seven of them (Megilla 14a). There were great female Torah scholars from the Mishnaic period (Beruriah, Ima Shalom) until today.

At stake is a more general distinction. Rabbi Eliyahu Bakshi-Doron in his responsa, *Binyan Av*, differentiates between formal or official authority (*samkhut*) and actual leadership (*hanhaga*).[5] There are figures who hold positions of authority – prime ministers, presidents, CEOs – who may not be leaders at all. They may have the power to force people to do what they say, but they have no followers. They excite no admiration. They inspire no emulation. And there may be leaders who hold no official position at all but who are consulted for advice and held up as role models. They have no power but great influence. Israel's prophets belonged to this category. So, often, did the *gedolei Yisrael*, the

---

3. Leviticus Rabba, 1:3.
4. *Derekh Eretz Zuta* 1.
5. Rabbi Eliyahu Bakshi-Doron, *Shut Binyan Av* (Jerusalem: Binyan Av Institute, 2009), no. 65.

great sages of each generation. Neither Rashi nor the Rambam held any official position (some scholars say that the Rambam was chief rabbi of Egypt but most maintain that he was not, though his descendants were). Wherever leadership depends on personal qualities – what Max Weber called "charismatic authority" – and not on office or title, there is no distinction between women and men.

Yokheved, Miriam, Shifra, Puah, Tzippora, and Bitya were leaders not because of any official position they held (in the case of Bitya she was a leader *despite* her official title as a princess of Egypt). They were leaders because they had courage and conscience. They refused to be intimidated by power or defeated by circumstance. They were the real heroes of the Exodus. Their courage is still a source of inspiration today.

Overcoming Setbacks

At first, Moses' mission seemed to be successful. He had feared that the people would not believe in him, but God had given him signs to perform, and his brother Aaron to speak on his behalf. Moses "performed the signs before the people, and they believed. And when they heard that the Lord was concerned about them and had seen their misery, they bowed down and worshipped" (Ex. 4:30–31).

But then things start to go wrong, and continue going wrong. Moses' first appearance before Pharaoh is disastrous. Pharaoh refuses to recognise God. He rejects Moses' request to let the people travel into the wilderness. He makes life worse for the Israelites. They must still make the same quota of bricks, but now they must also gather their own straw. The people turn against Moses and Aaron: "May the Lord look on you and judge you! You have made us obnoxious to Pharaoh and his officials and have put a sword in their hand to kill us" (Ex. 5:21).

Moses and Aaron return to Pharaoh to renew their request. They perform a sign – they turn a staff into a snake – but Pharaoh is unimpressed. His own magicians can do likewise. Next they bring the first of the plagues, but again Pharaoh is unmoved. He will not let the Israelites go. And so it goes, nine times. Moses does everything in his power and finds that nothing makes a difference. The Israelites are still slaves.

We sense the pressure Moses is under. After his first setback, at the end of *Parashat Shemot*, he turns to God and bitterly complains: "Why, Lord, why have You brought trouble on this people? Is this why You sent me? Ever since I went to Pharaoh to speak in Your name, he has brought trouble on this people, and You have not rescued Your people at all" (Ex. 5:22–23). In *Parashat Va'era*, even though God has reassured him that he will eventually succeed, he replies, "If the Israelites will not listen to me, why would Pharaoh listen to me, since I speak with faltering lips?" (Ex. 6:12).

There is an enduring message here. Leadership, even of the very highest order, is often marked by failure. The first Impressionists had to arrange their own exhibition because their work was rejected by the Paris salons. The first performance of Stravinsky's *The Rite of Spring* caused a riot, with the audience booing throughout. Van Gogh sold only one painting in his lifetime despite the fact that his brother Theo was an art dealer.

So it is with leaders. As we noted in our discussion of *Parashat Vayishlaḥ*, Lincoln and Churchill faced countless setbacks and were at times exceedingly unpopular. Gandhi failed in his dream of uniting Muslims and Hindus together in a single nation. Nelson Mandela spent twenty-seven years in prison, accused of treason and regarded as a violent agitator. Only in retrospect do heroes seem heroic; only in hindsight do the many setbacks they faced reveal themselves as stepping stones on the road to victory.

In our discussion of *Parashat Vayetzeh*, we saw that in every field – high or low, sacred or secular – leaders are tested not by their successes but by their failures. It can sometimes be easy to succeed. The conditions may be favourable. The economic, political, or personal climate is good. When there is an economic boom, most businesses flourish. In the first months after a general election, the successful leader carries the charisma of victory. In the first year, most marriages are happy. It takes no special skill to succeed in good times.

But then the climate changes. Eventually, it always does. That is when many businesses and politicians and marriages fail. There are times when even the greatest people stumble. At such moments, character is tested. The great human beings are not those who never fail. They are those who survive failure, who keep on going, who refuse to be defeated, who never give up or give in. They keep trying. They learn from every mistake. They treat failure as a learning experience. And from every refusal to be defeated, they become stronger, wiser, and more determined. That is the story of Moses' life in *Parashat Shemot* and *Parashat Va'era*.

Jim Collins, one of the great writers on leadership, puts it well:

> The signature of the truly great versus the merely successful is not the absence of difficulty, but the ability to come back from setbacks, even cataclysmic catastrophes, stronger than before.... The path out of darkness begins with those exasperatingly persistent individuals who are constitutionally incapable of capitulation. It's one thing to suffer a staggering defeat...and entirely another to give up on the values and aspirations that make the protracted struggle worthwhile. Failure is not so much a physical state as a state of mind; success is falling down, and getting up one more time, without end.[1]

Rabbi Yitzhak Hutner once wrote a powerful letter to a disciple who had become discouraged by his repeated failure to master Talmudic learning:

> A failing many of us suffer is that when we focus on the high attainments of great people, we discuss how they are complete in this or that area, while omitting mention of the inner struggles that had previously raged within them. A listener would get the impression that these individuals sprang from the hand of their creator in a state of perfection....
>
> The result of this feeling is that when an ambitious young man of spirit and enthusiasm meets obstacles, falls and slumps,

---

1. Jim Collins, *How the Mighty Fall: And Why Some Companies Never Give In* (New York: HarperCollins, 2009), 123.

69

he imagines himself as unworthy of being "planted in the house of God" (Ps. 92:13) ....

Know, however, my dear friend, that your soul is rooted not in the tranquillity of the good inclination, but in the battle of the good inclination .... The English expression, "Lose a battle and win the war," applies. Certainly you have stumbled and will stumble again, and in many battles you will fall lame. I promise you, though, that after those losing campaigns you will emerge from the war with laurels of victory on your head .... The wisest of men said, "A righteous man falls seven times, but rises again" (Prov. 24:16). Fools believe the intent of the verse is to teach us that the righteous man falls seven times and, despite this, he rises. But the knowledgeable are aware that the essence of the righteous man's rising again is *because of* his seven falls.[2]

Rabbi Hutner's point is that *greatness cannot be achieved without failure.* There are heights you cannot climb without first having fallen.

For many years, I kept on my desk a quote from Calvin Coolidge, sent by a friend who knew how easy it is to be discouraged. It said:

Nothing in this world can take the place of persistence. Talent will not; nothing is more common than unsuccessful men with talent. Genius will not; unrewarded genius is almost a proverb. Education will not; the world is full of educated derelicts. Persistence and determination alone are omnipotent.

I would only add, "And *siyata DiShmaya*, the help of Heaven." God never loses faith in us, even if we sometimes lose faith in ourselves.

The supreme role model is Moses who, despite all the setbacks chronicled in *Parashat Shemot* and *Parashat Va'era*, eventually became the man of whom it was said that he was "a hundred and twenty years old when he died, his eyes were undimmed and his natural energy unabated" (Deut. 34:7).

2. Rabbi Yitzhak Hutner, *Sefer Paḥad Yitzḥak: Iggerot UKetavim* (Gur Aryeh, 1981), no. 128, 217–18.

Defeats, delays, and disappointments hurt. They hurt even for Moses. So if there are times when we too feel discouraged and demoralised, it is important to remember that even the greatest people failed. What made them great is that they kept going. The road to success passes through many valleys of failure. There is no other way.

Bo

The Far Horizon

To gain insight into the unique leadership lesson of *Parashat Bo*, I often ask an audience to perform a thought experiment. Imagine you are the leader of a people that has suffered exile for more than two centuries, one that has been enslaved and oppressed. Now, after a series of miracles, it is about to go free. You assemble them and rise to address them. They are waiting expectantly for your words. This is a defining moment they will never forget. What will you speak about?

Most people answer: freedom. That was Abraham Lincoln's decision in the Gettysburg Address when he invoked the memory of "a new nation, conceived in liberty," and looked forward to "a new birth of freedom."[1] Some suggest that they would inspire the people by talking about the destination that lay ahead, the "land flowing with milk and honey." Yet others say they would warn the people of the dangers and challenges that they would encounter on what Nelson Mandela called "the long walk to freedom."[2]

---

1. Abraham Lincoln, "The Gettysburg Address" (Soldiers' National Cemetery in Gettysburg, Penn., Nov. 19, 1863).
2. Nelson Mandela, *Long Walk to Freedom: The Autobiography of Nelson Mandela* (Back Bay Books, 1995).

Any of these would have been the great speech of a great leader. Guided by God, Moses does none of these things. That is what made him a unique leader. If you examine the text in *Parashat Bo* you will see that three times he reverts to the same theme: children, education, and the distant future.

> And when your children ask you, "What do you mean by this rite?" you shall say, "It is the Passover sacrifice to the Lord, because He passed over the houses of the Israelites in Egypt when He smote the Egyptians, but saved our houses." (Ex. 12:26–27)

> And you shall explain to your child on that day, "It is because of what the Lord did for me when I went free from Egypt." (Ex. 13:8)

> And when, in time to come, your child asks you, saying, "What does this mean?" you shall say to him, "It was with a mighty hand that the Lord brought us out from Egypt, the house of bondage." (Ex. 13:14)

It is one of the most counterintuitive acts in the history of leadership. Moses does not speak about today or tomorrow. He speaks about the distant future and the duty of parents to educate their children. He even hints – and this is engrained in Jewish tradition – that we should encourage our children to ask questions, so that the handing on of the Jewish heritage would be not a matter of rote learning but of active dialogue between parents and children.

So Jews became the only people in history to predicate their very survival on education. The most sacred duty of parents was to teach their children. Passover itself became an ongoing seminar in the handing on of memory. Judaism became the religion whose heroes were teachers and whose passion was study and the life of the mind. The Mesopotamians built ziggurats. The Egyptians built pyramids. The Greeks built the Parthenon. The Romans built the Coliseum. Jews built schools. That is why they alone, of all the civilisations of the ancient world, are still alive and strong, still continuing their ancestors' vocation, their heritage intact and undiminished.

Moses' insight was profound. He knew that you cannot change the world by externalities alone – by monumental architecture, or armies and empires, or the use of force and power. How many empires have come and gone while the human condition remains untransformed and unredeemed?

There is only one way to change the world, and that is through education. Children must be taught the importance of justice, righteousness, kindness, and compassion. They must learn that freedom can only be sustained by the laws and habits of self-restraint. They must be continually reminded of the lessons of history, "We were slaves to Pharaoh in Egypt," because those who forget the bitterness of slavery eventually lose the commitment and courage to fight for freedom. And they must be empowered to ask, challenge, and argue. Children must be respected if they are to respect the values we wish them to embrace.

This is a lesson most cultures still have not learned after more than three thousand years. Revolutions, protests, and civil wars still take place, encouraging people to think that removing a tyrant or having a democratic election will end corruption, create freedom, and lead to justice and the rule of law – and still people are surprised and disappointed when it does not happen. All that happens is a change of faces in the corridors of power.

In one of the great speeches of the twentieth century, a distinguished American justice, Judge Learned Hand, said:

> I often wonder whether we do not rest our hopes too much upon constitutions, upon laws and upon courts. These are false hopes; believe me, these are false hopes. Liberty lies in the hearts of men and women; when it dies there, no constitution, no law, no court can save it; no constitution, no law, no court can even do much to help it.[3]

What God taught Moses was that the real challenge does not lie in gaining freedom; it lies in sustaining it, keeping the spirit of liberty

---

3. Learned Hand, "The Spirit of Liberty," "'I Am an American' Day" ceremony (Central Park, New York City, May 21, 1944).

alive in the hearts of successive generations. That can only be done through a sustained process of education. Nor is this something that can be delegated to teachers and schools. Some of it has to take place within the family, at home, and with the sacred obligation that comes from religious duty. No one ever saw this more clearly than Moses, and only because of his teachings have Jews and Judaism survived.

What makes leaders great is that they think ahead, worrying not about tomorrow but about the next year, or the next decade, or the next generation. In one of his finest speeches, Robert F. Kennedy spoke of the power of leaders to transform the world when they have a clear vision of a possible future:

> Some believe there is nothing one man or one woman can do against the enormous array of the world's ills – against misery, against ignorance, or injustice and violence. Yet many of the world's great movements, of thought and action, have flowed from the work of a single man. A young monk began the Protestant reformation, a young general extended an empire from Macedonia to the borders of the earth, and a young woman reclaimed the territory of France. It was a young Italian explorer who discovered the New World, and the thirty-two-year-old Thomas Jefferson who proclaimed that all men are created equal. "Give me a place to stand," said Archimedes, "and I will move the world." These men moved the world, and so can we all.[4]

Visionary leadership forms the text and texture of Judaism. It was the book of Proverbs that said, "Without a vision [*ḥazon*] the people perish" (29:18). That vision, in the minds of the prophets, was always of a long-term future. God told Ezekiel that a prophet is a watchman, one who climbs to a high vantage point and so can see the danger in the distance, before anyone at ground level is aware of it (Ezek. 33:1–6). The sages said, "Who is wise? One who sees the long-term consequences [*hanolad*]" (Tamid 32a). Two of the greatest leaders of the twentieth

---

4. The Poynter Institute, *The Kennedys: America's Front Page Family* (Kansas City, Mo.: Andrews McMeel, 2010), 112.

century, Churchill and Ben-Gurion, were also distinguished historians. Knowing the past, they could anticipate the future. They were like chess masters who, because they have studied thousands of games, recognise almost immediately the dangers and possibilities in any configuration of the pieces on the board. They know what will happen if you make this move or that.

If you want to be a great leader in any field, from prime minister to parent, it is essential to think long-term. Never choose the easy option because it is simple or fast or yields immediate satisfaction. You will pay a high price in the end.

Moses was the greatest leader because he thought further ahead than anyone else. He knew that real change in human behaviour is the work of many generations. Therefore we must place as our highest priority educating our children in our ideals so that what we begin they will continue until the world changes because we have changed. He knew: If you plan for a year, plant rice. If you plan for a decade, plant a tree. If you plan for posterity, educate a child.[5] Moses' lesson, thirty-three centuries old, is still compelling today.

5.   A statement attributed to Confucius.

Beshallaḥ

Looking Up

The Israelites had crossed the Red Sea. The impossible had happened. The mightiest army in the ancient world – the Egyptians with their horse-drawn chariots – had been defeated and drowned. The people were now free. But the relief proved short-lived. Almost immediately the Israelites faced attack by the Amalekites, and they had to fight a battle, this time with no apparent miracles from God. They did so and won. This was a decisive turning point in history, not only for the Israelites but for Moses and his leadership of the people.

The contrast between before and after the Red Sea could not be more complete. Before, facing the approaching Egyptians, Moses said to the people: "Stand still and you will see the deliverance the Lord will bring you today.... The Lord will fight for you; you need only be silent" (Ex. 14:13). In other words: do nothing. God will do it for you. And He did.

In the case of the Amalekites, however, Moses said to Joshua, "Choose men for us, and prepare for battle against Amalek" (Ex. 17:9). Joshua did so and the people waged war. This was the great transition: the Israelites moved from a situation in which the leader (with the help of God) did everything for the people, to one in which the leader empowered the people to do it for themselves.

As this happens, the Torah focuses our attention on one detail. As the battle begins Moses climbs to the top of a hill overlooking the battlefield, with a staff in his hand:

> As long as Moses held his hands up, the Israelites prevailed, but when he let his hands down, the Amalekites prevailed. When Moses' hands became weary, they took a stone and placed it under him, so that he would be able to sit on it. Aaron and Hur then held his hands, one on each side, and his hands remained steady until sunset. (Ex. 17:11–12)

What is going on here? The passage could be read in two ways. The staff in Moses' hand – with which he had performed miracles in Egypt and at the sea – might be a sign that the Israelites' victory was a miraculous one. Alternatively, it might simply be a reminder to the Israelites that God was with them, giving them strength.

Very unusually – since the Mishna in general is a book of law rather than biblical commentary – a mishna resolves the question: "Did the hands of Moses make or break [the course of the] war? Rather, the text implies that whenever the Israelites looked up and dedicated their hearts to their Father in heaven, they prevailed, but otherwise they fell" (Mishna Rosh HaShana 3:8). The mishna is clear. Neither the staff nor Moses' upraised hands were performing a miracle. They were simply reminding the Israelites to look up to heaven and remember that God was with them. This gave them the confidence and courage to win.

A fundamental principle of leadership is being taught here. A leader must empower the team. He cannot do the work for them; they must do it for themselves. But he must, at the same time, give them the absolute confidence that they can do it and succeed. The leader is responsible for their mood and morale. During the battle, he must betray no sign of weakness, doubt, or fear. That is not always easy. Moses' hands "became weary." All leaders have their moments of exhaustion. At such times the leader needs support – even Moses needed the help of Aaron and Hur. In the end, though, his upraised hands were the sign the Israelites needed that God was giving them the strength to prevail, and they did.

In today's terminology, a leader needs emotional intelligence. Daniel Goleman, best known for his work in this field, argues that one of the most important tasks of a leader is to shape and lift the mood of the team: "Great leaders move us. They ignite our passion and inspire the best in us. When we try to explain why they are so effective, we speak of strategy, vision, or powerful ideas. But the reality is much more primal: great leadership works through the emotions."[1]

Groups have an emotional temperature. As individuals they can be happy or sad, agitated or calm, fearful or confident. But when they come together as a group, a process of attunement – "emotional contagion" – takes place, and they begin to share the same feeling. Scientists have shown experimentally how, within fifteen minutes of starting a conversation, two people begin to converge in the physiological markers of mood, such as pulse rate. "When three strangers sit facing each other in silence for a minute or two, the one who is most emotionally expressive transmits his or her mood to the other two – without speaking a single word."[2] The physiological basis of this process, known as *mirroring*, has been much studied in recent years, and observed even among primates. It is the basis of empathy, through which we enter into and share other people's feelings.

This is the foundation of one of the most important roles of a leader. It is he or she who, more than others, determines the mood of the group. Goleman reports on several scientific studies showing how leaders play a key role in determining the group's shared emotions:

> Leaders typically talked more than anyone else, and what they said was listened to more carefully.... But the impact on emotions goes beyond what a leader says. In these studies, even when leaders were not talking, they were watched more carefully than anyone else in the group. When people raised a question for the

1. Daniel Goleman, *Primal Leadership* (Boston: Harvard Business Review Press, 2002), 3.
2. Ibid., 7.

group as a whole, they would keep their eyes on the leader to see his or her response. Indeed, group members generally see the leader's emotional reaction as the most valid response, and so model their own on it – particularly in an ambiguous situation, where various members react differently. In a sense, the leader sets the emotional standard.[3]

When it comes to leadership, even non-verbal cues are important. Leaders, at least in public, must project confidence even if inwardly they are full of doubts and hesitations. If they betray their private fears in word or gesture, they risk demoralising the group.

There is no more powerful example of this than the episode in which King David's son Absalom mounts a coup d'etat against his father, proclaiming himself king in his place. David's troops put down the rebellion, in the course of which Absalom dies, caught by his hair in a tree and stabbed to death by Joab, David's commander-in-chief.

When he hears the news, David is heartbroken. His son may have rebelled against him, but he is still his son. Devastated by his death, he covers his face and cries, "O my son Absalom! O Absalom, my son, my son!" (II Sam. 18:33). News of David's grief quickly spreads throughout the army, and they too – by emotional contagion – are overcome by mourning. Joab regards this as disastrous. The army has taken great risks to fight for David against his son. They cannot now start regretting their victory without creating confusion and fatefully undermining their morale:

> Then Joab went into the house to the king and said, "Today you have humiliated all your men, who have just saved your life and the lives of your sons and daughters and the lives of your wives and concubines. You love those who hate you and hate those who love you. You have made it clear today that the commanders and their men mean nothing to you. I see that you would be pleased if Absalom were alive today and all of us were dead. Now go out and encourage your men. I swear by the Lord that if you do not go out, not a man will be left with you by nightfall. This will be

---

3.   Ibid., 8.

worse for you than all the calamities that have come on you from your youth till now." (11 Sam. 19:6–8)

David does as Joab insists. He accepts that there is a time and place for grief, but not now, not here, and above all, not in public. Now is the time to thank the army for its courage in defence of the king.

Leaders must sometimes silence their private emotions if they are not to demoralise those they lead. In the case of the battle against Amalek, the first battle the Israelites had to fight for themselves, Moses had a vital role to perform. He had to give the people confidence by getting them to look up.

In 1875 an amateur archaeologist, Marcelino de Sautuola, began excavating the ground in a cave in Altamira near the north coast of Spain. At first he found little to interest him, but his curiosity was rekindled by a visit to the Paris exhibition of 1878 where a collection of Ice Age implements and art objects was on display. Determined to see whether he could find equally ancient relics, he returned to the cave in 1879.

One day he took his nine-year-old daughter Maria with him. While he was searching through the rubble, she wandered deeper into the cave and to her amazement saw something on the wall above her. "Look, papa, oxen," she said. They were, in fact, bison. She had made one of the great discoveries of prehistoric art of all time. The magnificent Altamira cave paintings, between twenty-five thousand and thirty-five thousand years old, were so unprecedented a finding that it took twenty-two years for their authenticity to be accepted. For four years Sautuola had been within a few feet of a monumental treasure, but he had missed it for one reason. He had forgotten to look up.

One of the ongoing themes of Tanakh is the need to look up. "Lift up your eyes on high, and see who has created these things," says Isaiah (40:26). "I lift up my eyes to the hills. From where will my help come," says King David (Ps. 121:1). In Deuteronomy, Moses tells the Israelites that the Promised Land will not be like the flat plain of the Nile Delta where water is plentiful and in regular supply. It will be a land of hills and valleys, entirely dependent on unpredictable rain (11:10–11). It will be a landscape that forces its inhabitants to look up. That is what Moses did for the people in their first battle. He taught them to look up.

No political, social, or moral achievement is without formidable obstacles. There are vested interests to be confronted, attitudes to be changed, resistances to be overcome. The problems are immediate, the ultimate goal often frustratingly far away. Every collective undertaking is like leading a nation across the wilderness towards a destination that is always more distant than it seems when you look at the map.

Look down at the difficulties and you can give way to despair. The only way to sustain energies, individual or collective, is to turn our gaze up towards the far horizon of hope. The philosopher Ludwig Wittgenstein once said that his aim in philosophy was "to show the fly the way out of the fly-bottle."[4] The fly is trapped in the bottle. It searches for a way out. Repeatedly it bangs its head against the glass until at last, exhausted, it dies. Yet the bottle has been open all the time. The one thing the fly forgets to do is to look up. So, sometimes, do we.

It is the task of a leader to empower, but it is also his or her task to inspire. That is what Moses did when, at the top of a hill, in full sight of the people, he raised his hands and his staff to heaven. When they saw this, the people knew they could prevail. "Not by might nor by power, but by My spirit," said the prophet (Zech. 4:6). Jewish history is a sustained set of variations on this theme. A small people that, in the face of difficulty, continues to look up will win great victories and achieve great things.

4. Ludwig Wittgenstein, *Philosophical Investigations*, trans. G. E. M. Anscombe (Blackwell Publishers, 2001), 309.

Yitro

A Nation of Leaders

P*arashat Yitro* consists of two episodes that seem to constitute a study in contrasts. The first is in chapter 18. Yitro, Moses' father-in-law and a Midianite priest, gives Moses his first lesson in leadership. In the second, the prime mover is God Himself who, at Mount Sinai, makes a covenant with the Israelites in an unprecedented and unrepeated epiphany. For the first and only time in history God appears to an entire people, making a covenant with them and giving them the world's most famous brief code of ethics, the Ten Commandments.

What can there be in common between the practical advice of a Midianite and the timeless words of Revelation itself? There is an intended contrast and it is an important one. The forms and structures of governance are not specifically Jewish. They are part of *ḥokhma*, the universal wisdom of humankind. Jews have known many forms of leadership: by prophets, elders, judges, and kings; by the *nasi* in Israel under Roman rule and the *resh galuta* in Babylon; by town councils (*shiva tuvei ha'ir*) and various forms of oligarchy; and by other structures up to and including the democratically elected Knesset. *The forms of government are not eternal truths, nor are they exclusive to Israel.* In fact, the Torah says about monarchy that a time will come when the people say, "Let us set a king over us *like all the nations around us*" – the only case in the entire Torah in which Israel is commanded (or permitted) to imitate other nations. There is nothing specifically Jewish about political structures.

What is specifically Jewish is the principle of the covenant at Sinai, that Israel is the only nation whose sole ultimate king and legislator is God Himself. "He has revealed His word to Jacob, His laws and decrees to Israel. He has done this for no other nation; they do not know His laws, Hallelujah" (Ps. 147:19–20). What the covenant at Sinai established for the first time was *the moral limits of power*. All human authority is delegated authority, subject to the overarching moral imperatives of the Torah itself. This side of heaven, there is no absolute power. That is what has always set Judaism apart from the empires of the ancient world and the secular nationalisms of the West. So Israel can learn practical politics from a Midianite but it must learn the limits of politics from God Himself.

Despite the contrast, however, there is one theme in common to Yitro and the Revelation at Sinai, namely the *delegation, distribution, and democratisation* of leadership. Only God can rule alone.

The theme is introduced by Yitro. He arrives to visit his son-in-law and finds him leading alone. He says, "What you are doing is not good" (Ex. 18:17). This is one of only two instances in the whole Torah in which the words *lo tov*, "not good," appear. The other is in Genesis (2:18), where God says, "It is not good [*lo tov*] for man to be alone." We cannot lead alone. We cannot live alone. To be alone is not good.

Yitro proposes delegation:

> You must be the people's representative before God and bring their disputes to Him. Teach them His decrees and instructions, and show them the way they are to live and how they are to behave. But select capable men from all the people – men who fear God, trustworthy men who hate dishonest gain – and appoint them as officials over thousands, hundreds, fifties, and tens. Have them serve as judges for the people at all times, but have them bring every difficult case to you; the simple cases they

can decide themselves. That will make your load lighter, because they will share it with you. (Ex. 18:19–22)

This is a significant devolution. It means that among every thousand Israelites, there are 131 leaders (one head of one thousand, ten heads of one hundred, twenty heads of fifty, and one hundred heads of ten). One in every eight adult male Israelites was expected to undertake some form of leadership role.

In the next chapter, prior to the Revelation at Mount Sinai, God commands Moses to propose a covenant with the Israelites. In the course of this, God articulates what is in effect the mission statement of the Jewish people:

> You yourselves have seen what I did to Egypt, and how I carried you on eagles' wings and brought you to Myself. Now if you obey Me fully and keep My covenant, then out of all nations you will be My treasured possession. Although the whole earth is Mine, you will be for Me a kingdom of priests and a holy nation. (Ex. 19:4–6)

This is a very striking statement. Every nation had its priests. In the book of Genesis, we encounter Melchizedek, Abraham's contemporary, described as "a priest of the most high God" (Gen. 14:18). The story of Joseph mentions the Egyptian priests, whose land was not nationalised during the famine (47:22). Yitro was a Midianite priest. In the ancient world there was nothing distinctive about priesthood. Every nation had its priests and holy men. What was distinctive about Israel was that *every one of its members was to be a priest; each of its citizens was called on to be holy.*

I vividly recall standing with Rabbi Adin Steinsaltz in the General Assembly of the United Nations in August 2000 at a unique gathering of two thousand religious leaders representing all the major faiths in the world. I pointed out that even in that distinguished company we were different. We were almost the only religious leaders wearing suits. All the others wore robes of office. It is an almost universal phenomenon that priests and holy people wear distinctive garments to indicate that they are set apart (the core meaning of the word *kadosh*, "holy"). In post-biblical Judaism there were no robes of office because everyone was expected to be holy.[1] (Theophrastus, a pupil of Aristotle, called Jews "a nation of philosophers," reflecting the same idea.[2])

Yet in what sense were Jews ever "a kingdom of priests" (Ex. 19:6)? The priests were an elite within the nation, members of the tribe of Levi, descendants of Aaron, the first high priest. There never was a full democratisation of *keter kehuna*, the crown of priesthood.

Faced with this problem, the commentators offer two solutions. The word *kohanim*, "priests," may mean "princes" or "leaders" (Rashi, Rashbam). Or it may mean "servants" (Ibn Ezra, Ramban). But this is precisely the point. The Israelites were called on to be *a nation of servant-leaders*. They were the people called on, by virtue of the covenant, to accept responsibility not only for themselves and their families, but for the moral-spiritual state of the nation as a whole. This is the principle that later became known as *kol Yisrael arevim zeh bazeh*, "All Israelites are responsible for one another" (Shevuot 39a). Jews were the people who did not leave leadership to a single individual, however holy or exalted, or to an elite. Instead, every one of them was expected to be both a prince and a servant; that is to say, every one of them was called on to be a leader. Never was leadership more profoundly democratised.

That is what made Jews historically hard to lead. As Chaim Weizmann, first president of Israel, famously said, "I head a nation of a million presidents." The Lord may be our shepherd, but no Jew was ever a sheep. At the same time, it is what led Jews to have an impact on the world out of all proportion to their numbers. Jews constitute only the tiniest fragment – one fifth of one per cent – of the population of the world, but an extraordinarily high percentage of leaders in any given field of human endeavour.

To be a Jew is to be called on to lead.[3]

---

1. This idea reappeared in Protestant Christianity in the phrase "the priesthood of all believers," during the age of the Puritans, the Christians who took most seriously the principles of what they called the Old Testament.
2. See Josephus, *Against Apion* 1:22.
3. On the role of the follower in Judaism, see the chapter on *Parashat Kedoshim* in this volume.

Mishpatim

Vision and Detail

This *parasha* takes us through a bewildering transition. Until now in the book of Exodus we have been carried along by the sweep and drama of the narrative: the Israelites' enslavement, their hope for freedom, the plagues, Pharaoh's obstinacy, the escape into the desert, the crossing of the Red Sea, the journey to Mount Sinai, and the great covenant with God.

Suddenly, now we find ourselves faced with a different kind of literature altogether: a law code covering a bewildering variety of topics, from responsibility for damages to protection of property, to laws of justice, to Shabbat and the festivals. Why here? Why not continue the story, leading up to the next great drama, the sin of the Golden Calf? Why interrupt the flow? And what does this have to do with leadership?

The answer is this: Great leaders, be they CEOs or simply parents, have the ability to connect a large vision with highly specific details. Without the vision, the details are merely tiresome. There is a well-known story of three men who are employed cutting blocks of stone. When asked what they are doing, one says, "Cutting stone"; the second says, "Earning a living"; and the third says, "Building a palace." Those who have the larger picture take more pride in their labour, and work harder and better. Great leaders communicate a vision.

But they are also painstaking, even perfectionists, when it comes to the details. Edison famously said, "Genius is 1 per cent inspiration and 99 per cent perspiration." It is attention to detail that separates the great artists, poets, composers, filmmakers, politicians, and heads of corporations from the merely average. Anyone who has read Walter Isaacson's biography of the late Steve Jobs knows that he had an attention to detail bordering on the obsessive. He insisted, for example, that all Apple stores should have glass staircases. When he was told that there was no glass strong enough, he insisted that it be invented, which it was (he held the patent).

The genius of the Torah was to apply this principle to society as a whole. The Israelites had come through a transformative series of events. Moses knew there had been nothing like it before. He also knew, from God, that none of it was accidental or incidental. The Israelites had experienced slavery to make them cherish freedom. They had suffered so that they would know what it feels like to be on the wrong side of tyrannical power. At Sinai, God, through Moses, had given them a mission statement: to become "a kingdom of priests and a holy nation" (Ex. 19:6), under the sovereignty of God alone. They were to create a society built on principles of justice, human dignity, and respect for life.

But neither historical events nor abstract ideals – not even the broad principles of the Ten Commandments – are sufficient to sustain a society in the long run. Hence the remarkable project of the Torah: to translate historical experience into detailed legislation, so that the Israelites would live what they had learned on a daily basis, weaving it into the very texture of their social life. In *Parashat Mishpatim*, vision becomes detail, and narrative becomes law.

So, for example: "If you buy a Hebrew servant, he is to serve you for six years. But in the seventh year, he shall go free, without paying anything" (Ex. 21:2–3). At a stroke, in this law, slavery is transformed from a condition of birth to a temporary circumstance – from who you are to what, for the time being, you do. Slavery, the bitter experience of the Israelites in Egypt, could not be abolished overnight. It was not abolished in the United States until the 1860s, and even then, not without a devastating civil war. But this opening law of *Parashat Mishpatim* is the start of that long journey.

Likewise, the *parasha* contains the law that "Anyone who beats their male or female slave with a rod must be punished if the slave dies as a direct result" (Ex. 21:20). A slave is not mere property. He has a right to life. Similarly, the law of Shabbat states: "Six days do your work, but on the seventh day do not work, so that your ox and your donkey may rest, and so that the slave born in your household and the foreigner living among you may be refreshed" (23:12). One day in seven, slaves were to breathe the air of freedom. All three laws prepared the way for the abolition of slavery, even though it would take more than three thousand years to reach that point.

There are two laws that have to do with the Israelites' experience of being an oppressed minority: "Do not mistreat or oppress a stranger, for you were strangers in Egypt" (Ex. 22:21) and "Do not oppress a stranger; you yourselves know how it feels to be foreigners, because you were foreigners in Egypt" (23:9). And there are laws that evoke other aspects of the people's experience in Egypt, such as, "Do not take advantage of the widow or the fatherless. If you do and they cry out to Me, I will certainly hear their cry" (22:21–22). This recalls the episode at the beginning of the Exodus, "The Israelites groaned in their slavery and cried out, and their cry for help because of their slavery went up to God. God heard their groaning and He remembered His covenant with Abraham, with Isaac, and with Jacob. So God looked on the Israelites and was concerned about them" (2:23–25).

In a famous article written in the 1980s, Yale law professor Robert Cover writes about "Nomos and Narrative."[1] Beneath the laws of any given society is a *nomos*, he asserts, a vision of an ideal social order that the law is intended to create. And behind every *nomos* is a narrative, that is, a story about why the shapers and visionaries of that society or group came to have that specific vision of the ideal order they sought to build. Cover's examples are largely taken from the Torah, and the truth is that

---

1. Robert Cover, "Nomos and Narrative," Foreword to the Supreme Court 1982 Term, Yale Faculty Scholarship Series, Paper 2705, 1983. The paper can be found at http:// digitalcommons.law.yale.edu/fss_papers/2705.

his analysis sounds less like a description of law as such than a description of that unique phenomenon we know as Torah.

The word "Torah" is untranslatable because it means several different things that only appear together in the book that bears that name. Torah means "law." But it also means "teaching," "instruction," "guidance," or more generally, "direction." It is also the generic name for the five books, from Genesis to Deuteronomy, that comprise both narrative and law.

In general, law and narrative are two distinct literary genres that have very little overlap. Most books of law do not contain narratives, and most narratives do not contain law. Besides which, as Cover himself notes, even if people in Britain or America today know the history behind a given law, there is no canonical text that brings the two together. In any case, in most societies there are many different ways of telling the story. Moreover, most laws are enacted without a statement of why they came to be, what they were intended to achieve, and what historical experience led to their enactment.

So the Torah is a unique combination of *nomos* and narrative, history and law, the formative experiences of a nation and the way that nation sought to live its collective life so as never to forget the lessons it learned along the way. It brings together vision and detail in a way that has never been surpassed.

That is how we must lead if we want people to come with us, giving of their best. There must be a vision to inspire us, telling us why we should do what we are asked to do. There must be a narrative: this is what happened, this is who we are, and this is why the vision is so important to us. Then there must be the law, the code, the fastidious attention to detail, that allow us to translate vision into reality and turn the pain of the past into the blessings of the future. That extraordinary combination, to be found in almost no other law code, is what gives Torah its enduring power. It is a model for all who seek to lead people to greatness.

Teruma

The Home We
Build Together

T he sequence of *parashot* – *Teruma, Tetzaveh, Ki Tissa, Vayak'hel,* and *Pekudei* – is puzzling in many ways. First, it outlines the construction of the Tabernacle, the portable house of worship the Israelites built and carried with them through the desert, in exhaustive and exhausting detail. The narrative takes almost the whole of the last third of the book of Exodus. Why so long? Why such detail? The Tabernacle was, after all, only a temporary home for the Divine Presence, eventually superseded by the Temple in Jerusalem.

Besides which, why is the making of the *Mishkan* in the book of Exodus at all? Its natural place seems to be in the book of Leviticus, which is overwhelmingly devoted to an account of the service of the *Mishkan* and the sacrifices that were offered there. The book of Exodus, by contrast, could be subtitled, "the birth of a nation." It is about the transition of the Israelites from a family to a people and their journey from slavery to freedom. It rises to a climax with the covenant made between God and the people at Mount Sinai. What has the Tabernacle to do with this? It seems an odd way to end the book.

The answer, it seems to me, is profound. First, recall the history of the Israelites until now. It has been a long series of complaints. They complained when Moses' first intervention made their situation worse. Then, at the Red Sea, they said to Moses,

> Was it because there were no graves in Egypt that you brought us to the desert to die? What have you done to us by bringing us out of Egypt? Did we not say to you in Egypt, "Leave us alone; let us serve the Egyptians"? It would have been better for us to serve the Egyptians than to die in the desert!" (Ex. 14:11–12)

After crossing the sea they continued to complain, first about the lack of water, then that the water was bitter, then regarding the lack of food, then about the lack of water again. Then, within weeks of the Revelation at Sinai – the only time in history God appeared to an entire nation – they made a Golden Calf. If an unprecedented sequence of miracles cannot bring about a mature response on the part of the people, what will?

It was then that God said: *Let them build something together.* This simple command transformed the Israelites. During the whole construction of the Tabernacle there were no complaints. The people contributed – some gold or silver or bronze, some brought skins and drapes, others gave their time and skill. They gave so much that Moses had to order them to stop. A remarkable proposition is being framed: *It is not what God does for us that transforms us. It is what we do for God.*

So long as every crisis was dealt with by Moses and miracles, the Israelites remained in a state of dependency. Their default response was complaint. For them to grow to adulthood and responsibility they had to undergo a transition from passive recipients of God's blessings to active creators. The people had to become God's "partners in the work of creation" (Shabbat 10a). That, I believe, is what the sages meant when they said, "Call them not 'your children' but 'your builders'" (Berakhot 64a). People have to become builders if they are to grow from childhood to adulthood.

Judaism is God's call to responsibility. He does not want us to rely on miracles. He does not want us to be dependent on others. He wants us to become His partners, recognising that what we have, we have from Him, but what we make of what we have is up to us, our choices and our effort. This is not an easy balance to achieve. It is easy to live a life of dependency. It is equally easy in the opposite direction to slip into the mistake of saying, "My power and the strength of my hands have produced this wealth for me" (Deut. 8:17). The Jewish view of the human condition is that everything we achieve is due to our own efforts, but equally and essentially the result of God's blessing.

The building of the Tabernacle was the first great project the Israelites undertook together. It involved their generosity and skill. It gave them the chance to give back to God a little of what He had given them. It conferred on them the dignity of labour and creative endeavour. It brought to closure their birth as a nation and it symbolised the challenge of the future. The society they were summoned to create in the land of Israel would be one in which everyone would play their part. It was to become – in the phrase I used as the title of one of my books – "the home we build together."[1]

From this we see that one of the greatest challenges of leadership is to give people the chance to give, to contribute, to participate. That requires self-restraint, *tzimtzum*, on the part of the leader, creating the space for others to lead. As the saying goes: "If the leader is good, the people say: 'The leader did it.' If the leader is great, they say: 'We did it ourselves.'"[2]

This brings us to the fundamental distinction in politics between state and society. The state represents what is *done for us* by the machinery of government, through the instrumentality of laws, courts, taxation, and public spending. Society is what we *do for one another* through communities, voluntary associations, charities, and welfare organisations. Judaism, I believe, has a marked preference for society rather than state, precisely because it recognises – and this is the central theme of the book of Exodus – that it is what we do for others, not what others do or

---

1. Jonathan Sacks, *The Home We Build Together: Recreating Society* (Bloomsbury Academic, 2009).
2. Attributed to Lao-Tzu.

what God does for us, that transforms us. The Jewish formula, I believe, is: small state, big society.

The person who had the deepest insight into the nature of democratic society was Alexis de Tocqueville. Visiting America in the 1830s, he saw that its strength lay in what he called the "art of association," the tendency of Americans to come together in communities and voluntary groups to help one another, rather than leave the task to a centralised government. Were it ever to be otherwise, were individuals to depend wholly on the state, then democratic freedom would be at risk.

In one of the most haunting passages of his masterwork, *Democracy in America*, he says that democracies are at risk of a completely new form of oppression for which there is no precedent in the past. It will happen, he says, when people exist solely in and for themselves, leaving the pursuit of the common good to the government. This is what life would be like:

> Above this race of men stands an immense and tutelary power, which takes upon itself alone to secure their gratifications and to watch over their fate. That power is absolute, minute, regular, provident, and mild. It would be like the authority of a parent if, like that authority, its object was to prepare men for manhood; but it seeks, on the contrary, to keep them in perpetual childhood: it is well content that the people should rejoice, provided they think of nothing but rejoicing. For their happiness such a government willingly labours, but it chooses to be the sole agent and the only arbiter of that happiness; it provides for their security, foresees and supplies their necessities, facilitates their pleasures, manages their principal concerns, directs their industry, regulates the descent of property, and subdivides their inheritances: what remains, but to spare them all the care of thinking and all the trouble of living?[3]

Tocqueville wrote these words in the 1830s, and there is a risk that this is what some European societies are becoming like today: all state,

---

3. Alexis De Tocqueville, *Democracy in America*, abridged and with an introduction by Thomas Bender (The Modern Library, 1981), 584.

no society; all government, little or no community.[4] Tocqueville was not a religious writer. He makes no reference to the Hebrew Bible. But the fear he has is precisely what the book of Exodus documents. When a central power – even when this is God Himself – does everything on behalf of the people, they remain in a state of arrested development. They complain instead of acting. They give way easily to despair. When the leader, in this case Moses, is missing, they do foolish things, none more so than making a Golden Calf.

There is only one solution: to make the people co-architects of their own destiny, to get them to build something together, to shape them into a team and show them that they are not helpless, that they are responsible and capable of collaborative action. Genesis begins with God creating the universe as a home for human beings. Exodus ends with human beings creating the *Mishkan* as a "home" for God.

Hence the basic principle of Judaism, that we are called on to become co-creators with God. And hence, too, the corollary: that leaders do not do the work on behalf of the people. They teach people how to do the work themselves. It is not what God does for us but what we do for God that allows us to reach dignity and responsibility.

---

4. This is not to imply that there is no role for governments, that all should be left to voluntary associations. Far from it. There are things – from the rule of law to the defence of the realm to the enforcement of ethical standards and the creation of an equitable distribution of the goods necessary for a dignified existence – that only governments can achieve. The issue is balance.

Tetzaveh

The Counterpoint of Leadership

One of the most important Jewish contributions to our understanding of leadership is its early insistence of what, in the eighteenth century, Montesquieu called "the separation of powers."[1] Neither authority nor power was to be located in a single individual or office. Instead, leadership was divided between different kinds of roles. One of the most important of these divisions – anticipating by millennia the "separation of church and state" – was between the king, the head of state, on the one hand, and the high priest, the most senior religious office, on the other.

This was revolutionary. The kings of Mesopotamian city-states and the pharaohs of Egypt were considered demigods or chief intermediaries with the gods. They officiated at supreme religious festivals. They were regarded as the representatives of heaven on earth. In Judaism, by stark contrast, monarchy had little or no religious function (other than

1.   Charles-Louis Montesquieu, *The Spirit of Laws* (Encyclopaedia Britannica, 1952).

the recital by the king of the book of the covenant every seven years in the ritual known as *hak'hel*). Indeed the chief objection to the Hasmonean kings on the part of the sages was that they broke this ancient rule, some of them declaring themselves high priests also. The Talmud records the objection: "Let the crown of kingship be sufficient for you. Leave the crown of priesthood to the sons of Aaron" (Kiddushin 66a). The effect of this principle was to *secularise power*.[2]

No less fundamental was the division of religious leadership itself into two distinct functions: that of the prophet and that of the priest. That is dramatised in *Parashat Tetzaveh*, focusing as it does on the role of the priest to the exclusion of that of the prophet. *Parashat Tetzaveh* is the first *parasha* since the beginning of the book of Exodus in which Moses' name is missing. It is supremely the priestly, as opposed to prophetic, *parasha*.

Priests and prophets were very different in their roles, despite the fact that some prophets, most famously Ezekiel, were priests also. The primary distinctions were:

1. The role of priest was dynastic, that of the prophet was charismatic. Priests were the sons of Aaron. They were born into the role. Parenthood had no part in the role of the prophet. Moses' own children were not prophets.

2. The priest wore robes of office. There was no official uniform for a prophet.

3. The priesthood was exclusively male; not so prophecy. As we noted earlier, the Talmud lists seven female prophets: Sarah, Miriam, Deborah, Hannah, Abigail, Huldah, and Esther (Megilla 14a).

4. The role of the priest did not change over time. There was a precise annual timetable of sacrifices that did not vary from year to year. The prophet, by contrast, could not know what his mission would be until God revealed it to him. Prophecy was never a matter of routine.

5. As a result, prophet and priest had different senses of time. Time for the priest was what it was for Plato: the "moving image of

---

2. In Judaism, power, except that exercised by God, is not holy.

eternity,"[3] a matter of everlasting recurrence and return. The prophet lived in historical time. His today was not the same as yesterday and tomorrow would be different again. One way of putting this is that the priest heard the word of God for *all* time. The prophet heard the word of God for *this* time.

6. The priest was "holy" and therefore set apart from the people. He had to eat his food in a state of purity and had to avoid contact with the dead. The prophet, by contrast, often lived among the people and spoke a language they understood. Prophets could come from any social class.

7. The keywords for the priest were *tahor, tamei, kodesh,* and *ḥol* – "pure," "impure," "sacred," and "secular." The keywords for the prophets were *tzedek, mishpat, ḥesed,* and *raḥamim* – "righteousness," "justice," "love," and "compassion." It is not that the prophets were concerned with morality while the priests were not. Some of the key moral imperatives, such as "You shall love your neighbour as yourself," come from priestly sections of the Torah. It is rather that priests thought in terms of a moral order embedded in the structure of reality, sometimes called a "sacred ontology."[4] Prophets tended to think not of things or acts in themselves but in terms of relationships between persons or social classes.

8. The task of the priest was *boundary maintenance.* The key priestly verbs were *lehavdil* and *lehorot,* to distinguish one thing from another and apply the appropriate rules. Priests gave rulings; prophets gave warnings.

9. There was nothing personal about the role of a priest. If one – even a high priest – was unable to officiate at a given service, another could be substituted. Prophecy was essentially personal. The sages said that "no two prophets prophesied in the same style"

---

3. Plato, *Timaeus* 37d.
4. On this rather difficult idea, see Philip Rieff, *My Life among the Deathworks* (Charlottesville, Va.: University of Virginia Press, 2006). Rieff was an unusual and insightful critic of modernity. For an introduction to his work, see Antonius A. W. Zondervan, *Sociology and the Sacred: An Introduction to Philip Rieff's Theory of Culture* (Toronto, Ontario: University of Toronto Press, 2005).

(Sanhedrin 89a). Hosea was not Amos. Isaiah was not Jeremiah. Each prophet had a distinctive voice.

10. Priests constituted a religious establishment. The prophets, at least those whose messages have been eternalised in Tanakh, were not an establishment but an anti-establishment, critical of the powers that be.

The roles of priest and prophet varied over time. The priests always officiated at the sacrificial service of the Temple. But they were also judges. The Torah says that if a case is too difficult to be dealt with by the local court, you should "Go to the priests, the Levites, and to the judge who is in office at that time. Inquire of them and they will give you the verdict" (Deut. 17:9). Moses blesses the tribe of Levi saying that "They will teach Your ordinances to Jacob and Your Torah to Israel" (33:10), suggesting that they had a teaching role as well.

Malachi, a prophet of the Second Temple period, says: "For the lips of a priest ought to preserve knowledge, because he is the messenger of the Lord Almighty and people seek instruction from his mouth" (Mal. 2:7). The priest was guardian of Israel's sacred social order. Yet it is clear throughout Tanakh that the priesthood was liable to corruption. There were times when priests took bribes, others when they compromised Israel's faith and performed idolatrous practices. Sometimes they became involved in politics. Some held themselves as an elite apart from and disdainful towards the people as a whole.

At such times the prophet became the voice of God and the conscience of society, reminding the people of their spiritual and moral vocation, calling on them to return and repent, reminding the people of their duties to God and to their fellow humans, and warning of the consequences if they did not heed the call.

The priesthood became massively politicised and corrupted during the Hellenistic era, especially under the Seleucids in the second century BCE. Hellenised high priests like Jason and Menelaus introduced idolatrous practices – even at one stage, a statue of Zeus – into the Temple. This provoked the internal revolt that led to the events we recall on the festival of Ḥanukka.

Yet despite the fact that the initiator of the revolt, Mattityahu, was himself a righteous priest, corruption re-emerged under the Hasmonean kings. The Qumran sect known to us through the Dead Sea Scrolls was particularly critical of the priesthood in Jerusalem. It is striking that the sages traced their spiritual ancestry to the prophets, not the priests (Mishna Avot 1:1). The priests were essential to ancient Israel. They gave the religious life its structure and continuity, its rituals and routines, its festivals and celebrations. Their task was to ensure that Israel remained a holy people with God in its midst. But they were an establishment, and like every establishment, at best they were the guardians of the nation's highest values, but at worst they became corrupt, using their position for power and engaging in internal politics for personal advantage. That is the fate of establishments, especially those whose membership is a matter of birth.

That is why the prophets were essential. They were the world's first social critics, mandated by God to speak truth to power. Still today, for good or otherwise, religious establishments always resemble Israel's priesthood. Who, though, are Israel's prophets at the present time?

The essential lesson of the Torah is that leadership can never be confined to one class or role. It must always be distributed and divided. In ancient Israel, kings dealt with power, priests with holiness, and prophets with the integrity and faithfulness of society as a whole. In Judaism, leadership is less a *function* than a *field of tensions* between different roles, each with its own perspective and voice.

Leadership in Judaism is *counterpoint*, a musical form defined as "the technique of combining two or more melodic lines in such a way that they establish a harmonic relationship while retaining their linear individuality."[5] It is this internal complexity that gives Jewish leadership its vigour, saving it from entropy, the loss of energy over time.

Leadership must always, I believe, be like this. Every team must be made up of people with different roles, strengths, temperaments, and perspectives. They must always be open to criticism and they must

5. *American Heritage Dictionary*, 5th ed., s.v. "Counterpoint" (Boston: Houghton Mifflin, 2011).

always be on the alert against groupthink. The glory of Judaism is its insistence that only in heaven is there one commanding voice. Down here on earth, no individual may ever hold a monopoly of leadership. Out of the clash of perspectives – king, priest, and prophet – comes something larger than any single role or individual could achieve.

Ki Tissa

How Leaders Fail

As we saw in *Parashat Vayetzeh* and *Parashat Va'era*, leadership is marked by failure; it is the recovery that is the true measure of the leader. Leaders can fail for two kinds of reason. The first is external. The time may not be right. The conditions may be unfavourable. There may be no one on the other side to talk to. Machiavelli called this *fortuna*: the power of bad luck that can defeat even the greatest individual. Sometimes despite your best efforts, you fail. Such is life.

The second kind of failure is internal. A leader can simply lack the courage to lead. Sometimes leaders have to oppose the crowd. They have to say no when everyone else is crying yes. That can be terrifying. Crowds have a will and momentum of their own. To say no may be to put your career, even your life, at risk. That is when courage is needed, and not showing it can constitute a moral failure of the worst kind.

The classic example is King Saul, who failed to carry out Samuel's instructions in his battle against the Amalekites. Saul was told to spare no one and nothing. This is what happened, as told in 1 Samuel 15:

> When Samuel reached him, Saul said, "The Lord bless you! I have carried out the Lord's instructions."

But Samuel said, "What then is this bleating of sheep in my ears? What is this lowing of cattle that I hear?"

Saul answered, "The soldiers brought them from the Amalekites; they spared the best of the sheep and cattle to sacrifice to the Lord your God, but we totally destroyed the rest."

"Enough!" Samuel said to Saul. "Let me tell you what the Lord said to me last night."

"Tell me," Saul replied.

Samuel said, *"Although you may be small in your own eyes, are you not head of the tribes of Israel?* The Lord anointed you king over Israel. And He sent you on a mission, saying, 'Go and completely destroy those wicked people, the Amalekites; wage war against them until you have wiped them out.' Why did you not obey the Lord? Why did you pounce on the plunder and do evil in the eyes of the Lord?"

"But I did obey the Lord," Saul said. "I went on the mission the Lord assigned me. I completely destroyed the Amalekites and brought back Agag their king. The soldiers took sheep and cattle from the plunder, the best of what was devoted to God, in order to sacrifice them to the Lord your God at Gilgal." (1 Sam. 15:13–21)

Saul makes excuses. The failure was not his; it was his soldiers'. Besides which, he and they had the best intentions. The sheep and cattle were spared to offer as sacrifices. Saul did not kill King Agag but brought him back as a prisoner. Samuel is unmoved. He says, "Because you have rejected the word of the Lord, He has rejected you as king" (1 Sam. 15:23). Only then does Saul admit, "I have sinned" (15:24). But by then it is too late. His career as a leader is at an end.

There is an apocryphal quote attributed to several politicians: "Of course I follow the party. After all, I am their leader."[1] There are leaders who follow instead of leading. Rabbi Yisrael Salanter compared them to a dog taken by its master for a walk. The dog runs on ahead, but keeps turning around to see whether it is going in the direction the master wants it to go. The dog may think it is leading but actually, it is following.

1.   The phrase has been attributed to Benjamin Disraeli and Stanley Baldwin.

That, on a plain reading of the text, was the fate of Aaron in *Parashat Ki Tissa*. Moses had been up the mountain for forty days. The people were afraid. Had he died? Where was he? Without Moses they felt bereft. He was their point of contact with God. He performed the miracles, divided the sea, gave them water to drink and food to eat. This is how the Torah describes what happened next:

> When the people saw that Moses was so long in coming down from the mountain, they gathered round Aaron and said, "Come, make us a god who will go before us. As for this man Moses who brought us up out of Egypt, we do not know what has happened to him." Aaron answered them, "Take off the gold earrings that your wives, your sons, and your daughters are wearing, and bring them to me." So all the people took off their earrings and brought them to Aaron. He took what they handed him and he fashioned it with a tool and made it into a molten calf. Then they said, "This is your god, Israel, who brought you up out of Egypt." (Ex. 32:1–4)

God becomes angry. Moses pleads with Him to spare the people. He then descends the mountain, sees what has happened, smashes the tablets of the law he brought down with him, burns the idol, grinds it to powder, mixes it with water, and makes the Israelites drink it. Then he turns to Aaron his brother and says, "What have you done?"

> "Do not be angry, my lord," Aaron answered. "You know how prone these people are to evil. They said to me, 'Make us a god who will go before us. As for this man Moses who brought us up out of Egypt, we do not know what has happened to him.' So I told them, 'Whoever has any gold jewellery, take it off.' Then they gave me the gold, and I threw it into the fire, and out came this calf!" (Ex. 32:22–24)

Aaron blames the people. It was they who made the illegitimate request. He denies responsibility for making the calf. It just happened. "I threw it into the fire, and out came this calf!" This is the same kind of denial of responsibility we recall from the story of Adam and Eve. The man says, "It was the woman." The woman says, "It was the serpent." It happened. It wasn't me. I was the victim, not the perpetrator. In anyone, such evasion is a moral failure; in a leader, all the more so.

The odd fact is that Aaron is not immediately punished. According to the Torah he was condemned for another sin altogether when, years later, he and Moses spoke angrily against the people complaining about the lack of water: "Aaron will be gathered to his people. He will not enter the land I give the Israelites, because both of you rebelled against My command at the waters of Meriba" (Num. 20:24).

It was only later still, in the last month of Moses' life, that Moses told the people a fact that he had kept from them until that point: "I feared the anger and wrath of the Lord, for He was angry enough with you to destroy you. But again the Lord listened to me. And the Lord was angry enough with Aaron to destroy him, but at that time I prayed for Aaron, too" (Deut. 9:19–20). God, according to Moses, was so angry with Aaron for the sin of the Golden Calf that He was about to kill him, and would have done so had it not been for Moses' prayer.

It is easy to be critical of people who fail the leadership test when it involves opposing the crowd, defying the consensus, blocking the path the majority is intent on taking. The truth is that it is hard to oppose the mob. They can ignore you, remove you, even assassinate you. When a crowd gets out of control there is no elegant solution. Even Moses was helpless in the face of the people during the later episode of the spies (Num. 14:5).

Nor is it easy for Moses to restore order now. He does so only by the most dramatic action: smashing the tablets and grinding the calf to dust. He then asks for support and is given it by his fellow Levites. They take reprisals against the crowd, killing three thousand people that day. History judges Moses a hero but he might well have been seen by his contemporaries as a brutal autocrat. We, thanks to the Torah, know what passed between God and Moses at the time. The Israelites at the foot of the mountain knew nothing of how close they had come to being utterly destroyed.

Tradition dealt kindly with Aaron. He is portrayed as a man of peace. Perhaps that is why he was made high priest. There is more than one kind of leadership, and priesthood involves following rules, not taking stands and swaying crowds. The fact that Aaron was not a leader from the same mould as Moses does not mean that he was a failure. It means that he was made for a different kind of role. There are times when you need someone with the courage to stand against the crowd, others when you need a peacemaker. Moses and Aaron were different types. Aaron failed when he was called on to be a Moses, but he became a great leader in his own right in a different capacity. Aaron and Moses complemented one another. No one person can do everything.

The truth is that when a crowd is out of control, there is no easy answer. That is why the whole of Judaism is an extended seminar in individual and collective responsibility. Jews do not, or should not, form crowds. When they do, it may take a Moses to restore order. But it may take an Aaron, at other times, to maintain the peace.

Vayak'hel

Team Building

How do you re-motivate a demoralised people? How do you put the pieces of a broken nation back together again? That is the challenge faced by Moses in *Parashat Vayak'hel*.

The key word here is *vayak'hel*, "and he gathered." *Kehilla* means community. A *kehilla* or *kahal* is a group of people assembled for a given purpose. That purpose can be positive or negative, constructive or destructive. The same word that appears at the beginning of this *parasha* as the beginning of the solution appeared in the previous *parasha* as the start of the problem: "When the people saw that Moses was so long in coming down from the mountain, they gathered (*vayikahel*) around Aaron and said, 'Come, make us a god who will go before us. As for this man Moses who brought us up out of Egypt, we do not know what has happened to him'" (Ex. 32:1).

The difference between the two kinds of *kehilla* is that one results in order, the other in chaos. Coming down the mountain to see the Golden Calf, we read that "Moses saw that the people were *running wild* and that Aaron had *let them get out of control* and so become a laughingstock to their enemies" (Ex. 32:25). The verb for "running wild" (P-R-A) means "loose," "unbridled," "unrestrained."

There is an assembly that is disciplined, task-oriented, and purposeful. And there is an assembly that is a mob. It has a will of its own. People in crowds lose their sense of self-restraint. They get carried along in a wave of emotion. Normal deliberative thought-processes become bypassed by the more primitive feelings of the group. There is, as neuroscientists put it, an "amygdala hijack." Passions run wild.

There have been famous studies of this: Charles Mackay's *Extraordinary Popular Delusions and the Madness of Crowds* (1841), Gustave Le Bon's *The Crowd: A Study of the Popular Mind* (1895), and Wilfred Trotter's *Instincts of the Herd in Peace and War* (1914). One of the most haunting works on the subject is Jewish Nobel prize-winner Elias Canetti's *Crowds and Power* (1960; English translation published in 1962).

Vayak'hel is Moses' response[1] to the wild abandon of the crowd that gathered around Aaron and made the Golden Calf. He does something fascinating. He does not oppose the people, as he did initially when he saw the Golden Calf. Instead, he uses the same motivation that drove them in the first place. They wanted to create something that would be a sign that God was among them – not on the heights of a mountain but in the midst of the camp. He appeals to the same sense of generosity that made them offer up their gold ornaments. The difference is that they are now acting in accordance with God's command, not their own spontaneous feelings.

He asks the Israelites to make voluntary contributions to the construction of the Tabernacle, the Sanctuary, the *Mishkan*. They do so with such generosity that Moses has to order them to stop. *If you want to bond human beings so that they act for the common good, get them to build something together.* Get them to undertake a task that they can only achieve together, that none can do alone.

---

1. I mean this only figuratively. The building of the Tabernacle was, of course, God's command, not Moses'. The fact that it is set out as a divine command before the story of the Golden Calf (in *Parashat Teruma*) is intended to illustrate the principle that "God creates the cure before the disease" (Megilla 13b).

The power of this principle was demonstrated in a famous social-scientific research exercise carried out in 1954 by Muzafer Sherif and others from the University of Oklahoma, known as the "Robbers Cave" experiment. Sherif wanted to understand the dynamics of group conflict and prejudice. To do so, he and his fellow researchers selected a group of twenty-two white, eleven-year-old boys, none of whom had met before. They were taken to a remote summer camp in Robbers Cave State Park, Oklahoma. They were randomly allocated into two groups.

Initially neither group knew of the existence of the other. They were staying in cabins far apart. The first week was dedicated to team building. The boys hiked and swam together. Each group chose a name for itself – they became the Eagles and the Rattlers. They stencilled the names on their shirts and flags.

Then, for four days, they were introduced to one another through a series of competitions. There were trophies, medals, and prizes for the winners and nothing for the losers. Almost immediately there was tension between them: name-calling, teasing, and derogatory songs. It got worse. Each burned the other's flag and raided their cabins. They objected to eating together with the others in the same dining hall.

Stage 3 was called the "integration phase." Meetings were arranged. The two groups watched films together. They lit Fourth-of-July fire-crackers together. The hope was that these face-to-face encounters would lessen tensions and lead to reconciliation. They did not. Several encounters broke up with the children throwing food at one another.

In stage 4, the researchers arranged situations in which a prob-lem arose that threatened both groups simultaneously. The first was a blockage in the supply of drinking water to the camp. The two groups identified the problem separately and gathered at the point where the blockage had occurred. They worked together to remove it, and cel-ebrated together when they succeeded.

In another, both groups voted to watch some films. The research-ers explained that the films would cost money to hire, and there was not enough in camp funds to do so. Both groups agreed to contribute an equal share to the cost. In a third, the coach on which they were travel-ling stalled, and the boys had to work together to push it. By the time the trials were over, the boys had stopped having negative images of the other side. On the final bus ride home, the members of one team used their prize money to buy drinks for everyone.

Similar outcomes have emerged from other studies. The conclusion is revolutionary. You can turn even hostile factions into a single cohesive group so long as they are faced with a shared challenge that all can overcome together but none can do alone.

Rabbi Norman Lamm, former president of Yeshiva University, once remarked that he knew of only one joke in the Mishna, the statement that "Scholars increase peace in the world" (Berakhot 64a). Rabbis are known for their disagreements. How then can they be said to increase peace in the world?

I suggest that the passage is not a joke but a precisely calibrated truth. To understand it we must read the continuation: "Scholars increase peace in the world, as it is said, 'All your children shall be learned of the Lord and great will be the peace of your children' (Is. 54:13). Read not 'your children' but 'your builders.'" When scholars become builders they create peace. If you seek to create a community out of strongly individualistic people, you have to turn them into builders. That is what Moses did in *Parashat Vayak'hel*.

Team building, even after a disaster like the Golden Calf, is neither a mystery nor a miracle. It is done by setting the group a task, one that speaks to their passions and one no subsection of the group can achieve alone. It must be constructive. Every member of the group must be able to make a unique contribution and then feel that it has been valued. Each must be able to say with pride: I helped make this.

That is what Moses understood and did. He knew: if you want to build a team, create a team that builds.

Pekudei

Celebrate

If leaders are to bring out the best in those they lead, they must give them the chance to show they are capable of great things, and *then they must celebrate their achievements.* That is what happens at a key moment towards the end of *Parashat Pekudei*, one that brings the book of Exodus to a sublime conclusion after all the strife that has gone before.

The Israelites have finally completed the work of building the Tabernacle. We then read:

> So all the *work* on the Tabernacle, the Tent of Meeting was *completed.* The Israelites did everything just as the Lord commanded Moses.... Moses inspected the *work* and saw that they had done it just as the Lord had commanded. So Moses *blessed* them. (Ex. 39:32, 43)

The passage sounds simple enough, but to the practised ear it recalls another biblical text from the end of the creation narrative in Genesis:

The heavens and the earth were *completed* in all their vast array. On the seventh day God finished the *work* He had been doing; so on the seventh day He rested from all His *work*. Then God *blessed* the seventh day and made it holy, because on it He rested from all the *work* of creating that He had done. (Gen. 2:1–3)

Three keywords appear in both passages: "work," "completed," and "blessed." These verbal echoes are not accidental. They are how the Torah signals intertextuality, hinting that one law or story is to be read in the context of another. In this case the Torah is emphasising that Exodus ends as Genesis began, with a work of creation. Note the difference as well as the similarity. Genesis began with an act of *divine* creation. Exodus ends with an act of *human* creation.

The closer we examine the two texts, the more we see how intricately the parallel has been constructed. The creation account in Genesis is tightly organised around a series of sevens. There are seven days of creation. The word "good" appears seven times, the word "God" thirty-five times, and the word "earth" twenty-one times. The opening verse of the Genesis passage contains seven words, the second contains fourteen, and the three concluding verses contain thirty-five words. The complete text is 469 (7 x 67) words.

The account of the construction of the Tabernacle in *parashot Vayak'hel* and *Pekudei* is similarly built around the number seven. The word "heart" appears seven times in Exodus 35:5–29, as Moses specifies the materials to be used in the construction, and seven times again in 35:34–36:8, the description of how the craftsmen Betzalel and Oholiav were to carry out the work. The word *teruma*, "contribution," appears seven times in this section. In chapter 39, which describes the making of the priestly vestments, the phrase "as God commanded Moses" occurs seven times. It occurs again seven times in chapter 40.

A remarkable parallel is being drawn between God's creation of the universe and the Israelites' creation of the Sanctuary. We now understand what the Sanctuary represented. It was a micro-cosmos, a universe in miniature, constructed with the same precision and wisdom as the universe itself, a place of order against the formlessness of the wilderness and the ever-threatening chaos of the human heart. The Sanctuary was a visible reminder of God's presence within the camp, itself a metaphor for God's presence within the universe as a whole.

A large and fateful idea is taking shape. The Israelites – who have been portrayed throughout much of Exodus as ungrateful and half-hearted – have now been given the opportunity, after the sin of the Golden Calf, to show that they are not irredeemable. They are capable of great things. They have shown they can be creative. They have used their generosity and skill to build a mini-universe. By this symbolic act they have shown they are capable of becoming, in the potent rabbinic phrase, "God's partners in the work of creation."

This was fundamental to their re-moralisation and to their self-image as the people of God's covenant. Judaism does not take a low view of human possibility. We do not believe we are tainted by original sin. We are not incapable of moral grandeur. To the contrary, the very fact that we are in the image of the Creator means that we – uniquely among life forms – have the ability to be creative. As Israel's first creative achievement reached its culmination, Moses blessed the Israelites, saying, according to the sages, "May it be God's will that His presence rests in the work of your hands."[1] Our potential greatness is that we can create structures, relationships, and lives that become homes for the Divine Presence.

Blessing them and celebrating their achievement, Moses showed them what they could be. That is potentially a life-changing experience. Here is a contemporary example: In 2001, shortly after 9/11, I received a letter from a woman in London whose name I did not immediately recognise. The morning of the attack on the World Trade Centre, I had been giving a lecture on ways to raise the status of the teaching profession, and she had seen a report about it in the press. This prompted her to write and remind me of a meeting we had had eight years earlier.

She was then, in 1993, head teacher of a school that was floundering. She had heard some of my broadcasts, felt a kinship with what I had to say, and thought that I might have the answer to her problem. I invited her, together with two of her deputies, to our house. The story she told me was this: morale within the school, among teachers, pupils,

---

1.   *Sifrei*, Numbers, *Pinḥas*, 143.

and parents alike, was at an all-time low. Parents had been withdrawing their children. The student roll had fallen from one thousand children to five hundred. Examination results were bad: only 8 per cent of students achieved high grades. It was clear that unless something changed dramatically, the school would have to close.

We talked for an hour or so on general themes: the school as a community, how to create an ethos, and so on. Suddenly, I realised that we were thinking along the wrong lines. The problem she faced was practical, not philosophical. I said: "I want you to live one word – *celebrate*." She turned to me with a sigh: "You don't understand – we have *nothing* to celebrate. Everything in the school is going wrong." "In that case," I replied, "*find* something to celebrate. If a single student has done better this week than last week, celebrate. If someone has a birthday, celebrate. If it's Tuesday, celebrate." She seemed unconvinced, but promised to give the idea a try.

Now, eight years later, she was writing to tell me what had happened since then. Examination results at high grades had risen from 8 to 65 per cent. The roll of pupils had risen from five hundred to one thousand. Saving the best news to last, she added that she had just been made a Dame of the British Empire – one of the highest honours the Queen can bestow – for her contribution to education. She ended by saying that she just wanted me to know how one word had changed the school and her life.

She was a wonderful teacher, and certainly did not need my advice. She would have discovered the answer on her own anyway. But I was never in any doubt that the strategy would succeed. We grow to fill other people's expectations of us. If they are low, we remain small. If they are high, we walk tall.

The idea that each of us has a fixed quantum of intelligence, virtue, academic ability, motivation, and drive is absurd. Not all of us can paint like Monet or compose like Mozart. But we each have gifts, capacities that can lie dormant throughout life until someone awakens them. We can achieve heights of which we never thought ourselves capable. All it takes is for us *to meet someone who believes in us, challenges us, and then, when we have responded to the challenge, blesses and celebrates our achievements.* That is what Moses did for the Israelites after the sin of the

Golden Calf. First he got them to create, and then he blessed them and their creation with one of the simplest and most moving of all blessings, that the *Shekhina* should dwell in the work of their hands.

Celebration is an essential part of motivating. It turned a school around. In an earlier age and in a more sacred context it turned the Israelites around. When we celebrate the achievements of others, we change lives.

Leviticus
ויקרא

Vayikra

The Sins of a Leader[1]

As we have seen many times in this book, leaders make mistakes. That is inevitable. So, strikingly, *Parashat Vayikra* implies. The real issue is how they respond to those mistakes.

The point is made by the Torah in a very subtle way. The *parasha* deals with sin offerings to be brought when people have made mistakes. The technical term for this is *shegaga*, meaning inadvertent wrongdoing (Lev. 4:1–35). You did something, not knowing it was forbidden, either because you forgot or did not know the law, or because you were unaware of certain facts. You may, for instance, have carried something in a public place on Shabbat, either because you did not know it was forbidden to carry or because you forgot it was Shabbat.

The Torah prescribes different sin offerings, depending on who made the mistake. It enumerates four categories. First is the high priest, second is "the whole community" (understood to mean the Great

1. For a fuller version of this essay, see "The Sins of a Leader" on my website at http://www.rabbisacks.org/covenant-conversation-5768-vayikra-the-sins-of-a-leader/.

Sanhedrin, the Supreme Court), third is "the leader" (*nasi*), and fourth is an ordinary individual.

In three of the four cases, the law is introduced by the word *im*, "if" – if such a person commits a sin (Lev. 4:2, 3, 13). In the case of the leader, however, the law is prefaced by the word *asher*, "when" (4:22). It is *possible* that a high priest, the Supreme Court, or an individual may err. But in the case of a leader, it is probable or even certain. Leaders make mistakes. It is an occupational hazard. Talking about the sin of a *nasi*, the Torah uses the word "when," not "if."

Nasi is the generic word for a leader: a ruler, king, judge, elder, or prince. Usually it refers to the holder of political power. In Mishnaic times, the *nesi'im*, the most famous of whom were leaders from the family of Hillel, had quasi-governmental roles as representatives of the Jewish people to the Roman government. Rabbi Moses Sofer (Bratislava, 1762–1839), in one of his responsa,[2] examines the question of why, when positions of Torah leadership were never dynastic, the role of *nasi* was an exception. Often it did pass from father to son. The answer he gives, and it is historically insightful, is that with the decline of monarchy in the Second Temple period and thereafter, the *nasi* took on many of the roles of a king. His role, internally and externally, was as much political and diplomatic as religious. That in general is what is meant by the word *nasi*.

Why does the Torah consider this type of leadership particularly prone to error? The commentators offer three possible explanations. Rabbi Ovadiah Sforno (to Lev. 4:21–22) cites the phrase, "But Yeshurun waxed fat, and kicked" (Deut. 32:15). Those who have advantages over others, whether of wealth or power, can lose their moral sense. Rabbenu Baḥya agrees, suggesting that rulers tend to become arrogant and haughty. Implicit in these commentators – it is in fact a major theme of Tanakh as a whole – is the idea later stated by Lord Acton in the aphorism, "Power tends to corrupt, and absolute power corrupts absolutely."[3]

---

2. *Shut Ḥatam Sofer, Oraḥ Ḥayim* 12.
3. This famous phrase comes from a letter written by Lord Acton in 1887. See Martin H. Manser and Rosalind Fergusson, *The Facts on File Dictionary of Proverbs* (New York: Facts on File, 2002), 225.

Rabbi Elie Munk, citing the Zohar, offers a second explanation. The high priest and the Sanhedrin were in constant contact with the holy. They lived in a world of ideals. The king or political ruler, by contrast, was involved in secular affairs: war and peace, the administration of government, and international relations. He was more likely to sin because his day-to-day concerns were not religious but pragmatic.[4]

Rabbi Meir Simcha HaKohen of Dvinsk[5] points out that a king was especially vulnerable to being led astray by popular sentiment. Neither a priest nor a judge in the Sanhedrin was answerable to the people. The king, however, relied on popular support. Without that he could be deposed. But this was laden with risk. Doing what the people want is not always doing what God wants. That, Rabbi Meir Simcha argues, is what led David to order a census (II Sam. 24) and Zedekiah to ignore the advice of Jeremiah and rebel against the king of Babylon (II Chr. 36). Thus, for a whole series of reasons, a political leader is more exposed to temptation and error than a priest or judge.

There are further reasons. One is that politics is an arena of conflict. It deals in matters – specifically wealth and power – that are in the short term zero-sum games. The more I have, the less you have. Seeking to maximise the benefits to myself or my group, I come into conflict with others who seek to maximise benefits to themselves or their group. The politics of free societies is always conflict-ridden. The only societies without conflict are tyrannical or totalitarian ones in which dissenting voices are suppressed – and Judaism is a standing protest against tyranny. So in a free society, whatever course a politician takes, it will please some and anger others. From this, there is no escape.

Politics involves difficult judgements. A leader must balance competing claims, and will sometimes get it wrong. One example – one of the most fateful in Jewish history – occurred after the death of King Solomon. People came to his son and successor, Rehoboam, complaining that Solomon had imposed unsustainable burdens on the population, particularly during the building of the Temple. Led by Jeroboam,

---

4. Elie Munk, *The Call of the Torah: Vayikra* (Brooklyn, N.Y.: Mesorah Publications, 1992), 33.
5. *Meshekh Ḥokhma*, ad loc.

they asked the new king to reduce the burden. Rehoboam asked his father's counsellors for advice. They told him to concede to the people's demand. Serve them, they said, and they will serve you. Rehoboam, however, turned to his own friends, who told him the opposite: Reject the request. Show the people you are a strong leader who cannot be intimidated (1 Kings 12:1–15).

It was disastrous advice, and the result was tragic. The kingdom split in two, the ten northern tribes following Jeroboam, leaving only the southern tribes, generically known as "Judah," loyal to the king. For Israel as a people in its own land, it was the beginning of the end. Always a small people surrounded by large and powerful empires, it needed unity, high morale, and a strong sense of destiny to survive. Divided, it was only a matter of time before both nations – Israel in the north, Judah in the south – fell to other powers.

The reason leaders – as opposed to judges and priests – cannot avoid making mistakes is that there is no textbook that infallibly teaches how to lead. Priests and judges follow laws. For leadership there are no laws because every situation is unique. As Isaiah Berlin put it in his essay "Political Judgement,"[6] in the realm of political action, there are few laws and what is needed instead is skill in reading a situation. Successful statesmen "do not think in general terms." Instead "they grasp the unique combination of characteristics that constitute this particular situation – this and no other."[7] Berlin compares this to the gift possessed by great novelists like Tolstoy and Proust.[8] Applying inflexible rules to a constantly shifting political landscape destroys societies. Communism was like that. In free societies, people change, culture changes, the

6. Isaiah Berlin, *The Sense of Reality* (Chatto and Windus, 1996), 40–53.
7. Ibid., 45.
8. Incidentally, this answers the point made by political philosopher Michael Walzer in his book on the politics of the Bible, *In God's Shadow* (New Haven, Conn.: Yale University Press, 2012). He is undeniably right when he points out that political theory, so significant in ancient Greece, is almost completely absent from the Hebrew Bible. I would argue, and so surely would Isaiah Berlin, that there is a reason for this. In politics there are few general laws, and the Hebrew Bible is interested in laws. But when it comes to politics – to Israel's kings, for example – it does not give laws but instead tells stories.

world beyond a nation's borders does not stand still. So a politician will find that what worked a decade or a century ago does not work now. In politics it is easy to get it wrong, hard to get it right.[9]

There is one more reason why leadership is so challenging. It is alluded to by the Mishnaic sage, R. Neḥemiah, commenting on the verse, "My son, if you have put up security for your neighbour, if you have struck your hand in pledge for another" (Prov. 6:1):

> So long as a man is an associate [i.e., concerned only with personal piety], he need not be concerned with the community and is not punished on account of it. But once a man has been placed at the head and has donned the cloak of office, he may not say: I have to look after my welfare, I am not concerned with the community. Instead, the whole burden of communal affairs rests on him. If he sees a man doing violence to his fellow, or committing a transgression, and does not seek to prevent him, he is punished on account of him, and the Holy Spirit cries out: "My son, if you have put up security for your neighbour" – meaning, you are responsible for him.... You have entered the gladiatorial arena, and he who enters the arena is either conquered or conquers.[10]

A private individual is responsible only for his own sins. A leader is held responsible for the sins of the people he leads – at least those he might have prevented (Shabbat 54b). With power comes responsibility: the greater the power, the greater the responsibility.

There are no universal rules, no fail-safe textbook, for leadership. Every situation is different and each age brings its own challenges. Rulers, in the best interests of their people, may sometimes have to take decisions that a conscientious individual would shrink from doing in private life. They may have to decide to wage a war, knowing that some will die. They may have to levy taxes, knowing that this will leave some

---

9. This, needless to say, is not the plain sense of the text. The sins for which leaders brought an offering were spiritual offences, not errors of political judgement.
10. Exodus Rabba, 27:9.

impoverished. Only after the event will the leader know whether the decision was justified, and it may depend on factors beyond his or her control.

The Jewish approach to leadership is thus an unusual combination of realism and idealism – realism in its acknowledgement that leaders inevitably make mistakes, idealism in its constant subordination of politics to ethics, power to responsibility, pragmatism to the demands of conscience. What matters is not that leaders never get it wrong – that is inevitable, given the nature of leadership – but that they are always exposed to prophetic critique and that they constantly study Torah to remind themselves of transcendent standards and ultimate aims. The most important thing from a Torah perspective is that a leader is sufficiently honest to admit his or her mistakes. Hence the significance of the sin offering.

R. Yoḥanan b. Zakkai summed it up with a brilliant double-entendre on the word *asher*, "*When* a leader sins." He relates it to the word *ashrei*, "happy," and says: "Happy is the generation whose leader is willing to bring a sin offering for his mistakes" (Tosefta Bava Kamma 7:5).

Leadership demands two kinds of courage: the strength to take a risk, and the humility to admit when a risk fails.

Tzav

On Not Trying to Be What You Are Not

The great leaders know their own limits. They do not try to do it all themselves. They build teams. They create space for people who are strong where they are weak. They understand the importance of checks and balances and the separation of powers. They surround themselves with people who are different from them. They understand the danger of concentrating all power in a single individual. But learning your limits, knowing there are things you cannot do – even things you cannot *be* – can be a painful experience. Sometimes it involves an emotional crisis.

The Torah contains four fascinating accounts of such moments. They are linked not by words but by music. From quite early on in Jewish history, the Torah was sung, not just read. Moses at the end of his life calls the Torah a song (Deut. 31:19). Different traditions grew up in Israel and Babylon, and from around the tenth century onwards the chant began to be systematised in the form of the musical notations known as *Taamei HaMikra*, cantillation signs, devised by the Tiberian Masoretes (guardians of Judaism's sacred texts). One very rare note, known as a *shalshelet* (chain), appears in the Torah four times only. Each time it is a sign of existential crisis. Three instances are in Genesis. The fourth is in *Parashat Tzav*. As we will see, the fourth is about leadership. In a broad sense, the other three are as well.

The first instance occurs in the story of Lot. Lot had separated from his uncle, Abraham, and settled in Sodom. There he had assimilated into the local population. His daughters had married local men. He himself sat at the city gate, a sign that he had been made a judge. Then two visitors come to tell him to leave – God is about to destroy the city. Yet Lot hesitates, and above the word for "hesitates" in the Torah – *vayitmama* – a *shalshelet* appears (Gen. 19:16). He is torn, conflicted. He senses that the visitors are right. The city is indeed about to be destroyed. But he has invested his whole future in the new identity he has been carving out for himself and his daughters. Had the angels not seized him and taken him to safety, he would have delayed until it was too late.

The second occurs when Abraham asks his servant – traditionally identified as Eliezer – to find a wife for his son Isaac. The commentators suggest that Eliezer feels a profound ambivalence about his mission. Were Isaac not to marry and have children, Abraham's estate would eventually pass to Eliezer or his descendants. Abraham had already said so before Isaac was born: "Sovereign Lord, what can You give me since I remain childless and the one who will inherit my estate is Eliezer of Damascus?" (Gen. 15:2). If Eliezer succeeds in his mission, bringing back a wife for Isaac, and if the couple has children, then his chances of one day acquiring Abraham's wealth would disappear completely. Two instincts war within him: loyalty to Abraham and personal ambition. The verse states: "And he said: Lord, the God of my master Abraham, send me … good speed this day, and show kindness to my master Abraham" (Gen. 24:12). Loyalty wins, but not without a deep struggle. Hence the *shalshelet*.

The third brings us to Egypt and the life of Joseph. Sold by his brothers as a slave, he is now working in the house of an eminent Egyptian, Potiphar. Left alone in the house with his master's wife, he finds himself the object of her desire. He is handsome. She wants him to sleep with her. He refuses. To do such a thing, he says, would be to betray his master, her husband. It would be a sin against God. Yet over "he refused" is a *shalshelet* (Gen. 39:8), indicating – as some rabbinic sources and mediaeval commentaries suggest – that he does so at the cost of considerable effort.[1] He nearly succumbs. This is more than the usual conflict between sin and temptation. It is a conflict of identity. Recall that Joseph is now living in, for him, a new and strange land. His brothers have rejected him. They made it clear that they did not want him as part of their family. Why then should he not, in Egypt, do as the Egyptians do? Why not yield to his master's wife if that is what she wants? The question for Joseph is not just, "Is this right?" but also, "Am I an Egyptian or a Jew?"

All three episodes are about inner conflict, and all three are about identity. There are times when each of us has to decide not just "What shall I do?" but "What kind of person shall I be?" That is particularly fateful in the case of a leader, which brings us to episode four, this time about Moses.

After the sin of the Golden Calf, Moses had, at God's command, instructed the Israelites to build a Sanctuary which would be, in effect, a permanent symbolic home of God in the midst of the people. The work is complete; all that remains is for Moses to induct his brother Aaron and his sons into office. He robes Aaron with the special garments of the high priest, anoints him with oil, and performs the various sacrifices appropriate to the occasion. Over the word *vayishḥat*, "and he slaughtered [the sacrificial ram]" (Lev. 8:23), there is a *shalshelet*. By now we know that this means there is an internal struggle in Moses' mind. But what was it? There is not the slightest sign in the text that suggests that he is undergoing a crisis.

Yet a moment's thought makes it clear what Moses' inner turmoil is about. Until now he has led the Jewish people. Aaron his older brother assisted him, accompanying him on his missions to Pharaoh, acting as his spokesman, aide, and second-in-command. Now, however, Aaron is about to undertake a new leadership role in his own right. No longer will he be a shadow of Moses. He will do what Moses himself cannot. He will preside over the daily offerings in the Tabernacle. He will

---

1. Tanḥuma, *Vayeshev* 8, cited by Rashi in his commentary to Genesis 39:8.

mediate the *avoda*, the Israelites' sacred service to God. Once a year on Yom Kippur he will perform the service that will secure atonement for the people from its sins. No longer in Moses' shadow, Aaron is about to become the one kind of leader Moses is not destined to be: a high priest.

The Talmud adds a further dimension to the poignancy of the moment. At the burning bush, Moses had repeatedly resisted God's call to lead the people. Eventually God told him that Aaron would go with him, helping him speak (Ex. 4:14–16). The Talmud says that at that moment Moses lost the chance to be a priest. "Originally [said God] I had intended that you would be the priest and Aaron your brother would be a Levite. Now he will be the priest and you will be a Levite" (Zevaḥim 102a).

That is Moses' inner struggle, conveyed by the *shalshelet*. He is about to induct his brother into an office he himself will never hold. Things might have been otherwise – but life is not lived in the world of "might have been." He surely feels joy for his brother, but he cannot altogether avoid a sense of loss. Perhaps he already senses what he will later discover, that though he is the prophet and liberator, Aaron will have a privilege Moses is denied, namely, seeing his children and their descendants inherit his role. The son of a priest is a priest. The son of a prophet is rarely a prophet.

What all four stories tell us is that there comes a time for each of us when we must make an ultimate decision as to who we are. It is a moment of existential truth. Lot is a Hebrew, not a citizen of Sodom. Eliezer is Abraham's servant, not his heir. Joseph is Jacob's son, not an Egyptian of loose morals. Moses is a prophet, not a priest. To say yes to who we are, we have to have the courage to say no to who we are not. Pain and conflict are involved. That is the meaning of the *shalshelet*. But we emerge less conflicted than we were before.

This applies especially to leaders, which is why the case of Moses in this *parasha* is so important. There were things Moses was not destined to do. He would not become a priest. That task fell to Aaron. He would not lead the people across the Jordan. That was Joshua's role. Moses had to accept both facts with good grace if he was to be honest with himself. And great leaders must be honest with themselves if they are to be honest with those they lead.

A leader should never try to be all things to all people. A leader should be content to be what he or she is. Leaders must have the strength to know what they cannot be if they are to have the courage to be themselves.

Shemini

Reticence vs. Impetuosity

Parashat Shemini begins with what should have been a day of joy. The Israelites had completed the *Mishkan*, the Sanctuary. For seven days Moses had made preparations for its consecration.[1] Now on the eighth day – the first of Nisan (Ex. 10:2), one year to the day since the Israelites had received their first command two weeks prior to the Exodus – the service of the Sanctuary was about to begin. The sages say that in heaven, it was the most joyous day since creation (Megilla 10b).

But tragedy struck. The two elder sons of Aaron "offered a strange fire that had not been commanded" (Lev. 10:1) and the fire from heaven that should have consumed the sacrifices consumed them as well. They died. Aaron's joy turned to mourning. *Vayidom Aharon*, "And Aaron was silent" (10:3). The man who had been Moses' spokesman could no longer speak. Words turned to ash in his mouth.

There is much in this episode that is hard to understand, much that has to do with the concept of holiness and the powerful energies it released that, like nuclear power today, could be deadly dangerous

1. As described in Exodus 40.

if not properly used. But there is also a more human story about two approaches to leadership that still resonates with us today.

First there is the story about Aaron. We read about how Moses told him to begin his role as high priest. "Moses [then] said to Aaron, 'Approach the altar, and prepare your sin offering and burnt offering, thus atoning for you and the people. Then prepare the people's offering to atone for them, as God has commanded'" (Lev. 9:7). The sages sense a nuance in the words, "Approach the altar," as if Aaron was standing at a distance from it, reluctant to come near. They said: "Initially Aaron was ashamed to come close. Moses said to him, 'Do not be ashamed. This is what you have been chosen to do.'"[2]

Why was Aaron ashamed? Tradition gives two explanations, both brought by Ramban in his commentary to the Torah. The first is that Aaron was simply overwhelmed by trepidation at coming so close to the Divine Presence. The rabbis likened it to the bride of a king, nervous at entering the bridal chamber for the first time. The second is that Aaron, seeing the "horns" of the altar, was reminded of the Golden Calf, his great sin. How could he, who had played a key role in that terrible event, now take on the role of atoning for the people's sins? That surely demanded an innocence he no longer had. Moses had to remind him that it was precisely to atone for sins that the altar had been made; the fact that he had been chosen by God to be high priest was an unequivocal sign that he had been forgiven.

There is perhaps a third explanation, albeit less spiritual. Until now Aaron had been in all respects second to Moses. Yes, he had been at his side throughout, helping him speak and lead. But there is vast psychological difference between being second-in-command and being a leader in your own right. We probably all know of examples of people who quite readily serve in an assisting capacity but who are terrified at the prospect of leading on their own.

Whichever explanation is true – and perhaps they all are – Aaron was reticent at taking on his new role, and Moses had to give him confidence. "This is what you have been chosen to do."

---

2. Rashi to Leviticus 9:7, quoting *Sifra*, Leviticus, *Shemini*, 9:8.

The other story is the tragic tale of Aaron's two sons, Nadav and Avihu, who "offered a strange fire that had not been commanded." The sages offer several readings of this episode, all based on a close reading of the several places in the Torah where their death is referred to. Some say they had been drinking alcohol.[3] Others maintain that they were arrogant, holding themselves up above the community; this was the reason they had never married.[4] Some say that they were guilty of giving a halakhic ruling about the use of man-made fire, instead of asking their teacher Moses whether it was permitted (Eiruvin 63a). Others claim they were restless in the presence of Moses and Aaron. They said: when will these two old men die so we can lead the congregation (Sanhedrin 52a)?

However we read the episode, it seems clear that they were all too eager to exercise leadership. Carried away by their enthusiasm to play a part in the inauguration, they did something they had not been commanded to do. After all, had Moses not done something entirely on his own initiative, namely breaking the tablets when he came down the mountain and saw the Golden Calf? If he could act spontaneously, why could not they?

They forgot the difference between a priest and a prophet. As we noted earlier, a prophet lives and acts in time – in this moment that is unlike any other. A priest acts and lives in eternity, by following a set of rules that never changes. Everything about "the holy," the realm of the priest, is precisely scripted in advance. The holy is the place where God, not man, decides.

Nadav and Avihu failed to fully understand that there are different kinds of leadership and they are not interchangeable. What is appropriate to one may be radically inappropriate to another. A judge is not a politician. A king is not a prime minister. A religious leader is not a celebrity seeking popularity. Confuse these roles and not only will you fail, you will also damage the very office you were chosen to hold.

The real contrast here, though, is the difference between Aaron and his two sons. They were, it seems, opposites. Aaron was overcautious and had to be persuaded by Moses even to begin. Nadav and

3. Leviticus Rabba, 12:1; Ramban to Leviticus 10:9.
4. Leviticus Rabba, 20:10.

Avihu were not cautious enough. So keen were they to put their own stamp on the role of priesthood that their impetuosity was their downfall.

These are, perennially, the two challenges leaders must overcome. The first is the reluctance to lead. Why me? Why should I get involved? Why should I undertake the responsibility and all that comes with it – the stress, the hard work, and the criticisms leaders always have to face? Besides which, there are other people better qualified and more suited than I am.

Even the greatest were reluctant to lead. Moses at the burning bush found reason after reason to show that he was not the man for the job. Isaiah and Jeremiah both felt inadequate. Summoned to lead, Jonah ran away. The challenge really is daunting. But when you feel as if you are being called to a task, if you know that the mission is necessary and important, then there is nothing you can do but say *Hineni*, "Here I am" (Ex. 3:4). In the words of a famous book title, you have to "feel the fear and do it anyway."[5]

The other challenge is the opposite. There are some people who simply see themselves as leaders. They are convinced that they can do it better. From a distance it seems so easy. Is it not obvious that the leader should do X, not Y? Homo sapiens contains many backseat drivers who know better than those whose hands are on the steering wheel. Put them in a position of leadership and they can do great damage. Never having sat in the driver's seat, they have no idea of how many considerations have to be taken into account, how many voices of opposition have to be overcome, how difficult it is at one and the same time to cope with the pressures of events while not losing sight of long-term ideals and objectives. The late John F. Kennedy said that the worst shock on being elected president was that "when we got to the White House we discovered that things were as bad as we'd been saying they were." Nothing prepares you for the pressures of leadership when the stakes are high.

Over-enthusiastic, over-confident leaders can do great harm. Before they became leaders they understood events through their own perspective. What they did not understand was that leadership involves relating to many perspectives, many interest groups and points of view.

5.   Susan Jeffers, *Feel the Fear and Do It Anyway* (New York: Ballantine Books, 2006).

That does not mean that you try to satisfy everyone. Those who do so end up satisfying no one. But you have to consult and persuade. Sometimes you need to honour precedent and the traditions of a particular institution. You have to know exactly when to behave as your predecessors did and when not to. These call for considered judgement, not wild enthusiasm in the heat of the moment.

Nadav and Avihu were surely great people. The trouble was that they believed they were great people. They were not like their father Aaron who had to be persuaded to come close to the altar because of his sense of inadequacy. The one thing Nadav and Avihu lacked was a sense of their own inadequacy.[6]

To do anything great, we have to be aware of these two temptations. One is the fear of greatness: Who am I? The other is being convinced of your greatness: Who are they? I can do it better. We can do great things if (a) the task matters more than the person; (b) we are willing to do our best without thinking ourselves superior to others; and (c) we are willing to take advice, the thing Nadav and Avihu failed to do.

People do not become leaders because they are great. They become great because they are willing to serve as leaders. It does not matter that we think ourselves inadequate. So did Moses. So did Aaron. What matters is the willingness, when challenge calls, to say *Hineni*, "Here I am."

---

6. The composer Berlioz once said of a young musician: "He knows everything. The one thing he lacks is inexperience."

Tazria

The Price of Free Speech

Hannah Smith was a fourteen-year-old schoolgirl living in Lutterworth, Leicestershire, UK. Bright and outgoing, she enjoyed an active social life and seemed to have an exciting future ahead of her. On the morning of August 2, 2013, Hannah was found hanged in her bedroom. She had committed suicide.

Seeking to unravel what had happened, her family soon discovered that she had been the target of anonymous abusive posts on a social network website. Hannah was a victim of the latest variant of the oldest story in human history: the use of words as weapons by those seeking to inflict pain. The new version is called cyberbullying.

The Jewish phrase for this kind of behaviour is *lashon hara*, evil speech, speech about people that is negative and derogatory. It means, quite simply, speaking badly about people, and is a subset of the biblical prohibition against spreading gossip (Lev. 19:16). Despite the fact that it is not singled out in the Torah as a prohibition in its own right, the sages regarded it as one of the worst of all sins. They said, astonishingly, that it is as bad as the three cardinal sins – idolatry, murder, and incest – combined. More significantly in the context of Hannah Smith, they said it kills three people, the one who says it, the one it is said about, and the one who listens in.[1]

The connection with *Parashat Tazria* is straightforward. *Parashot Tazria* and *Metzora* are about a condition called *tzaraat,* sometimes translated as leprosy. The commentators were puzzled as to what this condition is and why it should be given such prominence in the Torah. They concluded that it was precisely because it was a punishment for *lashon hara,* derogatory speech. Evidence for this is the story of Miriam, who spoke scornfully about her brother Moses "because of the Cushite woman whom he had married" (Num. 12:1). God Himself felt bound to defend Moses' honour, and as a punishment, turned Miriam leprous. Moses prayed for God to heal her. God mitigated the punishment to seven days, but did not annul it entirely. Clearly this was no minor matter, because Moses singles it out among the teachings he gives the next generation: "Remember what the Lord your God did to Miriam along the way after you came out of Egypt" (Deut. 24:9, see Ibn Ezra ad loc.).

Oddly enough Moses himself, according to the sages, had been briefly guilty of the same offence. At the burning bush when God challenged him to lead the people, Moses replied, "They will not believe in me" (Ex. 4:1). God then gave Moses three signs: water that turned to blood, a staff that became a snake, and his hand briefly turning leprous. We find reference later in the narrative to water turning to blood and a staff turning into a serpent, but none to a hand that turns leprous. The sages, ever alert to the nuances of the biblical text, say that the hand that turned leprous was not a sign but a punishment. Moses was being reprimanded for "casting doubts against the innocent" by saying that the Israelites would not believe in him. "They are believers the children of believers," said God according to the Talmud, "but in the end you will not believe" (Shabbat 97a).

How dangerous *lashon hara* can be is illustrated by the story of Joseph and his brothers. The Torah says that Joseph "brought an evil report" to his father about some of his brothers (Gen. 37:2). This was not the only provocation that led his brothers to plot to kill him and eventually sell him as a slave. There were several other factors. But his

---

1. See *Mishneh Torah, Hilkhot Deot* 7:3.

derogatory gossip did not endear him to his siblings. No less disastrous was the "evil report" (*diba*; the Torah uses the same word as it does in the case of Joseph) brought back by the spies about the land of Canaan and its inhabitants (Num. 13:32). Even after Moses' prayers to God for forgiveness, the report delayed entry to the land by almost forty years and condemned a whole generation to die in the wilderness.

Why is the Torah so severe about *lashon hara*, branding it as one of the worst sins? This has deep roots, in part, in the Jewish understanding of God and the human condition. Judaism is less a religion of holy people and holy places than it is a religion of holy words. God created the universe using words: "And God said, 'Let there be...' and there was." God reveals Himself in words. He spoke to the patriarchs and the prophets and, at Mount Sinai, to the whole nation. Our very humanity has to do with our ability to use language. The creation of Homo sapiens is described in the Torah thus: "Then the Lord God formed man from the dust of the ground and breathed into his nostrils the breath of life, and the man became a living soul" (Gen. 2:7), which, as we saw earlier, the *Targum* renders as "a *speaking* soul." Language is life. Words are creative but also destructive. If good words are holy then evil words are a desecration.

One sign of how seriously Judaism takes this is the prayer we say at the end of every *Amida*, at least three times a day: "My God, guard my tongue from evil and my lips from deceitful speech. To those who curse me, let my soul be silent; may my soul be to all like the dust." Having prayed to God at the beginning to "Open my lips so that my mouth may declare Your praise," we pray to Him at the end to help us close our lips so that we do not speak badly about others nor react when others speak badly about us.

Despite everything, however – despite the Torah's prohibition of gossip, despite its stories about Joseph, Moses, Miriam, and the spies, despite the unparalleled strictures against evil speech by the sages – *lashon hara* remained a problem throughout Jewish history and still does today. Every leader is subject to it. The sages said that when Moses left his tent early in the morning, people would say, "You see, he has had a row with his wife." If he left late they would say, "He is plotting against us" (Rashi to Deut. 1:12).

Any person who wants to lead, from CEO to parent, has to confront the issue of *lashon hara*. Firstly, he or she may have to put up with it as the price of any kind of achievement. Some people are envious. They gossip. They build themselves up by putting other people down. If you are in any kind of leadership position, you may have to live with the fact that behind your back – or even before your face – people will be critical, malicious, disdainful, vilifying, and sometimes downright dishonest. This can be hard to bear. Having known many leaders in many fields, I can testify to the fact that not all people in the public eye have a thick skin. Many of them are very sensitive and can find constant, unjust criticism deeply draining.

If you should ever suffer this, the best advice is given by the Rambam:

> If a person is scrupulous in his conduct, gentle in his conversation, pleasant towards his fellow creatures, affable in manner when receiving them, not responding even when affronted, but showing courtesy to all, even to those who treat him with disdain... such a person has sanctified God and about him Scripture says, "You are My servant, Israel, in whom I will be glorified" (Is. 49:3).[2]

That is in relation to *lashon hara* directed against the leader. As for the group as a whole, however, you should practise zero tolerance towards *lashon hara*. Allowing people to speak badly about one another will eventually destroy the integrity of the group. Evil speech generates negative energies. Within the group it sows the seeds of distrust and envy. Directed outside the group it can lead to arrogance, self-righteousness, racism, and prejudice, all of which are fatal to the moral credibility of any team. Whether or not you are the leader of such a group you must politely make it clear that you will have nothing to do with this kind of speech and that it has no place in your conversations.

Cyberbullying is the latest manifestation of *lashon hara*. In general the Internet is the most effective distributor of hate speech ever

2. *Mishneh Torah, Hilkhot Yesodei HaTorah* 5:11.

invented. Not only does it make targeted communication so easy, it also bypasses the face-to-face encounter that can sometimes induce shame, sensitivity, and self-control. Greek mythology told the story of Gyges' ring that had the magical property of making whoever wore it invisible, so that he could get away with anything.[3] Social media platforms that enable people to post anonymous comments or adopt false identities are as near as anyone has yet come to inventing a Gyges' ring. That is what is so dangerous about it.

The story of Hannah Smith is a tragic reminder of how right the sages were to reject the idea that "words can never harm me," and insist to the contrary that evil speech kills. Free speech is not speech that costs nothing. It is speech that respects the freedom and dignity of others. Forget this and free speech becomes very expensive indeed.

All of this helps us to understand the biblical idea of *tzaraat*. The peculiar property of *tzaraat* – whether as a skin disease, a discoloration of garments, or mould on the walls of a house – is that it was immediately and conspicuously visible. People engage in *lashon hara* because, like wearers of Gyges' ring, they think they can get away with it. "It wasn't me. I never said it. I didn't mean it. I was misunderstood." The Torah is telling us that malicious speech uttered in private is to be stigmatised in public, and those who engage in it are to be openly shamed.

To put it at its simplest: as we behave to others so God behaves to us. Do not expect God to be kind to those who are unkind to their fellow humans. Leaders have a responsibility to reflect those values – to react appropriately to *lashon hara* and create environments in which malicious speech is not tolerated.

3. See Plato, *The Republic*, 359a–360d.

Metzora

How to Praise

The sages were eloquent on the subject of *lashon hara*, evil speech, the sin they took to be the cause of *tzaraat*, the subject of *Parashat Metzora*. But there is a meta-halakhic principle: "From the negative you can infer the positive" (Nedarim 11a). So, for example, from the seriousness of the prohibition against *ḥillul Hashem*, desecrating God's name, one can infer the importance of the opposite, *kiddush Hashem*, sanctifying God's name.

It follows that there must in principle be a concept of *lashon hatov*, good speech, and it must be more than a mere negation of its opposite. The way to avoid *lashon hara* is to practise silence, and indeed the sages were also eloquent on the important of silence (see, for example, Mishna Avot 1:17; 3:13). Silence saves us from evil speech but in and of itself it achieves nothing positive. What then is *lashon hatov*?

Lashon hatov – one of the most important tasks of a leader, a parent, or a friend – is focused praise. The classic text on this is the mishna in Tractate Avot (2:11) in which R. Yoḥanan b. Zakkai enumerates the praises of his five beloved students (which we discussed in *Parashat Vayeshev*):

He used to recount their praise: Eliezer b. Hyrcanus: a plastered well that never loses a drop. Yehoshua b. Ḥanania: happy is the one who gave him birth. Yose the priest: a pious man. Shimon b. Netanel: a man who fears sin. Elazar b. Arakh: an ever-flowing spring.

This mishna is doing more than telling us that R. Yoḥanan b. Zakkai had disciples. Every rabbi had disciples. The imperative "Raise up many disciples" (Mishna Avot 1:1) is one of the oldest rabbinic teachings on record. What the mishna is telling us is *how* to create disciples. It is easy to have students who are uncritical devotees but never become creative intellects in their own right. It is not difficult to create followers. It is far harder to create leaders.

R. Yoḥanan b. Zakkai was a great teacher because five of his students became giants in their own right. The mishna is telling us how he did it: with focused praise. He showed each of his pupils where their particular strength lay. Eliezer b. Hyrcanus, the "plastered well that never loses a drop," was gifted with a superb memory – an important gift in an age in which manuscripts were rare and the Oral Law was not yet committed to writing. Shimon b. Netanel, the "man who fears sin," may not have had the intellectual brilliance of the others but his reverential nature was a reminder to others that they were not mere scholars but also holy men engaged in a sacred task. Elazar b. Arakh, the "ever-flowing spring," had a creative mind constantly giving rise to new interpretations of ancient texts.

I discovered the transformative power of focused praise from one of the more remarkable people I ever met, the late Lena Rustin. Lena was a speech therapist, specialising in helping stammering children. I came to know her through a television documentary I was making for the BBC about the state of the family in Britain. Lena believed that the young stammerers she was treating – they were, on average, around five years old – had to be understood in the context of their families. Families tend to develop an equilibrium. If a child stammers, everyone in the family adjusts to it. Therefore, if the child is to lose his or her stammer, all the relationships within the family will have to be renegotiated. Not only must the child change. So must everyone else.

By and large, we tend to resist change. We settle into patterns of behaviour until they become comfortable, like a well-worn armchair or a comfortable pair of shoes. How do you create an atmosphere within a family that encourages change and makes it unthreatening? The answer Lena discovered was praise. She told the families with whom she was working that every day they must catch each member of the family doing something right and say so – specifically, positively, and thankfully.

She did not go into deep explanations, but watching her at work I began to realise what she was doing. She was creating, within each home, an atmosphere of mutual regard and continuous positive reinforcement. She wanted the parents to shape an environment of self-respect and self-confidence, not just for the stammering child but for every member of the family, so that the entire atmosphere of the home was one in which people felt safe to change and help others to do so.

I suddenly realised that she had discovered a solution not just for stammering but for group dynamics as a whole. My intuition was soon confirmed in a surprising way. There had been tensions among the television crew with whom I was working. Various things had gone wrong and there was an atmosphere of mutual recrimination. After filming a session of Lena Rustin teaching parents how to give and receive praise, the crew started praising one another. Instantly the atmosphere was transformed. The tension dissolved, and filming became fun again. Praise gives people the confidence to let go of the negative aspects of their character and reach their full potential.

There is in praise a deep spiritual message. We think religion is about faith in God. What I had not fully understood before was that faith in God should lead us to have faith in people, for God's image is in each of us, and we have to learn how to discern it. I then understood that the repeated phrase in Genesis 1, "And God saw that it was good," was there to teach us to see the good in people and events, and by so doing, help to strengthen it. I also understood why God briefly punished Moses by turning his hand leprous – as mentioned in our study of *Parashat Tazria* – because he had said about the Israelites, "They will not believe in me" (Ex. 4:1). Moses was being taught a fundamental lesson of leadership: *It does not matter whether they believe in you. What matters is that you believe in them.*

It was from another wise woman that I learned another important lesson about praise. Stanford psychologist Carol Dweck, in her book *Mindset*,[1] argues that there is a decisive difference between two approaches: we might believe that our abilities are innate and determined once and for all (the "fixed" mindset) or we may assume that talent is something we achieve over time through effort, practice, and persistence (the "growth" mindset). People who take the former approach tend to be risk-averse, afraid that failure will show that they are not as good as they were thought to be. The latter embrace risk because they take failure as a learning experience from which they can grow. It follows that there is good praise and bad praise. Parents and teachers should not praise children in absolute terms: "You are gifted, brilliant, a star." They should praise effort: "You tried hard, you gave of your best." They should encourage a growth mindset, not a fixed one.

Perhaps this explains a sad aftermath in the lives of R. Yohanan b. Zakkai's two most gifted pupils. The mishna immediately following the one quoted above states:

> He [R. Yohanan b. Zakkai] used to say: If all the sages of Israel were in one scale of a balance and Eliezer b. Hyrcanus in the other, he would outweigh them all. However, Abba Shaul said in his name: If all the sages of Israel, including Eliezer b. Hyrcanus, were in one scale of a balance, and Elazar b. Arakh in the other, he would outweigh them all. (Mishna Avot 2:12)

Tragically, R. Eliezer b. Hyrcanus was eventually excommunicated by his colleagues for failing to accept the majority view on a matter of Jewish law (Bava Metzia 59b). As for R. Elazar b. Arakh, he became separated from his colleagues. When they went to the academy at Yavneh, he went to Emmaus, a pleasant place to live but lacking in other Torah scholars. Eventually he forgot his learning and became a pale shadow of his former self (Shabbat 147b). It may be that in praising his students for their innate abilities rather than their effort, R. Yohanan b. Zakkai inadvertently encouraged the two most talented of them to develop a fixed mindset rather than engage with colleagues and stay open to intellectual growth.

1. Carol Dweck, *Mindset* (New York: Ballantine Books, 2007).

Praise, and how we administer it, is a fundamental element in leadership of any kind. Recognising the good in people and saying so, we help bring people's potential to fruition. Praising their efforts rather than their innate gifts helps encourage growth, about which Hillel used to say: "He who does not increase his knowledge, loses it" (Mishna Avot 1:13). The right kind of praise changes lives. That is the power of *lashon hatov*. Bad speech diminishes us; good speech can lift us to great heights. Or as W. H. Auden said in a beautiful poem:

> In the prison of his days
> Teach the free man how to praise.[2]

---

2. W. H. Auden, "In Memory of W. B. Yeats," *Another Time* (New York: Random House, 1940).

Aḥarei Mot

Sprints and Marathons

It was a unique, unrepeatable moment of leadership at its highest height. For forty days Moses had been communing with God, receiving from Him the law written on tablets of stone. Then God informed him that the people had just made a Golden Calf. He was about to destroy them. It was the worst crisis of the wilderness years, and it called for every one of Moses' gifts as a leader.

First, Moses prayed to God not to destroy the people. God agreed. Then he went down the mountain and saw the people cavorting around the calf. Immediately, he smashed the tablets. Burning the calf, he mixed its ashes with water, and made the people drink. Then he called for people to join him. The Levites heeded the call, carrying out a bloody punishment in which three thousand people died. Then Moses went back up the mountain and prayed for forty days and nights; for a further forty days he stayed with God while a new set of tablets was engraved. Finally, he came down the mountain on the tenth of Tishrei carrying the new tablets with him as a visible sign that God's covenant with Israel remained.

This was an extraordinary show of leadership, at times bold and decisive, at others slow and persistent. Moses had to contend with both sides, inducing the Israelites to do *teshuva* and God to exercise forgiveness. At that moment he was the greatest-ever embodiment of the name Israel: one who wrestles with God and with people and prevails.

The good news is: there once was a Moses. Because of him, the people survived. The bad news is: what happens when there is no Moses? The Torah itself says: "No other prophet has risen in Israel like Moses" (Deut. 34:10). That is the problem faced by every nation, corporation, community, and family. What do you do in the absence of heroic leadership? It is easy to say, "Think what Moses would have done." But Moses did what he did because he was what he was. We are not Moses. That is why every human group that was once touched by greatness faces a problem of continuity. How does it avoid a slow decline?

The answer is given in *Parashat Aḥarei Mot*. The day Moses descended the mountain with the second tablets was to be immortalised when its anniversary became a holy day, Yom Kippur. On it, the drama of *teshuva* and *kappara*, repentance and atonement, was to be repeated annually. This time, though, the key figure would not be Moses but Aaron, not the prophet but the high priest.

That is how you perpetuate a transformative event: by turning it into a ritual. Max Weber called this "the routinisation of charisma."[1] A once-and-never-again moment becomes a once-and-ever-again ceremony. As James MacGregor Burns puts it in his classic work, *Leadership*: "The most lasting tangible act of leadership is the creation of an institution – a nation, a social movement, a political party, a bureaucracy – that continues to exert moral leadership and foster needed social change long after the creative leaders are gone."[2]

There is a remarkable midrash in which various sages put forward their idea of *klal gadol baTorah*, "the great principle of the Torah." Ben Azzai says it is the verse, "This is the book of the chronicles of man: On the day that God created man, He made him in the likeness

---

1. See Max Weber, *Economy and Society* (Oakland, Calif.: University of California Press, 1978), 246ff.

2. James MacGregor Burns, *Leadership* (New York: Harper, 1978), 454.

of God" (Gen. 5:1). Ben Zoma says that there is a more embracing principle, "Listen, Israel: The Lord our God, the Lord is one" (Deut. 6:4). Ben Nannas says there is a yet more comprehensive principle: "Love your neighbour as yourself" (Lev. 19:18). Ben Pazzi says we find a more inclusive principle still: "The first sheep shall be offered in the morning, and the second sheep in the afternoon" (Ex. 29:39) – or, as we might say today, Shaḥarit, Minḥa, and Maariv. In a word: "routine." The passage concludes: The law follows Ben Pazzi.[3]

The meaning of Ben Pazzi's statement is clear: all the high ideals in the world – the human as God's image, belief in God's unity, and the love of neighbours – count for little until they are turned into habits of action that become habits of the heart. We can all recall moments of insight or epiphany when we suddenly understood what life is about, what greatness is, and how we would like to live. A day, a week, or at most, a year later, the inspiration fades and becomes a distant memory and we are left as we were before, unchanged.

Judaism's greatness is that it gives space to both prophet and priest, to inspirational figures on the one hand, and on the other, daily routines – the halakha – that take exalted visions and turn them into patterns of behaviour that reconfigure the brain and change how we feel and who we are.

One of the most unusual passages I have ever read about Judaism written by a non-Jew occurs in William Rees-Mogg's book on macroeconomics, *The Reigning Error*.[4] Rees-Mogg (1928–2012) was a financial journalist who became editor of the *Times*, chairman of the Arts Council, and vice-chairman of the BBC. Religiously he was a committed Catholic. He begins the book with a completely unexpected paean of praise for halakhic Judaism. He explains his reason for doing so. Inflation, he says, is a disease of inordinacy, a failure of discipline – in this case in relation to money. What makes Judaism unique, he says, is its legal system. This

---

3. The passage is cited in the introduction to the *HaKotev* commentary on *Ein Yaakov*, the collected aggadic passages of the Talmud. It is also quoted by Maharal in *Netivot Olam, Ahavat Reʾa* 1.
4. William Rees-Mogg, *The Reigning Error: The Crisis of World Inflation* (London: Hamilton, 1974), 9–13.

has been wrongly criticised by Christians as drily legalistic. In fact, Jewish law was essential for Jewish survival because it "provided a standard by which action could be tested, a law for the regulation of conduct, a focus for loyalty and a boundary for the energy of human nature."

All sources of energy, most notably nuclear energy, need some form of containment. Without that, they become dangerous. Jewish law has always acted as a container for the spiritual and intellectual energy of the Jewish people. That energy "has not merely exploded or been dispersed; it has been harnessed as a continuous power." What Jews have, he argues, modern economies lack: a system of self-control that allows economies to flourish without booms and crashes, inflation and recession.

The same applies to leadership. In *Good to Great*, management theorist Jim Collins argues that what the great companies have in common is a *culture of discipline*. In *Great by Choice* he uses the phrase "the 20-Mile March" – outstanding organisations plan for the marathon, not the sprint. Confidence, he says, "comes not from motivational speeches, charismatic inspiration, wild pep rallies, unfounded optimism, or blind hope."[5] It comes from doing the deed, day after day, year after year. Great companies use disciplines that are specific, methodical, and consistent. They encourage their people to be self-disciplined and responsible. They do not overreact to change, be it for good or bad. They keep their eye on the far horizon. Above all, they do not depend on heroic, charismatic leaders who at best lift the company for a while but do not provide it with the in-depth strength it needs to flourish in the long run.

The classic instance of the principles articulated by Burns, Rees-Mogg, and Collins is the transformation that occurred between *Parashat Ki Tissa* and *Parashat Aharei Mot*, between the first Yom Kippur and the second, between Moses' heroic leadership and the quiet, understated priestly discipline of an annual day of repentance and atonement.

Turning ideals into codes of action that shape habits of the heart is what Judaism and leadership are about. Never lose the inspiration of the prophets, but never lose, either, the routines that turn ideals into acts and dreams into achieved reality.

5. Jim Collins, *Good to Great* (New York: HarperBusiness, 2001); *Great by Choice* (New York: HarperCollins, 2011), 55.

Kedoshim

Followership

There is a fascinating sequence of commands in the great "holiness code" with which *Parashat Kedoshim* begins that sheds light on the nature, not just of leadership in Judaism, but also of followership. Here is the command in context:

> Do not hate your brother in your heart. *Reprove [or reason with] your neighbour frankly so you will not bear sin because of him.* Do not seek revenge or bear a grudge against anyone among your people, but love your neighbour as yourself. I am the Lord. (Lev. 19:17–18)

There are two completely different ways of understanding the italicised words. The Rambam brings them both as legally binding.[1] Ramban includes them both in his commentary to the Torah (Ramban to Lev. 19:17).

The first way to understand the phrase is to read the command in terms of interpersonal relations. Someone, you believe, has done you

1.   *Mishneh Torah, Hilkhot Deot 6:6–7.*

harm. In such a case, says the Torah, do not remain in a state of silent resentment. Do not give way to hate, do not bear a grudge, and do not take revenge. Instead, reprove him, reason with him, tell him what you believe he has done and how you feel it has harmed you. He may apologise and seek to make amends. Even if he does not, at least you have made your feelings known to him. That in itself is cathartic. It will help you to avoid nursing a grievance.

The second interpretation, though, sees the command in impersonal terms. It has nothing to do with you being harmed. It refers to someone you see acting wrongly, committing a sin or a crime. You may not be the victim. You may be just an observer. The command tells us not to be content with passing a negative judgement on his behaviour (i.e., with "hate your brother in your heart"). You must get involved. You should remonstrate with him, pointing out in as gentle and constructive a way as you can that what he is doing is against the law, civil or moral. If you stay silent and do nothing, you will become complicit in his guilt (i.e., "bear sin because of him") because you saw him do wrong and you did nothing to protest.

This second interpretation is possible only because of Judaism's fundamental principle that *kol Yisrael arevim zeh bazeh*, "All Israelites are responsible for one another" (Shevuot 39a). However, the Talmud makes a fascinating observation about the scope of the command:

[The Torah says] *hokhe'aḥ tokhiaḥ*, meaning, "you shall reprove your neighbour repeatedly...." Why...does it add the word *tokhiaḥ*? Had there been only a single verb I would have known that the law applies to a master reproving his disciple. How do we know that it applies even to a disciple reproving his master? From the phrase, *hokhe'aḥ tokhiaḥ*, implying: under all circumstances. (Bava Metzia 31a)

This is significant because it establishes a principle of *critical followership*. So far in these essays we have been looking at the role of the leader in Judaism. But what about that of the follower? On the face of it, the duty of the follower is to follow, and that of the disciple to learn. After all, Judaism commands almost unlimited respect for teachers. "Let reverence for your teacher be as great as your reverence for Heaven," said the sages (Mishna Avot 4:12). Despite this the Talmud understands the Torah to be commanding us to remonstrate even with our teacher or leader, should we see him doing something wrong.

Supposing a leader commands you to do something you know to be forbidden by Jewish law. Should you obey? The answer is a categorical no. The Talmud puts this in the form of a rhetorical question: "Faced with a choice between obeying the master [God] or the disciple [a human leader], whom should you obey?" (Kiddushin 42b). The answer is obvious. Obey God. Here in Jewish law is the logic of civil disobedience, the idea that we have a duty to disobey an immoral order.

Then there is the great Jewish idea of active questioning and "argument for the sake of Heaven" (Mishna Avot 5:21). Parents are obliged, and teachers encouraged, to train students to ask questions. Traditional Jewish learning is designed to make teacher and disciple alike aware of the fact that more than one view is possible on any question of Jewish law and that there can be multiple interpretations (the traditional number is seventy) of any biblical verse. Judaism is unique in that virtually all of its canonical texts – Midrash, Mishna, and Gemara – are anthologies of arguments (Rabbi X said this, Rabbi Y said that) or are surrounded by multiple commentaries, each with its own perspective.

The very act of learning in rabbinic Judaism is conceived as active debate, a kind of gladiatorial contest of the mind: "Even a teacher and disciple, even a father and son, when they sit to study Torah together, become enemies to one another. But they do not move from there until they have become beloved to one another" (Kiddushin 30b). Hence the Talmudic saying, "I learned much from my teachers, more from my colleagues, but most of all from my students" (Taanit 7a). Therefore, despite the reverence we owe our teachers, we owe them also our best efforts at questioning and challenging their ideas. This is essential to the rabbinical ideal of learning as a collaborative pursuit of truth.

The idea of critical followership gave rise in Judaism to the world's first social critics, the prophets, mandated by God to speak truth to power and to summon even kings to the bar of justice and right conduct. That is what Samuel did to Saul, Elijah to Ahab, and Isaiah to Hezekiah. None did so more effectively than the prophet Nathan when, with immense skill, he got King David to appreciate the enormity of his sin in sleeping with another man's wife. David immediately recognised his wrong and said, "*Ḥatati* [I have sinned]" (II Sam. 12:13).

Exceptional though the prophets of Israel were, even their achievement takes second place to one of the most remarkable phenomena in the history of religion, namely that God chooses as His most beloved disciples the very people who are willing to challenge Heaven itself. Abraham says, "Shall the Judge of all the earth not do justice?" (Gen. 18:25). Moses says, "Why have You done evil to this people?" (Ex. 5:22). Jeremiah and Habakkuk challenge God on the apparent injustices of history. Job, who argues with God, is eventually vindicated by God, while his comforters, who defended God, are deemed by God to have been in the wrong. In short, God Himself chooses active, critical followers rather than those who silently obey.

Hence the unusual conclusion that *in Judaism, followership is as active and demanding as leadership.* We can put this more strongly: leaders and followers do not sit on opposite sides of the table. They are on the same side, the side of justice and compassion and the common good. No one is above criticism, and no one too junior to administer it, if done with due grace and humility. A disciple may criticise his teacher; a child may challenge a parent; a prophet may challenge a king; and all of us, simply by bearing the name Israel, are summoned to wrestle with God and our fellow humans in the name of the right and the good.

Uncritical followership and habits of silent obedience give rise to the corruptions of power, or sometimes simply to avoidable catastrophes. For example, a series of fatal accidents occurred between 1970 and 1999 to planes belonging to Korean Air. One in particular, Korean Air Flight 8509 in December 1999, led to a review that suggested that Korean culture, with its tendency towards autocratic leadership and deferential followership, may have been responsible for the first officer not warning the pilot that he was off course.[2] John F. Kennedy assembled one of the most talented groups of advisers ever to serve an American president, yet in the Bay of Pigs invasion of Cuba in 1961 committed

2. Malcolm Gladwell, *Outliers: The Story of Success* (New York: Little, Brown and Co., 2008), 177–223.

one of the most foolish mistakes. Subsequently, one of the members of the group, Arthur Schlesinger Jr., attributed the error to the fact that the atmosphere within the group was so convivial that no one wanted to disturb it by pointing out the folly of the proposal.[3]

Groupthink and conformism are perennial dangers within any closely knit group, as a series of famous experiments by Solomon Asch, Stanley Milgram, Philip Zimbardo, and others have shown (we took a closer look at some of these in our study of *Parashat Lekh Lekha*). This is why, in Cass Sunstein's words, "societies need dissent."[4] My favourite example is one given by James Surowiecki in *The Wisdom of Crowds*. He tells the story of how an American naturalist, William Beebe, came across a strange sight in the Guyana jungle. A group of army ants was moving in a huge circle. The ants went round and round in the same circle for two days until most of them dropped dead. The reason is that when a group of army ants is separated from their colony, they obey a simple rule: follow the ant in front of you.[5] The trouble is that if the ant in front of you is lost, so will you be.

Surowiecki's argument is that we need dissenting voices, people who challenge the conventional wisdom, resist the fashionable consensus, and disturb the intellectual peace. "Follow the person in front of you" is as dangerous to humans as it is to army ants. To stand apart and be willing to question where the leader is going is the task of the critical follower. Great leadership happens when there is strong and independently minded followership. Hence, when it comes to constructive criticism, a disciple may challenge a teacher and a prophet may reprimand a king.

---

3. See Cass Sunstein, *Why Societies Need Dissent* (Cambridge, Mass.: Harvard University Press, 2003), 2–3.
4. Ibid.
5. James Surowiecki, *The Wisdom of Crowds* (New York: Doubleday, 2004), 40–41.

Emor

On Not Being Afraid of Greatness

Embedded in *Parashat Emor* are two of the most fundamental commands of Judaism – commands that touch on the very nature of Jewish identity: "Do not desecrate My holy name. I must be sanctified among the Israelites. I am the Lord, who made you holy and who brought you out of Egypt to be your God. I am the Lord" (Lev. 22:32). The two commands are respectively the prohibition against desecrating God's name, *ḥillul Hashem*, and the positive corollary, *kiddush Hashem*, that we are commanded to sanctify God's name. We discussed both of these earlier in the chapters on *parashot Tazria* and *Metzora*. But in what sense can we sanctify or desecrate God's name?

First we have to understand the concept of "name" as it applies to God. A name is how we are known to others. God's "name" is therefore His standing in the world. Do people acknowledge Him, respect Him, honour Him?

The commands of *kiddush Hashem* and *ḥillul Hashem* locate that responsibility in the conduct and fate of the Jewish people. This is what Isaiah meant when he said: "You are My witnesses, says God, that I am God" (Is. 43:10). The God of Israel is the God of all humanity. He created the universe and life itself. He made all of us – Jew and non-Jew alike – in His image. He cares for all of us: "His tender mercies are on all His works" (Ps. 145:9).

Yet the God of Israel is radically unlike the gods in which the ancients believed, and the reality in which today's scientific atheists believe. He is not identical with nature. He created nature. He is not identical with the physical universe. He transcends the universe. He is not capable of being mapped by science – observed, measured, quantified. He is not that kind of thing at all. How then is He known?

The radical claim of Torah is that He is known, not exclusively but primarily, through Jewish history and through the ways Jews live. As Moses says at the end of his life:

> Ask now about the former days, long before your time, from the day God created human beings on the earth; ask from one end of the heavens to the other. Has anything so great as this ever happened, or has anything like it ever been heard of? Has any other people heard the voice of God speaking out of fire, as you have, and lived? Has any god ever tried to take for himself one nation out of another nation, by tests, by signs and wonders, by war, by a mighty hand and an outstretched arm, or by great and awesome deeds, like all the things the Lord your God did for you in Egypt before your very eyes? (Deut. 4:32–34)

Thirty-three centuries ago, Moses already knew that Jewish history was and would continue to be unique. No other nation has survived such trials. The Revelation of God to Israel was unique. No other religion is built on a direct Revelation to an entire people as happened at Mount Sinai. Therefore God – the God of revelation and redemption – is known to the world through Israel. In ourselves we are testimony to something beyond ourselves. We are God's ambassadors to the world.

When we behave in such a way as to evoke admiration for Judaism as a faith and a way of life, that is a *kiddush Hashem*, a sanctification of

God's name. When we do the opposite – when we betray that faith and way of life, causing people to have contempt for the God of Israel – that is a *ḥillul Hashem*, a desecration of God's name. That is what Amos means when he says: "They trample on the heads of the poor as on the dust of the ground, and deny justice to the oppressed … to desecrate My holy name" (Amos 2:7).

When Jews behave badly, unethically, unjustly, they create a *ḥillul Hashem*. People say: I cannot respect a religion or a God that inspires people to behave in such a way. The same applies on a larger, more international scale. The prophet who never tired of pointing this out was Ezekiel, the man who went into exile to Babylon after the destruction of the First Temple. This is what he hears from God:

> I dispersed them among the nations, and they were scattered through the countries; I judged them according to their conduct and their actions. And wherever they went among the nations they profaned My holy name, for it was said of them, "These are the Lord's people, and yet they had to leave His land." (Ezek. 36:19)

When Jews are defeated and sent into exile, it is not only a tragedy for them. It is a tragedy for God. He feels like a parent would feel when he sees a child of his disgraced and sent to prison. He feels a sense of shame and, worse than that, of inexplicable failure. "How is it that, despite all I did for him, I could not save my child from himself?" When Jews are faithful to their mission, when they live and lead and inspire as Jews, then God's name is exalted. That is what Isaiah means when he says, "You are My servant, Israel, in whom I will be glorified" (Is. 49:3).

That is the logic of *kiddush Hashem* and *ḥillul Hashem*. The fate of God's "name" in the world is dependent on us and how we behave. No nation has ever been given a greater or more fateful responsibility. And it means that we each have a share in this task.

When a Jew behaves badly – acts unethically in business, or is guilty of sexual abuse, or utters a racist remark, or acts with contempt for others – it reflects badly on all Jews and on Judaism itself. And when a Jew acts well – develops a reputation for acting honourably in business, or caring for victims of abuse, or showing conspicuous generosity of spirit – not only does it reflect well on Jews, it increases the respect people have for religion in general, and thus for God.

In the passage from his law code (cited above in *Parashat Tazria*), the Rambam, speaking of *kiddush Hashem*, adds: "And doing more than his duty in all things, while avoiding extremes and exaggerations – such a person has sanctified God."[1]

Rabbi Norman Lamm tells the amusing story of Mendel the waiter. When the news came through to a cruise liner about the daring Israeli raid on Entebbe in 1976, the passengers wanted to pay tribute, in some way, to Israel and the Jewish people. A search was made to see if there was a Jewish member of the crew. Only one could be found: Mendel the waiter. So, at a solemn ceremony, the captain offered his congratulations on behalf of the passengers to Mendel, who suddenly found himself elected de facto as the ambassador of the Jewish people. We are all, like it or not, ambassadors of the Jewish people, and how we live, behave, and treat others reflects not only on us as individuals but on Jewry as a whole, and thus on Judaism and the God of Israel.

"Be not afraid of greatness. Some are born great, some achieve greatness, and others have greatness thrust upon 'em," wrote Shakespeare in *Twelfth Night*.[2] Throughout history, Jews have had greatness thrust upon them. As the late Milton Himmelfarb wrote: "The number of Jews in the world is smaller than a small statistical error in the Chinese census. Yet we remain bigger than our numbers. Big things seem to happen around us and to us."[3]

God trusted us enough to make us His ambassadors to an often faithless, brutal world. The choice is ours. Will our lives be a *kiddush Hashem*, or, God forbid, the opposite? To have done something, even one act in a lifetime, to make someone grateful that there is a God in heaven who inspires people to do good on earth is perhaps the greatest

1. *Mishneh Torah, Hilkhot Yesodei HaTorah* 5:11.
2. Shakespeare, *Twelfth Night*, act 2, scene 5.
3. Milton Himmelfarb, *Jews and Gentiles* (New York: Encounter Books, 2007), 141.

achievement to which anyone can aspire. Shakespeare rightly defined the challenge: be not afraid of greatness. A great leader has the responsibility to both be an ambassador and inspire his or her people to be ambassadors as well.

Behar

Think Long

In *Parashat Emor* and *Parashat Behar* there are two quite similar commands, both of which have to do with counting time. In *Parashat Emor* we read about the counting of the Omer, the forty-nine days between the second day of Passover and Shavuot:

> From the day after the Shabbat, the day you brought the sheaf of the wave offering, count off seven full weeks. Count off fifty days up to the day after the seventh Shabbat, and then present an offering of new grain to the Lord. (Lev. 23:15-16)

In *Parashat Behar* we read about the counting of the years to the Jubilee:

> Count off seven Sabbath years – seven times seven years – so that the seven Sabbath years amount to a period of forty-nine years. Then have the trumpet sounded everywhere on the tenth day of the seventh month; on the Day of Atonement sound the trumpet throughout your land. Consecrate the fiftieth year and

proclaim liberty throughout the land to all its inhabitants. It shall be a Jubilee for you; each of you is to return to your family property and to your own clan. (Lev. 25:8–10)

There is, though, one significant difference between the two acts of counting, and it tends to be missed in translation. The counting of the Omer is in the plural: *usefartem lakhem*. The counting of the years is in the singular: *vesafarta lekha*. Oral tradition interpreted the difference as referring to who is to do the counting. In the case of the Omer, the counting is the duty of each individual (Menaḥot 65b); hence the use of the plural. In the case of the Jubilee, the counting is the responsibility of the beit din, specifically the Supreme Court, the Sanhedrin.[1] It is the duty of the Jewish people as a whole, performed centrally on their behalf by the court; hence the singular.

Implicit here is an important principle of leadership. As individuals we count the days, but as leaders we must count the years. As private persons we can think about tomorrow, but in our role as leaders we must think long-term, focusing our eyes on the far horizon. "Who is wise?" asked Ben Zoma, and answered: "One who foresees the consequences" (Tamid 32a). Leaders, if they are wise, think about the impact of their decisions many years from now. Famously, when asked in the 1970s what he thought about the French Revolution in 1789, Chinese leader Zhou Enlai replied: "Too soon to say."[2]

Jewish history is replete with just such long-term thinking. As we saw in our discussion of *Parashat Bo*, when Moses, on the eve of the Exodus, focused the attention of the Israelites on how they would tell the story to their children in the years to come, he was taking the first step to making Judaism a religion built on education, study, and the life of the mind, one of its most profound and empowering insights.

Throughout the book of Deuteronomy, Moses exhibits stunning insight: he says that the Israelites will find that their real challenge will

1.   *Sifra*, Leviticus, *Behar*, 2:2; *Mishneh Torah, Hilkhot Shemitta VeYovel* 10:1.
2.   Truth to tell, the conversation was probably not about the Revolution in 1789 but about the Paris students' revolt of 1968, just a few years earlier. Still, as they say, some stories are true even if they did not happen.

be not slavery but freedom, not poverty but affluence, and not home-lessness but home. Anticipating by two millennia the theory of the fourteenth-century Islamic historian Ibn Khaldun, he predicts that over the course of time, precisely as they succeed, the Israelites will be at risk of losing their *asabiyah*, or social cohesion and solidarity as a group. To prevent this he sets forth a way of life built on covenant, memory, col-lective responsibility, justice, welfare, and social inclusion – still, to this day, the most powerful formula ever devised for a strong civil society.

When the people of the Southern Kingdom of Judah went into exile to Babylon, it was the foresight of Jeremiah, expressed in his letter to the exiles (Jer. 29:1–8), that became the first-ever expression of the idea of a creative minority. The people could maintain their identity there, he said, while working for the benefit of society as a whole, and eventu-ally they would return. It was a remarkable prescription, and has guided Jewish communities in the Diaspora for the twenty-six centuries since.

When Ezra and Nehemiah gathered the people to the Water Gate in Jerusalem in the mid-fifth century BCE and gave them the world's first adult education seminar (Neh. 8), they were signalling a truth that would only become apparent several centuries later in Hellenistic times – that the real battle that would determine the future of the Jewish people was cultural rather than military. The Maccabees won the military struggle against the Seleucids, but the Hasmonean monarchy that ensued even-tually became Hellenised itself.

When R. Yoḥanan b. Zakkai said to Vespasian, the Roman gen-eral leading the siege against Jerusalem, "Give me Yavneh and its sages" (Gittin 56b), he was saving the Jewish future by ensuring that an ongoing source of spiritual and intellectual leadership would remain.

Among the most prescient of all Jewish leaders were the rabbis of the first two centuries of the Common Era. It was they who ordered the great traditions of the Oral Law into the disciplined structure that became the Mishna and subsequently the Talmud; they who developed textual study into an entire religious culture; they who developed the architectonics of prayer into a form eventually followed by Jewish com-munities throughout the world; and they who developed the elaborate system of rabbinic halakha as a "fence around the law" (Mishna Avot 1:1). They did what no other religious leadership has ever succeeded in doing, honing and refining a way of life capable of sustaining a nation in exile and dispersion for two thousand years.

In the early nineteenth century, when rabbis like Zvi Hirsch Kalischer and Yehuda Alkalai began to argue for a return to Zion, they inspired secular figures like Moses Hess (and later Yehudah Leib Pinsker and Theodor Herzl), and even non-Jews like George Eliot, whose *Daniel Deronda* (1876) was one of the first Zionist novels. That movement ensured that there was a Jewish population there, able to settle and build the land so that there could one day be a State of Israel.

When the yeshiva heads and hasidic leaders who survived the Holocaust encouraged their followers to marry and have children and rebuild their shattered worlds, they gave rise to what has become the single fastest growing element in Jewish life. Because of them there are now, within living memory of the almost total destruction of the great centres of Jewish learning in Eastern Europe, more Jews studying at yeshiva or seminary than at any time in the whole of Jewish history – more than in the great days of the nineteenth-century yeshivas at Volozhin, Ponevez, and Mir; more even than in the days of the academies at Sura and Pumbedita that produced the Babylonian Talmud.

Great leaders think long-term and build for the future. That has become all too rare in contemporary secular culture with its relentless focus on the moment, its short attention spans, its fleeting fashions and flash mobs, its texts and tweets, its fifteen minutes of fame, and its fixation with today's headlines and "the power of now."

Nonetheless, the real business leaders of today are those who play the longest of long games. Bill Gates of Microsoft, Jeff Bezos of Amazon. com, Larry Page and Sergei Brin of Google, and Mark Zuckerberg of Facebook were all prepared to wait a long time before monetising their creations. Amazon.com, for example, was launched in 1995 and did not show a profit until the last quarter of 2001. Even by historic standards, these were exceptional instances of long-term thinking and planning.

Though they are secular examples, and though in any case we have not had prophets since the Second Temple, there is nothing intrinsically mysterious about being able to foresee the consequences of choosing this way rather than that. Understanding the future is based on deep study of the past. Warren Buffett spent so many hours and years as a young man reading corporate annual accounts that he developed a finely honed ability to pick companies poised for growth. Already in 2002, five years before the financial collapse actually came, he was warning that derivatives and the securitisation of risk were "financial weapons of mass destruction,"[3] a secular prophecy that was both true and unheeded.

Throughout my years in the Chief Rabbinate, our team – and I believe leadership must always be a team enterprise – would always ask: how will this affect the Jewish community twenty-five years from now? Our task was to build not for us but for our children and grandchildren. The great systemic challenge was to move from a community proud of its past to one focused on its future. That is why we chose to express our mission in the form of a question: will we have Jewish grandchildren?

The leadership challenge of *Parashat Behar* is: count the years, not the days. Keep faith with the past but keep your eyes firmly fixed on the future.

3. Warren Buffet, "What Worries Me," *Fortune*, March 3, 2003, available at http:// www.tilsonfunds.com/BuffettWorries.pdf.

Beḥukkotai

"We the People"

In *Parashat Beḥukkotai*, in the midst of one of the most searing curses ever to have been uttered to a nation by way of warning, the sages found a fleck of pure gold.

Moses is describing a nation in flight from its enemies:

> I will bring despair into the hearts of those of you who survive in enemy territory. Just the sound of a windblown leaf will put them to running, and they will run scared as if running from a sword. They will fall even when no one is chasing them. *They will stumble over each other* as they would before a sword, even though no one is chasing them. You will have no power to stand before your enemies. (Lev. 26:36–37)

There is on the face of it nothing positive in this nightmare scenario. But the sages said: "'They will stumble over each other' – read this as 'stumble because of one another': this teaches that all Israelites are responsible for one another."[1]

---

1.   *Sifra* ad loc.; Sanhedrin 27b; Shevuot 39a.

This is an exceedingly strange passage. Why locate this principle here? Surely the whole Torah testifies to it. When Moses speaks about the reward for keeping the covenant he does so collectively. There will be rain in its due season. You will have good harvests. And so on. The principle that Jews have collective responsibility, that their fate and destiny are interlinked – this could have been found in the Torah's blessings. Why search for it among its curses?

The answer is that there is nothing unique to Judaism in the idea that we are all implicated in one another's fate. That is true of the citizens of any nation. If the economy is booming, most people benefit. If there is a recession many people suffer. If a neighbourhood is scarred by crime, people are scared to walk the streets. If there is law and order, if people are polite to one another and come to one another's aid, there is a general sense of well-being. We are social animals, and our horizons of possibility are shaped by the society and culture within which we live.

All of this applied to the Israelites so long as they were a nation in their own land. But what about when they suffered defeat and exile and were eventually scattered across the earth? They no longer had any of the conventional lineaments of a nation. They were not living in the same place. They did not share the same language of everyday life. While Rashi and his family were living in Christian northern Europe and speaking French, the Rambam was living in Muslim Egypt, speaking and writing Arabic.

Nor did Jews share a fate. While those in northern Europe were suffering persecution and massacres during the Crusades, the Jews of Spain were enjoying their Golden Age. While the Jews of Spain were being expelled and compelled to wander round the world as refugees, the Jews of Poland were enjoying a rare sunlit moment of tolerance. In what sense therefore were they responsible for one another? How did they constitute a nation? How – as the author of Psalm 137 put it – could they sing God's song in a strange land?

There are only two texts in the Torah that speak to this situation, namely the two sections of curses, one in *Parashat Beḥukkotai*, and the other in Deuteronomy in *Parashat Ki Tavo*. Only these speak about a time when Israel is exiled and dispersed, scattered, as Moses later put it, "to the most distant lands under heaven" (Deut. 30:4). There are three major differences between the two curses, however. The passage in Leviticus is in the plural, that in Deuteronomy in the singular. The curses in Leviticus are the words of God; in Deuteronomy they are the words of Moses. And the curses in Deuteronomy do not end in hope. They conclude in a vision of unrelieved bleakness:

> You will try to sell yourselves as slaves – both male and female – but no one will want to buy you. (Deut. 28:68)

Those in Leviticus end with a momentous hope:

> But despite all that, when they are in enemy territory, I will not reject them or despise them to the point of totally destroying them, breaking My covenant with them by doing so, because I am the Lord their God. But for their sake I will remember the covenant with the first generation, the ones I brought out of Egypt's land in the sight of all the nations, in order to be their God; I am the Lord. (Lev. 26:44–45)

Even in their worst hours, according to Leviticus, the Jewish people will never be destroyed. Nor will God reject them. The covenant will still be in force and its terms still operative. That means that Jews will still be linked to one another by the same ties of mutual responsibility that they had in the land – for it was the covenant that formed them as a nation and bound them to one another even as it bound them to God. Therefore, even when falling over one another in flight from their enemies they will still be bound by mutual responsibility. They will still be a nation with a shared fate and destiny.

This is a rare and special idea, and it is the distinctive feature of the politics of covenant. Covenant became a major element in the politics of the West following the Reformation. It shaped political discourse in Switzerland, Holland, Scotland, and England in the seventeenth century as the invention of printing and the spread of literacy made people familiar for the first time with the Hebrew Bible (or the "Old Testament," as they called it). There they learned that tyrants are to be resisted, that immoral orders should not be obeyed, and that kings did not rule by divine right but only by the consent of the governed.

The same convictions were held by the Pilgrim Fathers as they set sail for America, but with one difference: they did not disappear over time as they did in Europe. The result is that the United States is the only country today whose political discourse is framed by the idea of covenant.

Two textbook examples of this are Lyndon Baines Johnson's Inaugural of 1965, and Barack Obama's Second Inaugural of 2013. Both use the biblical device of significant repetition (always an odd number, three or five or seven). Johnson invokes the idea of covenant five times. Obama begins five paragraphs with a key phrase of covenant politics – words never used by British politicians – namely, "We the people."

In covenant societies it is the people as a whole who are responsible, under God, for the fate of the nation. As Johnson put it, "Our fate as a nation and our future as a people rest not upon one citizen but upon all citizens."[2] In Obama's words, "You and I, as citizens, have the power to set this country's course."[3] That is the essence of covenant: we are all in this together. There is no division of the nation into rulers and ruled. We are conjointly responsible, under the sovereignty of God, for one another.

This is not open-ended responsibility. There is nothing in Judaism like the tendentious and ultimately meaningless idea set out by Jean-Paul Sartre in *Being and Nothingness* of "absolute responsibility": "The essential consequence of our earlier remarks is that man, being condemned to be free, carries the weight of the whole world on his shoulders; he is responsible for the world and for himself as a way of being."[4]

In Judaism we are responsible only for what we could have prevented but did not. This is how the Talmud puts it:

> Whoever can forbid his household [to commit a sin] but does not, is seized for [the sins of] his household. [If he can forbid]

---

2. Lyndon B. Johnson, Inaugural Address (United States Capitol, January 20, 1965).
3. Barack Obama, Second Inaugural Address (United States Capitol, January 21, 2013).
4. Jean-Paul Sartre, *Being and Nothingness*, trans. Hazel Barnes (New York: Washington Square Press, 1966), 707.

his fellow citizens [but does not], he is seized for [the sins of] his fellow citizens. [If he can forbid] the whole world [but does not], he is seized for [the sins of] the whole world. (Shabbat 54b)

This remains a powerful idea and an unusual one. What makes it unique to Judaism is that it applied to a people scattered throughout the world, united only by the terms of a covenant our ancestors made with God at Mount Sinai. But it continues, as I have argued, to drive American political discourse likewise even today. It tells us that we are all equal citizens in the republic of faith and that responsibility cannot be delegated away to governments or presidents; it belongs inalienably to each of us. We *are* our brothers' and sisters' keepers.

That is what I mean by the strange, seemingly self-contradictory idea I have argued throughout these essays: that *we are all called on to be leaders*. Surely this cannot be so: if everyone is a leader, then no one is. If everyone leads, who is left to follow?

The concept that resolves the contradiction is covenant. Leadership is, I have argued, the acceptance of responsibility. Therefore if we are all responsible for one another, we are all called on to be leaders, each within our sphere of influence – be it within the family, the community, the organisation, or a larger grouping still.

This can sometimes make an enormous difference. In late summer of 1999 I was in Pristina making a BBC television programme about the aftermath of the Kosovo campaign. I interviewed General Sir Michael Jackson, then head of the NATO forces. To my surprise, he thanked me for what "my people" had done. The Jewish community had taken charge of the city's twenty-three primary schools. It was, he said, the most valuable contribution to the city's welfare. When eight hundred thousand people have become refugees and then return home, the most reassuring sign that life has returned to normal is that the schools open on time. That, he said, we owe to the Jewish people.

Meeting the head of the Jewish community later that day, I asked him how many Jews there were currently in Pristina. His answer? Eleven. The story, as I later uncovered it, was this. In the early days of the conflict, Israel had, along with other international aid agencies, sent a field medical team to work with the Kosovo Albanian refugees. They noticed that while other agencies were concentrating on the adults, there was no one working with the children. Traumatised by the conflict and far from home, the children were running wild.

The team phoned back to Israel and asked for young volunteers. Every youth movement in Israel, from the most secular to the most religious, sent out teams of youth leaders at two-week intervals. They worked with the children, organising summer camps, sports competitions, drama and music events, and whatever else they could think of to make their temporary exile less traumatic. The Kosovo Albanians were Muslims, and for many of the Israeli youth workers, it was their first contact and friendship with children of another faith.

Their effort won high praise from UNICEF, the United Nations' children's organisation. It was in the wake of this that "the Jewish people" – Israel, the American-based Joint Distribution Committee, and other Jewish agencies – were asked to supervise the return to normality of the school system in Pristina.

That episode taught me the power of *ḥesed*, acts of kindness, when extended across the borders of faith. It also showed the practical difference collective responsibility makes to the scope of the Jewish deed. World Jewry is small, but the invisible strands of mutual responsibility mean that even the smallest Jewish community can turn to the Jewish people worldwide for help and achieve things that would be exceptional for a nation many times its size. When the Jewish people join hands in collective responsibility, they become a formidable force for good.

Numbers
במדבר

Bemidbar

Leading a Nation
of Individuals

The book of Numbers begins with a census of the Israelites – hence its name. What is the significance of this act of counting? And why here at the beginning of the book? Besides which, there have already been two previous censuses of the people and this is the third within the space of a single year. Surely one would have been sufficient. Additionally, does counting have anything to do with leadership?

The place to begin is to note what looks like a contradiction. On the one hand, Rashi says that the acts of counting in the Torah are gestures of love on the part of God:

> Because they [the Children of Israel] are dear to Him, God counts them often. He counted them when they were about to leave Egypt. He counted them after the Golden Calf to establish how many were left. And now that He was about to cause His presence to rest on them [with the inauguration of the Sanctuary], He counted them again. (Rashi to Num. 1:1)

When God initiates a census of the Israelites it is to show that He loves them.

On the other hand, the Torah is explicit in saying that taking a census of the nation is fraught with risk: "Then God said to Moses, 'When you take a census of the Israelites to count them, each must give to God a ransom for his life at the time he is counted. Then no plague will come on them when you number them'" (Ex. 30:11–12). When, centuries later, King David counted the people, there was divine anger and seventy thousand people died (II Sam. 24; I Chr. 21). How can this be if counting is an expression of love?

The answer lies in the phrase the Torah uses to describe the act of counting: *se'u et rosh*, literally, "lift the head" (Num. 1:2). This is a strange, circumlocutory expression. Biblical Hebrew contains many verbs meaning "to count": *limnot, lifkod, lispor, laḥshov*. Why does the Torah not use these simple words, choosing instead the roundabout expression, "lift the heads" of the people?

The short answer is this: In any census, count, or roll call there is a tendency to focus on the total – the crowd, the multitude, the mass. Here is a nation of sixty million people, or a company with one hundred thousand employees, or a sports crowd of sixty thousand fans. Any total tends to value the group or nation as a whole. The larger the total, the stronger is the army, the more popular the team, and the more successful the company.

Counting devalues the individual, and tends to make him or her replaceable. If one soldier dies in battle, another will take his place. If one person leaves the organisation, someone else can be hired to do his or her job.

Notoriously, too, crowds have the effect of tending to make the individual lose his or her independent judgement and follow what others are doing, as we have noted before. We call this "herd behaviour," and it sometimes leads to collective madness. In 1841, Charles Mackay published his classic study, *Extraordinary Popular Delusions and the Madness of Crowds*,[1] which tells of the South Sea Bubble that cost thousands their money in the 1720s, and the tulip mania in Holland when fortunes were

---

1. Hertfordshire, England: Wordsworth, 1999.

spent on single tulip bulbs. The Great Crashes of 1929 and 2008 had the same crowd psychology.

Another great work, Gustav Le Bon's *The Crowd: A Study of the Popular Mind* (1895) showed how crowds exercise a "magnetic influence" that transmutes the behaviour of individuals into a collective "group mind." As he put it, "An individual in a crowd is a grain of sand amid other grains of sand, which the wind stirs up at will." People in a crowd become anonymous. Their conscience is silenced. They lose a sense of personal responsibility. Crowds are peculiarly prone to regressive behaviour, primitive reactions, and instinctual behaviour. They are easily led by figures who are demagogues, playing on people's fears and sense of victimhood. Such leaders, he says, are "especially recruited from the ranks of those morbidly nervous, excitable, half-deranged persons who are bordering on madness,"[2] a remarkable anticipation of Hitler. It is no accident that Le Bon's work was published in France at a time of rising anti-Semitism and the Dreyfus trial.

Hence the significance of one remarkable feature of Judaism: its principled insistence – like no other civilisation before – on the dignity and integrity of the individual. We believe that every human being is in the image and likeness of God. The sages said that every life is like an entire universe (Mishna Sanhedrin 4:4). The Rambam says that each of us should see ourselves as if our next act could change the fate of the world.[3] Every dissenting view is carefully recorded in the Mishna, even if the law is otherwise. Every verse of the Torah is capable, said the sages, of seventy interpretations. No voice, no view, is silenced. Judaism never allows us to lose our individuality in the mass.

There is a wonderful blessing mentioned in the Talmud to be said on seeing six hundred thousand Israelites together in one place. It is: "Blessed are You, Lord...who discerns secrets" (Berakhot 58a). The Talmud explains that every person is different. We each have different attributes. We all think our own thoughts. Only God can enter the minds of each of us and know what we are thinking, and this is what the blessing refers to. In other words, even in an enormous crowd

2. Gustav Le Bon, *The Crowd* (London: Fisher Unwin, 1896), 134.
3. *Mishneh Torah, Hilkhot Teshuva* 3:4.

where, to human eyes, faces blur into a mass, God still relates to us as individuals.

That is the meaning of the phrase, "lift the head," used in the context of a census. God tells Moses that there is a danger, when counting a nation, that each individual will feel insignificant. "What am I? What difference can I make? I am only one of millions, a mere wave in the ocean, a grain of sand on the seashore, dust on the surface of infinity."

Against that, God tells Moses to lift people's heads by showing that they each count; they matter as individuals. Indeed in Jewish law a *davar shebeminyan*, something that is counted, sold individually rather than by weight, is never nullified even in a mixture of a thousand or a million others (Beitza 3b). In Judaism, taking a census must always be done in such a way as to signal that we are valued as individuals. We each have unique gifts. There is a contribution only I can bring. To lift someone's head means to show them favour, to recognise them. It is a gesture of love.

There is, however, all the difference in the world between *individuality* and *individualism*. Individuality means that I am a unique and valued member of a team. Individualism means that I am not a team player at all. I am interested in myself alone, not the group. Harvard sociologist Robert Putnam gave this a famous name, noting that more people than ever in the United States are going ten-pin bowling but fewer than ever are joining teams. He called it "bowling alone."[4] MIT professor Sherry Turkle calls our age of Twitter, Facebook, and electronic rather than face-to-face friendships, "alone together."[5] Judaism values individuality, not individualism. As Hillel said, "If I am only for myself, what am I?" (Mishna Avot 1:14).

All this has implications for Jewish leadership. We are not in the business of counting numbers. The Jewish people always was small and yet achieved great things. Judaism has a profound mistrust of demagogic leaders who manipulate the emotions of crowds. Moses at the burning bush spoke of his inability to be eloquent. "I am not a man of words"

---

4. Robert Putnam, *Bowling Alone* (New York: Simon & Schuster, 2000).
5. Sherry Turkle, *Alone Together: Why We Expect More from Technology and Less from Each Other* (New York: Basic Books, 2011).

(Ex. 4:10). He thought this was a failing in a leader. In fact it was the opposite. Moses did not sway people by his oratory. Rather, he lifted them by his teachings.

A Jewish leader has to respect individuals. He or she must "lift their heads." However large the group you lead, you must always communicate the value you place on everyone, including those others exclude: the widow, the orphan, and the stranger. You must never attempt to sway a crowd by appealing to the primitive emotions of fear or hate. You must never ride roughshod over the opinions of others.

It is hard to lead a nation of individuals, but this is the most challenging, empowering, inspiring leadership of all.

The Politics of Envy

Few things in the Torah are more revolutionary than its conception of leadership.

Ancient societies were hierarchical. The masses were poor and prone to hunger and disease. They were usually illiterate. They were used by rulers as a means to wealth and power rather than people with individual rights – a concept born only in the seventeenth century. At times they formed a corvée, a vast conscripted labour force, often used to construct monumental buildings intended to glorify kings. At others they were dragooned into the army to further the ruler's imperial designs.

Rulers often had absolute power of life and death over their subjects. Not only were kings and pharaohs heads of state; they also held the highest religious rank, as children of the gods or demigods themselves. Their power had nothing to do with the consent of the governed. It was seen as written into the fabric of the universe. Just as the sun ruled the sky and the lion ruled the animal realm, so kings ruled their populations. That was how things were in nature, and nature itself was sacrosanct.

The Torah is a sustained polemic against this way of seeing things. Not just kings but all of us, regardless of colour, culture, creed, or class, are in the image and likeness of God. In the Torah, God summons His special people, Israel, to take the first steps to what might eventually become a truly egalitarian society – or to put it more precisely, a society in which dignity, *kavod*, does not depend on power or wealth or an accident of birth.

Hence the concept, which we will explore more fully in *Parashat Korah*, of *leadership as service*. The highest title accorded to Moses in the Torah is that of *eved Hashem*, "a servant of God" (Deut. 34:5). His highest praise is that he was "very humble, more so than anyone else on earth" (Num. 12:3). To lead is to serve. Greatness is humility. As the book of Proverbs puts it, "A man's pride will bring him low, but the humble in spirit will retain honour" (29:23).

The Torah points us in the direction of an ideal world, but it does not assume that we have reached it yet or are within striking distance. The people Moses led, like many of us today, were still prone to ambition, aspiration, vanity, and self-esteem. They still had the human desire for honour, status, and respect. And Moses had to recognise that fact. It would be a major source of conflict in the months and years ahead. It is one of the primary themes of the book of Numbers.

Of whom were the Israelites jealous? Most of them did not aspire to be Moses. He was, after all, the man who spoke to God and to whom God spoke. He performed miracles, brought plagues against the Egyptians, divided the Red Sea, and gave the people water from a rock and manna from heaven. Few would have had the hubris to believe they could do any of these things.

But they did have reason to resent the fact that religious leadership seemed to be confined to one tribe, Levi, and one family within that tribe, the priests or *kohanim*, male descendants of Aaron. Now that the Tabernacle was to be consecrated and the people were about to begin the second half of their journey, from Sinai to the Promised Land, there was a real risk of envy and animosity.

That is a constant throughout history. Aeschylus said, "It is in the character of very few men to honour without envy a friend who has prospered."[1] Goethe warned that although "hatred is active, and envy

---

1. Aeschylus, *Agamemnon* l.832.

passive dislike, there is but one step from envy to hate." Jews should know this in their very bones. We have often been envied, and all too frequently that envy has turned to hate with tragic consequences.

Leaders need to be aware of the perils of envy, especially within the people they lead. This is one of the unifying themes of the long and apparently disconnected *parasha* of *Naso*. In it we see Moses confronting three potential sources of envy. The first lay within the tribe of Levi. Its members had reason to resent the fact that priesthood had gone to just one man and his descendants: Aaron, Moses' brother. The second had to do with individuals who were neither of the tribe of Levi nor of the family of Aaron but who felt that they had the right to be holy in the sense of having a special, intense relationship with God in the way that the priests had. The third had to do with the leadership of the other tribes who might have felt left out of the service of the Tabernacle. We see Moses dealing sequentially with all these potential dangers.

First, Moses gives each Levitical clan a special role in carrying the vessels, furnishings, and framework of the Tabernacle whenever the people journeyed from place to place. The most sacred objects were to be carried by the clan of Kehat. The Gershonites were to carry the cloths, coverings, and drapes. The Merarites were to carry the planks, bars, posts, and sockets that made up the Tabernacle's framework. Each clan was, in other words, to have a special role in place in the solemn procession as the House of God was carried through the desert.

Next Moses deals with individuals who aspire to a higher level of holiness. This, it seems, is the underlying logic of the Nazirite, the individual who vows to set himself apart for the Lord (Num. 6:2). He was not to drink wine or any other grape product, he was not to have his hair cut, and he was not to defile himself through contact with the dead. Becoming a Nazirite was, it seems, a way of temporarily assuming the kind of set-apartness associated with the priesthood, a voluntary extra degree of holiness.[2]

Lastly, he turns to the leadership of the tribes. The highly repetitive chapter 7 of this *parasha* itemises the offerings of each of the tribes on the occasion of the dedication of the altar. Their offerings were identical,

---

2. See *Mishneh Torah, Hilkhot Shemitta VeYovel* 13:13.

and the Torah could have abbreviated its account by describing the gifts brought by one tribe and stating that each of the other tribes did likewise. Yet the sheer repetition has the effect of emphasising the fact that each tribe had its moment of glory. Each, by giving to the house of God, acquired its own share of honour.

These episodes are not the whole of *Naso* but enough of it to signal something that every leader and every group needs to take seriously. Even when people accept in principle the equal dignity of all, and even when they see leadership as service, the old dysfunctional passions die hard. People still resent the success of others. They still feel that honour has gone to others when it should have gone to them. R. Elazar HaKappar said: "Envy, lust, and the pursuit of honour drive a person out of the world" (Mishna Avot 4:21).

The fact that these are destructive emotions does not stop some people – perhaps most of us – from feeling them from time to time, and nothing does more to put at risk the harmony of the group. That is one reason why a leader must be humble. He or she should feel none of these things. But a leader must also be aware that not everyone is humble. Every Moses has a Korah, every Julius Caesar a Cassius, every Duncan a Macbeth, every Othello an Iago. In many groups there is a potential troublemaker driven by a sense of injury to his self-esteem. These are often a leader's deadliest enemies and they can do great damage to the group.

There is no way of eliminating the danger entirely, but Moses in *Parashat Naso* tells us how to behave. Honour everyone equally. Pay special attention to potentially disaffected groups. Make each feel valued. Give everyone a moment in the limelight, if only in a ceremonial way. Set a personal example of humility. Make it clear to all that leadership is service, not a form of status. Find ways in which those with a particular passion can express it, and ensure that everyone has a chance to contribute.

There is no fail-safe way to avoid the politics of envy but there are ways of minimising it, and this *parasha* is an object lesson in how to do so.

Behaalotekha

Power or Influence?

There is a lovely moment in *Parashat Behaalotehka* that shows Moses at the height of his generosity as a leader. It comes after one of his deepest moments of despair. The people, as is their wont, have been complaining, this time about the food. They are tired of the manna. They want meat instead. Moses, appalled that they have not yet learned to accept the hardships of freedom, prays to die. "If this is how You are going to treat me," he says to God, "please go ahead and kill me right now – if I have found favour in Your eyes – and do not let me face my own ruin" (Num. 11:15).

God tells him to appoint seventy elders to help him with the burdens of leadership. He does so, and the divine spirit rests on them. But it also rests on two other men, Eldad and Medad, who were not among the chosen seventy. Evidently Moses had selected six men out of each of the twelve tribes, making seventy-two, and then removed Eldad and Medad by lot. Nonetheless, they too were caught up in the moment of inspiration (Sanhedrin 17a).

Joshua, Moses' deputy, sees this as a potential threat. Moses replies with splendid magnanimity: "Are you jealous for my sake? I wish that all the Lord's people were prophets and that the Lord would put His spirit on them!" (Num. 11:29).

This contrasts sharply with his conduct later when his leadership is challenged by Korah and his followers. On that occasion he shows no gentleness or generosity. To the contrary, in effect he prays that the ground swallow them up, that "they go down alive into the realm of the dead" (Num. 16:28–30). He is sharp, decisive, and unforgiving. Why the difference between Korah, on the one hand, and Eldad and Medad, on the other?

To understand it, it is essential to grasp the difference between two concepts often confused, namely power and influence. We tend to think of them as similar if not identical. People of power have influence. People of influence have power. But it is not so. The two are quite distinct and operate by a different logic, as a simple thought experiment will show.

Imagine you have total power. Whatever you say goes. Then one day you decide to share your power with nine others. You now have at best one-tenth of the power you had before. Now imagine that you have a certain measure of influence. Then you decide to share that influence with nine others whom you make your partners. You now have ten times the influence you had before, because instead of just you there are now ten people delivering the same message.

Power works by division, influence by multiplication. Power, in other words, is a zero-sum game: the more you share, the less you have. Influence is a non-zero-sum game: the more you share, the more you have.

Throughout his forty years at the head of the nation, Moses held two different leadership roles. He was a prophet, teaching Torah to the Israelites and communicating with God. He was also the functional equivalent of a king, leading the people on their journeys, directing their destiny, and supplying them with their needs. The one leadership role he did not have was that of high priest, which went to his brother Aaron.

We can see this duality later in the narrative when he inducts Joshua as his successor. God commands him: "Take Joshua son of Nun, a man of spirit, and *lay your hand on him.... Give him some of your honour* (*hod*) *so that the whole Israelite community will obey him*" (Num. 27:18–20).

Note the two different acts. One, "lay your hand [*vesamakhta*] on him," is the origin of the term *semikha*, whereby a rabbi ordains a pupil, granting him the authority to make rulings in his own right. The rabbis saw their role as a continuation of that of the prophets ("Moses received the Torah from Sinai and transmitted it to Joshua; Joshua to the elders; the elders to the prophets; and the prophets handed it down to the men of the Great Assembly," Mishna Avot 1:1). By this act of *semikha*, Moses was handing on to Joshua his role as prophet.

By the other act, "Give him some of your honour," he was inducting him into the role of king. The Hebrew word *hod*, honour, is associated with kingship, as in the biblical phrase *hod malkhut*, "the honour of kingship" (Dan. 11:21; 1 Chr. 29:25).

Kings had power – including that of life and death (see Josh. 1:18). Prophets had none, but they had influence, not just during their lifetimes but, in many cases, to this day. To paraphrase Kierkegaard: When a king dies his power ends. When a prophet dies his influence begins.

Now we see exactly why Moses' reaction was so different in the cases of Eldad and Medad and that of Korah and his followers. Eldad and Medad sought and received no power. They merely received the same influence – the divine spirit that emanated from Moses. They became prophets. That is why Moses said, "I wish that all the Lord's people were prophets and that the Lord would put His spirit on them" (Num. 11:29). Prophecy is not a zero-sum game. When it comes to leadership as influence, the more we share, the more we have.

Korah, or at least some of his followers, sought power, and power is a zero-sum game. When it comes to *malkhut*, the leadership of power, the rule is: "There is one leader for the generation, not two" (Sanhedrin 8a). In kingship, a bid for power is an attempted coup d'etat and has to be resisted by force. Otherwise the result is a division of the nation into two, as happened after the death of King Solomon. Moses could not let the challenge of Korah go unopposed without fatefully compromising his own authority.

So Judaism clearly demarcates between leadership as influence and leadership by power. It is unqualified in its endorsement of the first, and deeply ambivalent about the second. Tanakh is a sustained polemic against the use of power. All power, according to the Torah, rightly belongs to God. The Torah recognises the need, in an imperfect world, for the use of coercive force in maintaining the rule of law and the defence of the realm. Hence its endorsement of the appointment of a king should the people so desire it (Deut. 17:15–20; 1 Sam. 8). But this is clearly a concession, not an ideal.[1]

The real leadership embraced by Tanakh and by rabbinic Judaism is that of influence, above all that of prophets and teachers. That is the ultimate accolade given to Moses by tradition. We know him as *Moshe Rabbenu,* Moses our teacher. Moses was the first of a long line of figures in Jewish history – among them Ezra, Hillel, R. Yoḥanan b. Zakkai, R. Akiva, the sages of the Talmud, and the scholars of the Middle Ages – who represent one of Judaism's most revolutionary ideas: *the teacher as hero.*

Judaism was the first and greatest civilisation to predicate its very survival on education, houses of study, and learning as a religious experience higher even than prayer (see Shabbat 10a). The reason is this: leaders are people able to mobilise others to act in certain ways. If they achieve this only because they hold power over them, this means treating people as means, not ends – as things, not persons. Not accidentally, the single greatest writer on leadership as power was Machiavelli.

The other way to achieve it is to speak to people's needs and aspirations and teach them how to achieve these things together as a group. That is done through the power of a vision, force of personality, the ability to articulate shared ideals in a language with which people can identify, and the capacity to "raise up many disciples" who will continue the work into the future. Power diminishes those on whom it is exercised. Influence and education lift and enlarge them.

Judaism is a sustained protest against what Hobbes called the "general inclination of all mankind," namely "a perpetual and restless desire of power after power, that ceaseth only in death."[2] That may be the reason why Jews have seldom exercised power for prolonged periods

---

1.   So, at any rate, is the view of Ibn Ezra, Rabbenu Baḥya, and Abrabanel to Deuteronomy 17:15.
2.   Hobbes, *The Leviathan,* part 1, ch. 11.

of time but have had an influence on the world out of all proportion to their numbers.

Not all of us have power, but we all have influence. That is why we can each be a leader. The most important forms of leadership come not with position, title, or robes of office, not with prestige and power, but with the willingness to work with others to achieve what we cannot do alone; to speak, to listen, to teach, to learn, to treat other people's views with respect even if they disagree with us; to explain patiently and cogently why we believe what we believe and do what we do; to encourage others, praise their best endeavours, and challenge them to do better still. Always choose influence rather than power. It helps change people into people who can change the world.

Shelaḥ

Confidence

It was perhaps the single greatest collective failure of leadership in the Torah. Ten of the spies whom Moses had sent to scout out the land came back with a report calculated to demoralise the nation.

> We came to the land to which you sent us. It flows with milk and honey, and this is its fruit. However, the people who dwell in the land are strong, and the cities are fortified and very large.... We are not able to go up against the people, for they are stronger than we are.... The land, through which we have gone to spy it out, is a land that devours its inhabitants, and all the people that we saw in it are of great height.... We seemed to ourselves like grasshoppers, and so we seemed to them. (Num. 13:27–33)

This was nonsense, and they should have known it. They had left Egypt, the greatest empire of the ancient world, after a series of plagues that brought that great country to its knees. They had crossed the seemingly impenetrable barrier of the Red Sea. They had fought and defeated the Amalekites, a ferocious warrior nation. They had even sung, along with their fellow Israelites, a song at the sea that contained the words:

> The peoples have heard; they tremble;
> pangs have seized the inhabitants of Philistia.
> Now are the chiefs of Edom dismayed;
> trembling seizes the leaders of Moab;
> all the inhabitants of Canaan have melted away. (Ex. 15:14–15)

They should have known that the people of the land were afraid of them, not the other way round. And so it was, as Rahab told the spies sent by Joshua forty years later:

> I know that the Lord has given you the land, and that the fear of you has fallen upon us, and that all the inhabitants of the land melt away before you. For we have heard how the Lord dried up the water of the Red Sea before you when you came out of Egypt, and what you did to the two kings of the Amorites who were beyond the Jordan, to Sihon and Og, whom you utterly destroyed. And as soon as we heard it, our hearts melted, and there was no spirit left in any man because of you, for the Lord your God, He is God in the heavens above and on the earth beneath. (Josh. 2:9–11)

Only Joshua and Caleb among the twelve showed leadership. They told the people that the conquest of the land was eminently achievable because God was with them. The people did not listen. But the two leaders received their reward. They alone of their generation lived to enter the land. More than that: their defiant statement of faith and their refusal to be afraid shines as brightly now as it did thirty-three centuries ago. They are eternal heroes of faith.

One of the fundamental tasks of any leader from president to parent is to give people a sense of confidence – in themselves, in the group of which they are a part, and in the mission itself. A leader must have faith in the people he leads, and inspire that faith in them. As Rosabeth Moss Kanter of the Harvard Business School writes in her book *Confidence*, "Leadership is not about the leader, it is about how he or she builds the confidence of everyone else."[1] Confidence, by the way, is Latin for "having faith together."

The truth is that in no small measure, a law of self-fulfilling prophecy applies in the human arena. Those who say, "We cannot do it" are probably right, as are those who say, "We can." If you lack confidence you will lose. If you have it – solid, justified confidence based on preparation and past performance – you will win. Not always, but often enough to triumph over setbacks and failures. That, as mentioned in our discussion of *Parashat Beshallah*, is what the story of Moses' hands is about, during the battle against the Amalekites. When the Israelites look up, they win. When they look down they start to lose.

That is why the negative definition of Jewish identity that has so often prevailed in modern times (Jews are the people who are hated, Israel is the nation that is isolated, to be Jewish is to refuse to grant Hitler a posthumous victory) is so misconceived, and why one in two Jews who have been brought up on this doctrine choose to marry out and discontinue the Jewish journey.[2]

Harvard economic historian David Landes in his *The Wealth and Poverty of Nations* explores the question of why some countries fail to grow economically while others succeed spectacularly. After more than five hundred pages of close analysis, he reaches this conclusion:

> In this world, the optimists have it, not because they are always right, but because they are positive. Even when wrong, they are positive, and that is the way of achievement, correction, improvement, and success. Educated, eyes-open optimism pays; pessimism can only offer the empty consolation of being right.[3]

I prefer the word "hope" to "optimism." Optimism is the belief that things will get better; hope is the belief that together we can make

---

1. Rosabeth Moss Kanter, *Confidence* (New York: Random House, 2005), 325.
2. *National Jewish Population Survey 1990: A Portrait of Jewish Americans*, Pew Research Center, October 1, 2013.
3. David Landes, *The Wealth and Poverty of Nations* (New York: Little, Brown and Co., 1998), 524.

things better. No Jew, knowing Jewish history, can be an optimist, but no Jew worthy of the name abandons hope. The most pessimistic of the prophets, from Amos to Jeremiah, were still voices of hope. By their defeatism, the spies failed as leaders and as Jews. To be a Jew is to be an agent of hope.

The most remarkable by far of all the commentators on the episode of the spies was the Lubavitcher Rebbe, Rabbi Menachem Mendel Schneerson. He raised the obvious question. The Torah emphasises that the spies were all leaders, princes, heads of tribes. They knew that God was with them, and that with His help there was nothing they could not do. They knew that God would not have promised them a land they could not conquer. Why then did they come back with a negative report?

His answer turns the conventional understanding of the spies upside down. They were, he said, not afraid of defeat. They were afraid of victory. What they said to the people was one thing, but what led them to say it was another entirely.

What was their situation now, in the wilderness? They lived in close and continuous proximity to God. They drank water from a rock. They ate manna from heaven. They were surrounded by the Clouds of Glory. Miracles accompanied them along the way.

What would be their situation in the land? They would have to fight wars, plough the land, plant seeds, gather harvests, and create and sustain an army, an economy, and a welfare system. They would have to do what every other nation does: live in the real world of empirical space. What then would happen to their relationship with God? Yes, He would still be present in the rain that made crops grow, in the blessings of field and town, and in the Temple in Jerusalem that they would visit three times a year, but not visibly, intimately, miraculously, as He was in the desert. This is what the spies feared: not failure but success.

This, said the Rebbe, was a noble sin but still a sin. God wants us to live in the real world of nations, economies, and armies. God wants us, as He put it, to create "a dwelling place in the lower world." He wants us to bring the *Shekhina*, the Divine Presence, into everyday life. It is easy to find God in total seclusion and escape from responsibility. It is hard to find God in the office, in business, in farms and fields and factories and finance. But it is that challenge to which we are summoned: to create a space for God in the midst of this physical world that He created and seven times pronounced good. That is what ten of the spies failed to understand, and it was a spiritual failure that condemned an entire generation to forty years of futile wandering.

The Rebbe's words ring true today even more loudly than they did when he first spoke them. They are a profound statement of the Jewish task. They are also a fine exposition of a concept that entered psychology only relatively recently – *fear of success*.[4] We are all familiar with the idea of fear of failure. It is what keeps many of us from taking risks, preferring instead to stay within our comfort zone.

No less real, though, is fear of success. We want to succeed, so we tell ourselves and others. But often unconsciously we fear what success may bring: new responsibilities, expectations on the part of others that we may find hard to fulfil, and so on. So we fail to become what we might have become had someone given us faith in ourselves.

The antidote to fear, both of failure and success, lies in the passage with which the *parasha* ends: the command of *tzitzit* (Num. 15:38–41). We are commanded to place fringes on our garments, among them a thread of blue. Blue is the colour of the sky and of heaven. Blue is the colour we see when we look up (at least in Israel; in Britain, more often than not we see clouds). When we learn to look up, we overcome our fears. Leaders give people confidence by teaching them to look up. We are not grasshoppers unless we think we are.

---

4. Sometimes called the "Jonah complex," after the prophet. See Abraham Maslow, *The Farther Reaches of Human Nature* (New York: Penguin Books, 1977), 35–40.

Koraḥ

Servant Leadership

You have gone too far! The whole community are holy, every one of them, and the Lord is with them. Why then do you set yourselves above God's congregation? (Num. 16:3)

What exactly was wrong in what Korah and his motley band of fellow agitators said? We know that Korah was a demagogue, not a democrat. He wanted power for himself, not for the people. We know also that the protestors were disingenuous. Each had his own reasons to feel resentful towards Moses or Aaron or fate. Set these considerations aside for a moment and ask: was what they said true or false?

They were surely right to say, "The whole community are holy." That, after all, is what God asked the people to be: a kingdom of priests and a holy nation (Ex. 19:6), meaning, a kingdom all of whose members are (in some sense) priests, and a nation all of whose citizens are holy.[1]

---

1. Some suggest that the mistake they made was to say, "The whole congregation *are* holy" (*kulam kedoshim*), instead of "All the congregation *is* holy" (*kula kedosha*). The holiness of the congregation is collective rather than individual. Others say that

They were equally right to say, "The Lord is with them." That was the point of the making of the Tabernacle: "Have them make My Sanctuary for Me, and I will dwell among them" (Ex. 25:8). Exodus ends with the words: "So the cloud of the Lord was over the Tabernacle by day, and fire was in the cloud by night, in the sight of all the Israelites during all their travels" (40:38). The Divine Presence was visibly with the people wherever they went.

What was wrong was their last remark: "Why then do you *set yourselves above* God's congregation?" This was not a small mistake. It was a fundamental one. Moses represents the birth of a new kind of leadership. That is what Korah and his followers did not understand. Many of us do not understand it still.

The most famous buildings in the ancient world were the Mesopotamian ziggurats and Egyptian pyramids. These were more than just buildings. They were statements in stone of a hierarchical social order. They were wide at the base and narrow at the top. At the top was the king or pharaoh – at the point, so it was believed, where heaven and earth met. Beneath was a series of elites, and beneath them the labouring masses.

This was believed to be not just one way of organising a society but the only way. The very universe was organised on this principle, as was the rest of life. The sun ruled the heavens. The lion ruled the animal kingdom. The king ruled the nation. That is how it was in nature. That is how it must be. Some are born to rule, others to be ruled.[2]

Judaism is a protest against this kind of hierarchy. Every human being, not just the king, is in the image and likeness of God. Therefore no one is entitled to rule over any other without his or her assent. There is still a need for leadership, because without a conductor an orchestra would lapse into discord. Without a captain, a team might have brilliant players and yet not be a team. Without generals, an army would be a mob. Without government, a nation would lapse into anarchy. "In those days there was no king in Israel. Everyone did what was right in his own eyes" (Judges 17:6; 21:25).

they should have said, "is called on to be holy" rather than "is" holy. Holiness is a vocation, not a state.

2.   Aristotle, *Politics*, book 1, 1254a21–24.

In a social order in which everyone has equal dignity in the eyes of Heaven, a leader does not stand *above* the people. He serves the people, and he serves God. The great symbol of biblical Israel, the menora, is an *inverted* pyramid or ziggurat, broad at the top, narrow at the base. The greatest leader is therefore the most humble. "Moses was very humble, more so than anyone else on earth" (Num. 12:3).

The name given to this is *servant leadership,*[3] and its origin is in the Torah. The highest accolade given to Moses is that he was "the servant of the Lord" (Deut. 34:5). Moses is given this title eighteen times in Tanakh as a whole. Only one other leader merits the same description: Joshua, who is described this way twice.

No less fascinating is the fact that only one person in the Torah is *commanded* to be humble, namely the king:

> When he takes the throne of his kingdom, he is to write for himself on a scroll a copy of this law, taken from that of the Levitical priests. It is to be with him, and he is to read it all the days of his life so that he may learn to revere the Lord his God and follow carefully all the words of this law and these decrees *and not consider himself better than his fellow Israelites.* (Deut. 17:18–20)

This is how the Rambam describes the proper conduct of a king:

> Just as the Torah has granted him the great honour and obligated everyone to revere him, so too it has commanded him to be lowly and empty at heart, as it says: "My heart is a void within me" (Ps. 109:22). Nor should he treat Israel with overbearing haughtiness, as it says, "He should not consider himself better than his fellows" (Deut. 17:20).

---

3. The well-known text on this theme is Robert K. Greenleaf, *Servant Leadership: A Journey into the Nature of Legitimate Power and Greatness* (New York: Paulist Press, 1977). Greenleaf does not, however, locate this idea in Torah. Hence it is important to see that it was born here, with Moses.

He should be gracious and merciful to the small and the great, involving himself in their good and welfare. He should protect the honour of even the humblest of people.

When he speaks to the people as a community, he should speak gently, as in, "Listen my brothers and my people ...." [King David's words in 1 Ch. 28:2]. Similarly, 1 Kings 12:7 states, "If today you will be a servant to these people ...."

He should always conduct himself with great humility. There is none greater than Moses, our teacher. Yet, he said: "What are we? Your complaints are not against us" (Ex. 16:8). He should bear the nation's difficulties, burdens, complaints, and anger as a nurse carries an infant.[4]

The same applies to all positions of leadership. The Rambam lists among those who have no share in the World to Come someone who "imposes a rule of fear on the community, not for the sake of Heaven." Such a person "rules over a community by force, so that people are greatly afraid and terrified of him," doing so "for his own glory and personal interests." The Rambam adds to this last phrase: "like heathen kings."[5] The polemical intent is clear. It is not that no one behaves this way. It is that this is not a Jewish way to behave.

When R. Gamliel acted in what his colleagues saw as a high-handed manner, he was deposed as *nasi*, head of the community, until he acknowledged his fault and apologised (Berakhot 27b). R. Gamliel learned the lesson. He later said to two people who declined his offer to accept positions of leadership: "Do you think that I am offering you authority [*serara*]? I am offering you the chance to serve [*avdut*]" (Horayot 10a–b). As Martin Luther King Jr. once said, "Everybody can be great ... because anybody can serve."[6]

C. S. Lewis rightly defined humility not as *thinking less of yourself* but as *thinking of yourself less*. The great leaders respect others. They

4. *Mishneh Torah, Hilkhot Melakhim* 2:6.
5. *Mishneh Torah, Hilkhot Teshuva* 3:13.
6. Martin Luther King Jr., Nobel Prize Acceptance Speech (Oslo, Norway, December 10, 1964).

honour them, lift them, inspire them to reach heights they might never have reached otherwise. They are motivated by ideals, not by personal ambition. They do not succumb to the arrogance of power.

Sometimes the worst mistakes we make are when we project our feelings onto others. Korah was an ambitious man, so he saw Moses and Aaron as two people driven by ambition, "setting themselves above God's congregation." He did not understand that in Judaism, to lead is to serve. Those who serve do not lift themselves high. They lift other people high.

Miriam, Moses' Friend

I t is one of the great mysteries of the Torah. Arriving at Kadesh, the people find themselves without water. They complain to Moses and Aaron. The two leaders go to the Tent of Meeting and there they are told by God to take the staff and speak to the rock, and water will emerge.

Moses' subsequent behaviour is extraordinary. He takes the staff. He and Aaron gather the people. Then Moses says: "Listen now, you rebels, shall we bring you water out of this rock?" Then "Moses raised his arm and struck the rock twice with his staff" (Num. 20:10–11).

This was the behaviour that cost Moses and Aaron their chance of leading the people across the Jordan into the Promised Land. "Because you did not have enough faith in Me to sanctify Me in the sight of the Israelites, you will not bring this community into the land I have given them" (Num. 10:12).

The commentators disagree as to which aspect of Moses' behaviour was wrong. His anger? His act of striking the rock instead of speaking to it? The implication that it was he and Aaron, not God, who were bringing water from the rock? I have contended in the past that Moses neither sinned nor was punished. He merely acted as he had done almost forty years earlier when God told him to hit the rock (Ex. 17:6), and thereby showed that though he was the right leader for the people who had been slaves in Egypt, he was not the leader for their children who were born in freedom and would conquer the land.

This time, though, I want to pose a different question. Why then? Why did Moses fail this particular test? After all, he had been in a similar situation twice before. After emerging from the Red Sea the people had travelled for three days without finding water. Then they found some, but it was bitter and they complained. God showed Moses how to make the water sweet (Ex. 15:22–26). Arriving at Rephidim, again they found no water and complained. Despairing, Moses said to God, "What am I to do with these people? They are almost ready to stone me." God patiently instructed Moses as to what to do, and water flowed from the rock (Ex. 17:1–7).

So Moses had successfully overcome two similar challenges in the past. Why on this third occasion did he lose emotional control? What was different? The answer is stated explicitly in the text, but in so understated a way that we may fail to grasp its significance. Here it is: "In the first month the whole Israelite community arrived at the Desert of Zin, and they stayed at Kadesh. There Miriam died and was buried" (Num. 20:1). Immediately after this we read: "Now there was no water for the community, and the people gathered in opposition to Moses and Aaron" (20:2). A famous Talmudic passage (Taanit 9a) explains that it was in Miriam's merit that the Israelites had a well of water that miraculously accompanied them through their desert journeys. When Miriam died, the water ceased. This interpretation reads the sequence of events simply and supernaturally. Miriam died. Then there was no water. From this, one can infer that until then there was water because Miriam was alive. It was a miracle in her merit.

However, there is another way of reading the passage, naturally and psychologically. The connection between Miriam's death and the events that followed had less to do with a miraculous well and more to do with Moses' response to the complaints of the Israelites. This was the first trial he had to face as leader of the people without the presence of his sister. Let us recall who Miriam was, for Moses. She was his elder sister, his oldest sibling. She had watched over his fate as he floated down the

Nile in a pitched basket. She had the presence of mind, and the audacity, to speak to Pharaoh's daughter and arrange for the child to be nursed by an Israelite woman, that is, by Moses' own mother Yokheved. Without Miriam, Moses would have grown up not knowing who he was and to which people he belonged. Miriam is a background presence throughout much of the narrative. We see her leading the women in song at the Red Sea, so it is clear that she, like Aaron, had a leadership role. We gain a sense of how much she meant to Moses when, in an obscure passage, she and Aaron "spoke against Moses because of the Cushite woman whom he had married, for he had married a Cushite woman" (Num. 12:1). We do not know exactly what the issue was, but we do know that Miriam is smitten with leprosy. Aaron turns helplessly to Moses and asks him to intervene on her behalf, which he does with simple eloquence in the shortest prayer on record – five Hebrew words – "Please, God, heal her now" (Num. 12:13). Moses still cares deeply for her, despite her negative talk.

It is only in *Parashat Ḥukkat* that we begin to get a full sense of her influence, and this only by implication. For the first time Moses faces a challenge without her, and for the first time Moses loses emotional control in the presence of the people. This is one of the effects of bereavement, and those who have suffered it often say that the loss of a sibling is harder to bear than the loss of a parent. The loss of a parent is part of the natural order of life. The loss of a sibling can be less expected and more profoundly disorienting. And Miriam was no ordinary sibling. Moses owed her his entire relationship with his natural family, as well as his identity as one of the Children of Israel.

It is a cliché to say that leadership is a lonely undertaking. But at the same time no leader can truly survive on his or her own. Yitro told Moses this many years earlier. Seeing him leading the people alone he said, "You and these people who come to you will only wear yourselves out. The work is too heavy for you; you cannot handle it alone" (Ex. 18:18). Leaders need three kinds of support: (1) allies who will fight alongside them, (2) troops or teams to whom they can delegate, and (3) a soulmate or soulmates to whom they can confide their doubts and fears, who will listen without an agenda other than being a supportive presence, and who will give them the courage, confidence, and sheer resilience to carry on.

Having known, through personal friendship, many leaders in many fields, I can say with certainty that it is false to suppose that people in positions of high leadership have thick skins. Most of those I have known have not. They are often intensely vulnerable. They can suffer deeply from doubt and uncertainty. They know that a leader must often make a choice between two evils, and he never knows in advance how a decision will work out. Leaders can be hurt by criticism and the betrayal of people they once considered friends. Because they are leaders, they rarely show any signs of vulnerability in public. They have to project a certainty and confidence they do not feel. But Ronald Heifetz and Marty Linsky, the Harvard leadership experts, are right to say, "The hard truth is that it is not possible to experience the rewards and joy of leadership without experiencing the pain as well."[1]

Leaders need confidants, people who "will tell you what you do not want to hear and cannot hear from anyone else, people in whom you can confide without having your revelations spill back into the work arena."[2] A confidant cares about you more than about the issues. He or she lifts you when you are low, and gently brings you back to reality when you are in danger of self-congratulation or complacency. Heifetz and Linsky write, "Almost every person we know with difficult experiences of leadership has relied on a confidant to help them get through."[3]

The Rambam in his commentary to the Mishna[4] counts this as one of the four kinds of friendship. He calls it the "trusted friend" (*ḥaver habitaḥon*) and describes it as having someone in whom "you have absolute trust and with whom you are completely open and unguarded," hiding neither the good news nor the bad, knowing that the other person will neither take advantage of the confidences shared nor share them with others.

A careful reading of this famous episode in the context of Moses' early life suggests that Miriam was Moses' "trusted friend," his confidante,

---

1. Ronald Heifetz and Marty Linsky, *Leadership on the Line* (Boston: Harvard Business School Press, 2002), 227.
2. Ibid., 200.
3. Ibid.
4. Commentary to Mishna Avot 1:6.

the source of his emotional stability; when she was no longer there, he could not cope with crisis as he had done until then.

Those who are a source of strength to others need their own source of strength. The Torah is explicit in telling us how often for Moses that source of strength was God Himself. But even Moses needed a human friend, and it seems, by implication, that this was Miriam. A leader in her own right, she was also one of her brother's sources of strength.

Even the greatest cannot lead alone.

Balak

Leadership and Loyalty

I s leadership a set of skills, the ability to summon and command power? Or does it have an essentially moral dimension also? Can a bad man be a good leader, or does his badness compromise his leadership? That is the question raised by the key figure in *Parashat Balak*, the pagan prophet Balaam.

First, by way of introduction, we have independent evidence that Balaam actually existed. An archaeological discovery in 1967 at Deir 'Alla, at the junction of the Jordan and Jabbok rivers, uncovered an inscription on the wall of a pagan temple, dated to the eighth century BCE, which makes reference to a seer named Balaam ben Beor, in terms remarkably similar to those of *Parashat Balak*. Balaam was a well-known figure in the region.

His skills were clearly impressive. He was a religious virtuoso, a sought-after shaman, magus, spell-binder, and miracle worker. Balak says, on the basis of experience or reputation, "I know that whomever you bless is blessed, and whomever you curse is cursed" (Num. 22:6). The rabbinic literature does not call this into question. On the phrase "No prophet has risen in Israel like Moses, whom the Lord knew face to face" (Deut. 34:10), the sages went so far as to say: "*In Israel* there was no other prophet as great as Moses, but among the nations there was. Who was he? Balaam."[1]

Another midrashic source says that "there was nothing in the world that the Holy One, Blessed Be He, did not reveal to Balaam, who surpassed even Moses in the wisdom of sorcery."[2] At a technical level, Balaam had all the skills.

Yet the ultimate verdict on Balaam is negative. In chapter 25, we read of the ironic sequel to the episode of the curses/blessings. The Israelites, having been saved by God from the would-be curses of Moab and Midian, suffer a self-inflicted tragedy by allowing themselves to be enticed by the women of the land. God's anger burns against them. Several chapters later (Num. 31:16) it emerges that it was Balaam who devised this strategy: "They were the ones *who followed Balaam's advice and were the means of turning the Israelites away from the Lord* in what happened at Peor, so that a plague struck the Lord's people." Having failed to curse the Israelites, Balaam eventually succeeds in doing them great harm.

So the picture that emerges from the Jewish sources is of a man with great gifts, a genuine prophet, a man whom the sages compared with Moses himself. Yet at the same time he is a figure of flawed character, which eventually leads to his downfall and to his reputation as an evildoer, one of those mentioned by the Mishna as being denied a share in the World to Come (Mishna Sanhedrin 10:2).

What was his flaw? There are many speculations, but one suggestion given in the Talmud infers the answer from his name. What is the meaning of "Balaam"? Answers the Talmud: it means, "a man without a people" – *belo am* (Sanhedrin 105a). This is a fine insight. Balaam is a man without loyalties. Balak sent for him saying: "Now come and put a curse on these people, because they are too powerful for me…. For I know that whomever you bless is blessed, and whomever you curse is cursed" (Num. 22:6). Balaam was a prophet for hire. He had supernatural powers.

---

1. *Sifrei*, Deuteronomy, *VeZot HaBerakha*, 357.
2. *Tanna DeVei Eliyahu Rabba* 28; see also Numbers Rabba, 14:20; Berakhot 7a; Avoda Zara 4a.

He could bless someone and that person would succeed. He could curse someone and that person would be blighted by misfortune. But there is no hint in any of the reports, biblical or otherwise, that Balaam was a prophet in the *moral* sense: that he was concerned with justice, desert, the rights and wrongs of those whose lives he affected. Like a contract killer of a later age, Balaam was a loner. His services could be bought. He had skills and used them to devastating effect. But he had no commitments, no loyalties, no rootedness in humanity. He was the man *belo am*, without a people.

Moses was the opposite. God Himself says of him, "He is [supremely] loyal in all My house" (Num. 12:7). However disappointed Moses was with the Israelites, he never ceased to argue their cause before God. When his initial intervention on their behalf with Pharaoh worsened their condition, he said to God, "O Lord, why do You mistreat Your people? Why did You send me?" (Ex. 5:22). When the Israelites made the Golden Calf and God threatened to destroy the people and begin again with Moses, he said, "Now, if You would, please forgive their sin. If not, then blot me out from the book that You have written" (Ex. 32:32). When the people, demoralised by the report of the spies, wanted to return to Egypt and God's anger burned against them, Moses said, "With Your great love, forgive the sin of this nation, just as You have forgiven them from [the time they left] Egypt until now" (Num. 14:19). When God threatened punishment during the Korah rebellion, Moses prayed, "Will You be angry with the entire assembly when only one man sins?" (Num. 16:22). Even when his own sister Miriam spoke badly about him and was punished by leprosy, Moses prayed to God on her behalf, "Please God, heal her now" (Num. 12:13). Moses never ceased to pray for his people, however much they had sinned, however audacious the prayer, however much he was putting his own relationship with God at risk. Knowing their faults, he remained utterly loyal to them.

The Hebrew word *emuna* is usually translated as "faith," and that is what it came to mean in the Middle Ages. But in biblical Hebrew it is better translated as "faithfulness," "reliability," "loyalty." It means not walking away from the other party when times are tough. It is a key covenantal virtue.

There are people with great gifts, intellectual and sometimes even spiritual, who nonetheless fail to achieve what they might have done. They lack the basic moral qualities of integrity, honesty, humility, and – above all – loyalty. What they do, they do brilliantly. But often they do the wrong things. Conscious of their unusual endowments, they tend to look down on others. They give way to pride, arrogance, and a belief that they can somehow get away with great crimes. Balaam is the classic example, and the fact that he planned to entice the Israelites into sin even after he knew that God was on their side is a measure of how the greatest can sometimes fall to become the lowest of the low.

Those who are loyal to other people find that other people are loyal to them. Those who are disloyal are eventually distrusted and lose whatever authority they might once have had. Leadership without loyalty is not leadership. Skills alone cannot substitute for the moral qualities that make people follow those who demonstrate them. We follow those we trust, because they have acted so as to earn our trust. That was what made Moses the great leader Balaam might have been but never was. Always be loyal to the people you lead.

Pinḥas

Lessons of a Leader

P arashat *Pinḥas* contains a mini-essay on leadership, as Moses confronts his own mortality and asks God to appoint a successor. The great leaders care about succession. In *Ḥayei Sara* we see Abraham instruct his servant to find a wife for Isaac so that the family of the covenant will continue. David chooses Solomon. Elijah, at God's bidding, appoints Elisha to carry on his work.

In the case of Moses, the sages sense a certain sadness at his realisation that he would not be succeeded by either of his sons, Gershom or Eliezer.[1] As we have noted before, such is the case with *keter Torah*, the invisible crown of Torah worn by the prophets and the sages. Unlike the crowns of priesthood and kingship, it does not pass dynastically from father to son. Charisma rarely does. What is instructive, though, is the language Moses uses in framing his request:

> May the Lord, God of the spirits of all flesh, choose a man over the congregation who will go out before them and come in

---

1. That is the implication of the statement that "Moses longed to die as did Aaron," *Sifrei*, Numbers, *Pinḥas*, 136, s.v. *vayomer*.

before them, who will lead them out and bring them in, so that the congregation of the Lord will not be like sheep without a shepherd." (Num. 27:16–17)

There are three basic leadership lessons to be learned from this choice of words. The first, noted by Rashi, is implicit in the unusually long description of God as "the Lord, God of the spirits of all flesh." This means, he says, "Master of the universe, the character of each person is revealed to You, and no two are alike. Appoint over them a leader who will tolerate each person according to his individual character."[2]

The Rambam in *The Guide for the Perplexed* says that this is a basic feature of the human condition. Homo sapiens is the most diverse of all life forms. Therefore cooperation is essential – because we are different, others are strong where we are weak and vice versa – but it is also difficult, because we respond to challenges in different ways. That is what makes leadership necessary, but also demanding:

This great variety and the necessity of social life are essential elements in man's nature. But the well-being of society demands that there should be a leader able to regulate the actions of man; he must complete every shortcoming, remove every excess, and prescribe for the conduct of all, so that the natural variety should be counterbalanced by the uniformity of legislation, and the order of society be well established.[3]

Leaders respect differences but, like the conductor of an orchestra, integrate them, ensuring that the many different instruments play their part in harmony with the rest. True leaders do not seek to impose uniformity. They honour diversity.

The second hint is contained in the word *ish*, "a man" who is placed over the congregation. God responds, "Take for yourself Joshua, a man [*ish*] of spirit" (Num. 27:18). The word *ish* here indicates something other than gender. It is to be found in the two places in the Torah that use the

2. Rashi to Numbers 27:16, based on Tanḥuma, *Pinḥas* 11.
3. *The Guide for the Perplexed*, II:40.

phrase *ha'ish Moshe,* "the man Moses." The first is in Exodus: "The man Moses was highly respected [*gadol meod,* literally, "very great"] in the land of Egypt, in the eyes of Pharaoh's servants and the people" (Ex. 11:3). The second appears in Numbers: "Now the man Moses was very humble [*anav meod*], more so than anyone else on earth" (Num. 12:3).

Note the two characteristics, seemingly opposed – great and humble – both of which Moses had in high degree (*meod,* "very"). This is the combination of attributes R. Yoḥanan attributed to God Himself: "Wherever you find God's greatness, there you find His humility."[4] Here is one of his prooftexts: "For the Lord your God is God of gods and Lord of lords, the great God, mighty and awesome, who shows no partiality and accepts no bribes. He defends the cause of the fatherless and the widow, and loves the stranger residing among you, giving them food and clothing" (Deut. 10:17–18).

An *ish* in the context of leadership is not a male but rather someone who is a *mensch,* a person whose greatness is lightly worn, who cares about the people others often ignore, "the fatherless, the widow, and the stranger," who spends as much time with the people at the margins of society as with the elites, who is courteous to everyone equally and who receives respect because he gives respect.

The real puzzlement, however, lies in the third clause: "Choose a man over the congregation *who will go out before them and come in before them, who will lead them out and bring them in*" (Num. 27:16–17). This sounds like saying the same thing twice, which the Torah tends not to do. What does it mean?

The Torah is hinting here at one of the most challenging aspects of leadership, namely timing and pace. The first phrase is simple: "who will go out before them and come in before them." This means that a leader must lead from the front. He cannot be like the apocryphal British politician who we quoted earlier: "Of course I follow the party. After all, I am their leader."

It is the second phrase that is vital: "who will lead them out and bring them in." This means: leaders must lead from the front, but they must not be so far out in front that when they turn around they find

---

4. From the liturgy on Saturday night. The source is *Pesikta Zutreta, Ekev.*

that no one is following. Pace is of the essence. Sometimes a leader can go too fast. That is when tragedies occur.

To take two very different examples: When Margaret Thatcher was prime minister, she knew she was going to have to confront the miners' union in a long and bitter struggle. In 1981 they went on strike for a pay rise. Mrs Thatcher immediately made enquiries about the size of coal stocks. She wanted to know how long the country could survive without new supplies of coal. As soon as she discovered that stocks were low, she in effect conceded victory to the miners. She then, very quietly, arranged for coal to be stockpiled. The result was that when the miners went on strike again in 1983, she resisted their demands. There was a prolonged strike, and this time it was the miners who conceded defeat. A battle she could not win in 1981 she was able to win in 1983.

A very different example is that of Yitzhak Rabin. The peace process he engaged in with the Palestinians between 1993 and 1995 was deeply controversial, in Israel and outside of it. There was some support but also much opposition. The tension mounted in 1995. In September of that year, I wrote an article in the press giving him my own personal support. At the same time, however, I wrote to him privately saying that I was deeply worried about internal opposition to the plan, and urged him to spend as much time negotiating with his fellow Israeli citizens – specifically the religious Zionists – as with the Palestinians. I did not receive a reply.

On Motza'ei Shabbat, November 4, 1995, the world heard the news that Prime Minister Rabin had been assassinated at a peace rally by a young religious Zionist. I attended the funeral in Jerusalem. Returning the next day, I went straight from the airport to the Israeli ambassador to tell him about the funeral, which he had not been able to attend, having had to stay in London to deal with the media.

As I entered his office, he handed me an envelope. "This has just arrived for you in the diplomatic bag." It was Yitzhak Rabin's reply to my letter – perhaps one of the last letters he wrote. It was a moving reaffirmation of his faith, but by the time it was delivered he was no longer alive. He had pursued peace, as we are commanded to do, but he had gone too fast.

Moses knew this himself from the episode of the spies. As the Rambam says in *The Guide for the Perplexed*,[5] the task of fighting battles and conquering the land was just too much for a generation born into slavery. It could only be done by their children, born in freedom. Sometimes a journey that seems small on the map takes forty years.

Respect for diversity, care for the lowly and powerless as well as the powerful and great, and a willingness to go no faster than people can bear – these are three essential attributes of a leader, as Moses knew from experience, and as Joshua learned through his long apprenticeship to the great man himself.

5. *The Guide for the Perplexed*, III:32.

Matot

Conflict Resolution

One of the hardest tasks of leaders – from prime ministers to parents – is conflict resolution. Yet it is also the most vital. Where there is leadership, there is long-term cohesiveness within the group, whatever the short-term problems. Where there is a lack of leadership – where leaders lack authority, grace, generosity of spirit, or the ability to respect positions other than their own – then there is divisiveness, rancour, back-biting, resentment, internal politics, and a lack of trust. Leaders are people who put the interests of the group above those of any subsection of the group. They care for, and inspire others to care for, the common good.

That is why an episode in *Parashat Matot* is of the highest consequence. It arose like this: The Israelites were on the last stage of their journey to the Promised Land. They were now situated on the east bank of the Jordan, within sight of their destination. Two of the tribes who had large herds and flocks of cattle, Reuben and Gad, felt that the land they were currently on was ideal for their purposes. It was good grazing country. So they approached Moses and asked for permission to stay there rather than take up their share in the land of Israel. They said: "If we have found favour in your eyes, let this land be given to your servants as our possession. Do not make us cross the Jordan" (Num. 32:5).

Moses was instantly alert to the danger. The two tribes were putting their own interests above those of the nation as a whole. They would be seen as abandoning the nation at the very time they were needed most. There was a war – in fact a series of wars – to be fought if the Israelites were to inherit the Promised Land. As Moses put it to the tribes: "Should your fellow Israelites go to war while you sit here? Why do you discourage the Israelites from crossing over into the land the Lord has given them?" (32:6–7).

The proposal was potentially disastrous. Moses reminded the men of Reuben and Gad what had happened in the incident of the spies. The spies demoralised the people, ten of them saying that they could not conquer the land. The inhabitants were too strong. The cities were impregnable. The result of that one moment was the condemning of an entire generation to die in the wilderness and to delay the eventual conquest by forty years. "And here you are, a brood of sinners, standing in the place of your fathers and making the Lord even angrier with Israel. If you turn away from following Him, He will again leave all this people in the wilderness, and you will be the cause of their destruction" (Num. 32:14–15). Moses was blunt, honest, and confrontational.

What then follows is a role model in negotiation and conflict resolution. The Reubenites and Gadites recognise the claims of the people as a whole and the justice of Moses' concerns. They propose a compromise. Let us make provisions for our cattle and our families, they say, and the men will then accompany the other tribes across the Jordan. They will fight alongside them. They will even go ahead of them. They will not return to their cattle and families until all the battles have been fought, the land has been conquered, and the other tribes have received their inheritance. Essentially they invoke what would later become a principle of Jewish law: *zeh neheneh vezeh lo ḥaser*, meaning, an act is permissible if "one side gains and the other side does not lose" (Bava Kamma 20b). We will gain, say the two tribes, by having good land for our cattle, but the nation as a whole will not lose because we will be in the army, we will be on the front line, and we will stay there until the war has been won.

Moses recognises the fact that they have met his objections. He restates their position to make sure he and they have understood the proposal and they are ready to stand by it. He extracts from them agreement to a *tenai kaful*, a double condition, both positive and negative: if we do this, these will be the consequences, but if we fail to do this, those will be the consequences. He leaves them no escape from their commitment. The two tribes agree. Conflict has been averted. The Reubenites and Gadites achieve what they want but the interests of the other tribes and of the nation as a whole have been secured. It is a model negotiation.

The extent to which Moses' concerns were justified became apparent many years later. The Reubenites and Gadites did indeed fulfil their promise in the days of Joshua. The rest of the tribes conquered and settled Israel while they (together with half the tribe of Menashe) established their presence in Transjordan. Despite this, within a brief space of time there was almost civil war.

Joshua 22 describes how, returning to their families and settling their land, the Reubenites and Gadites built "an altar to the Lord" on the east side of the Jordan. Seeing this as an act of secession, the rest of the Israelites prepared to do battle against them. Joshua, in a striking act of diplomacy, sent Pinhas, the former zealot, now a man of peace, to negotiate. He warned them of the terrible consequences of what they had done by, in effect, creating a religious centre outside the land of Israel. It would split the nation in two.

The Reubenites and Gadites made it clear that this was not their intention at all. To the contrary, they themselves were worried that in the future, the rest of the Israelites would see them living across the Jordan and conclude that they no longer wanted to be part of the nation. That is why they had built the altar, not to offer sacrifices, not as a rival to the nation's Sanctuary, but merely as a symbol and a sign to future generations that they too were Israelites. Pinhas and the rest of the delegation were satisfied with this answer, and once again civil war was averted.

The negotiation between Moses and the two tribes in this *parasha* follows closely the principles arrived at by the Harvard Negotiation Project, set out by Roger Fisher and William Ury in their classic text,

Getting to Yes.[1] Essentially, they came to the conclusion that a successful negotiation must involve four processes:

1. *Separate the people from the problem.* There are all sorts of personal tensions in any negotiation. It is essential that these be cleared away first so that the problem can be addressed objectively.
2. *Focus on interests, not positions.* It is easy for any conflict to turn into a zero-sum game: if I win, you lose; if you win, I lose. That is what happens when you focus on positions and the question becomes, "Who wins?" By focusing not on positions but on interests, the question becomes, "Is there a way of achieving what each of us wants?"
3. *Invent options for mutual gain.* This is the idea expressed halakhically as *zeh neheneh vezeh neheneh,* "both sides benefit." This comes about because the two sides usually have different objectives, neither of which excludes the other.
4. *Insist on objective criteria.* Make sure that both sides agree in advance to the use of objective, impartial criteria to judge whether what has been agreed is achieved. Otherwise, despite all apparent agreement, the dispute will continue, both sides insisting that the other has not done what was promised.

Moses does all four. First he separates the people from the problem by making it clear to the Reubenites and Gadites that the issue has nothing to do with who they are, and everything to do with the Israelites' experience in the past, specifically the episode of the spies. Regardless of who the ten negative spies were and which tribes they came from, everyone suffered. No one gained. The problem is not about this tribe or that but about the nation as a whole.

Second, he focuses on interests, not positions. The two tribes have an interest in the fate of the nation as a whole. If they put their personal interests first, God will become angry and the entire people will be punished, the Reubenites and Gadites among them. It is striking

---

1. Roger Fisher and William Ury, *Getting to Yes: Negotiating Agreement Without Giving In* (New York: Penguin Books, 2011).

how different this negotiation is from that of Korah and his followers. There, the whole argument was about positions, not interests – about who was entitled to be a leader. The result was collective tragedy.

Third, the Reubenites and Gadites then invent an option for mutual gain. If you allow us to make temporary provisions for our cattle and children, they say, we will not only fight in the army. We will be its advance guard. We will benefit, knowing that our request has been granted. The nation will benefit by our willingness to take on the most demanding military task.

Fourth, there is an agreement on objective criteria. The Reubenites and Gadites will not return to the east bank of the Jordan until all the other tribes are safely settled in their territories. And so it happens, as narrated in the book of Joshua:

> Then Joshua summoned the Reubenites, the Gadites, and the half-tribe of Menashe and said to them, "You have done all that Moses the servant of the Lord commanded, and you have obeyed me in everything I commanded. For a long time now – to this very day – you have not deserted your fellow Israelites but have carried out the mission the Lord your God gave you. Now that the Lord your God has given them rest as He promised, return to your homes in the land that Moses the servant of the Lord gave you on the other side of the Jordan." (Josh. 22:1–4)

This was, in short, a model negotiation, a sign of hope after the many destructive conflicts in the book of Numbers, as well as a standing alternative to the many later conflicts in Jewish history that had such appalling outcomes.

Note that Moses succeeds, not because he is weak, not because he is willing to compromise on the integrity of the nation as a whole, not because he uses honeyed words and diplomatic evasions, but because he is honest, principled, and focused on the common good. We all face conflicts in our lives. This is how to resolve them.

Masei

Leadership at a Time of Crisis

Parashat Masei always occurs at the heart of the Three Weeks. This is the time when we engage in an act of collective recall of our two greatest defeats as a nation. The symbol of the nation was the Temple in Jerusalem. So the symbol of the nation's defeat was the destruction of the Temple. It happened twice, once in the sixth century BCE, the second time in the first century of the Common Era. In both cases it happened because of poor leadership.

The first defeat was set in motion some three centuries before it happened by a disastrous decision on the part of King Solomon's son Rehoboam, which we discussed earlier in *Parashat Vayikra*. The people were restless during the latter part of Solomon's reign. They felt he had placed too heavy a burden on them, particularly during the building of the Temple. When he died they came to his son and successor and asked him to lighten the load. His father's counsellors told him to accede to their request. They gave him one of the finest pieces of advice ever given to a leader: if you serve the people they will serve you (I Kings 12:7). Rehoboam did not listen. The kingdom split. Defeat of both halves – the northern and southern kingdoms – was inevitable and only a matter of time. As Abraham Lincoln said, "A house divided against itself cannot stand."[1]

The second defeat, in the days of the Romans, was the result of a complete collapse of leadership during the late Second Temple period. The Hasmonean kings, having defeated Hellenism, then succumbed to it. The priesthood became politicised and corrupt. The Rambam wrote, in his letter to the sages of Marseilles,[2] that the Second Temple fell because Jews had not learned military strategy and the laws of conquest. The Talmud says it fell because of gratuitous hatred (Yoma 9b). Josephus tells us it fell because of conflicts within the forces defending Jerusalem.[3] All three explanations are true and part of the same phenomenon. When there is no effective leadership, divisions open up within the group. There is internal conflict, energy is wasted, and no coherent strategy emerges. Again defeat becomes inevitable.

In Judaism, leadership is not a luxury but a necessity. Ours is a small and intensely vulnerable people. Inspired, we rise to greatness. Uninspired, we fall.

But there is, oddly enough, a deeply positive message about the Three Weeks. For the fact is that the Jewish people survived those defeats. They did not *merely* survive – they recovered and grew stronger. They became in the most positive sense a nation of survivors. Who gave them that strength and courage?

The answer is three leaders whose names are indelibly associated with the Three Weeks: Moses, whose message to the generations at the beginning of Deuteronomy is always read on the Shabbat before Tisha B'Av; Isaiah, whose vision gives that day its name as *Shabbat Ḥazon*, and Jeremiah, the prophet who foresaw the destruction and whose words form the *haftarot* for two of the Three Weeks.

What made these men great leaders? They were all critical of their contemporaries – but then, so are most people. It takes no skill

---

1. Abraham Lincoln, Republican Party Nomination Acceptance Speech (Springfield, IL, June 16, 1858).
2. English translation available in Isidore Twersky, *A Maimonides Reader* (Springfield, N.J.: Behrman House, 1976), 463ff.
3. See *Flavius Josephus: Translation and Commentary*, vol. 1b, *Judean War*, trans. Steve Mason (Leiden, Netherlands; Boston: Brill, 2008).

whatsoever to be a critic. All three predicted doom. But Jeremiah himself pointed out that predicting doom is a no-risk option. If bad things happen, you are proved right. If they do not – well, clearly God decided to have compassion.[4]

So what made Moses, Isaiah, and Jeremiah different? What made them great leaders? Specifically, what made them leaders in hard times, and thus leaders for all time? Three things set them apart.

The first is that they were all *prophets of hope*. Even in their darkest moments they were able to see through the clouds of disaster to the clear sky beyond. They were not optimists. We talked earlier about the difference between optimism and hope: optimism is the belief that things will *get* better. Hope is the belief that if we work hard enough together, we can *make* things better. It takes no courage to be an optimist, but it takes courage, wisdom, a deep understanding of history and possibility, as well as the ability to communicate, to be a prophet of hope. That is what Moses, Isaiah, and Jeremiah all were. Here is Moses:

> When all these blessings and curses I have set before you come on you and you take them to heart wherever the Lord your God disperses you among the nations, and when you and your children return to the Lord your God and obey Him with all your heart and with all your soul according to everything I command you today, *then the Lord your God will restore your fortunes and have compassion on you and gather you again from all the nations where He scattered you.* Even if you have been banished to the most distant land under the heavens, from there the Lord your God will gather you and bring you back. (Deut. 30:1–4)

Here is Isaiah:

> *I will restore your leaders as in days of old,* your rulers as at the beginning. Afterwards you will be called the City of Righteousness, the Faithful City. (Is. 1:26)

---

4. See Jeremiah 28; *Mishneh Torah, Hilkhot Yesodei HaTorah* 10:4.

And this is Jeremiah:

> This is what the Lord says: "Restrain your voice from weeping and your eyes from tears, for your work will be rewarded," says the Lord. "They will return from the land of the enemy. *There is hope for your descendants*," says the Lord. "Your children will return to their land." (Jer. 31:15–16)

The point about all three of these prophecies is that they were delivered knowing that bad things were about to happen to the Jewish people. They are not easy hope; they express hope rescued from the valley of despair.

The second characteristic that made Moses, Isaiah, and Jeremiah different was that they delivered their criticism in love. Isaiah said in the name of God perhaps the loveliest words ever spoken to the Jewish people: "Though the mountains be shaken and the hills be removed, My unfailing love for you will not be shaken nor My covenant of peace be removed" (Is. 54:10). Jeremiah, in the midst of his critique of the nation, said in the name of God, "I remember the kindness of your youth, how as a bride you loved Me and followed Me through the wilderness, through a land not sown" (Jer. 2:2). Moses' love for the people was evident in every prayer he said on their behalf, especially after they had made the Golden Calf. On that occasion he said to God: "Now, if You would, please forgive their sin. If not, then blot me out of the book that You have written" (Ex. 32:32). He was prepared to give his life for his people. It is easy to be a critic, but the only effective critics are those who truly love – and *show* they love – those whom they criticise.

Third, Moses, Isaiah, and Jeremiah were the three prophets who, more than any others, spoke about the role of Jews and Israel in the context of humanity as a whole. Moses directed the people to keep the commands "for they are *your wisdom and understanding in the eyes of the nations*" (Deut. 4:6). Isaiah said in God's name: "You are My witnesses … that I am God" (Is. 43:12), and "I created you and appointed you a covenant people, a light of nations, opening eyes deprived of light, rescuing prisoners from confinement, from the dungeon those who sit in darkness" (42:6–7). Jeremiah was the leader who defined for all time the role of Jews in the Diaspora: "Seek the welfare of the city to which I have exiled you and pray to the Lord on its behalf, for in its prosperity you shall prosper" (Jer. 29:7) – the first statement in history of what it is to be a creative minority.

Why did this universal perspective matter? Because those who care only for their own people are chauvinists. They create false expectations, narrow and self-regarding emotions, and bravado rather than real courage.

Moses had to show (as he did when he rescued Yitro's daughters from the local shepherds, Ex. 2:17) that he cared for non-Israelites as well as Israelites. Jeremiah was told by God to become a "prophet to the nations," not just to Israel (Jer. 1:5). Isaiah, in one of the most remarkable prophecies of all time, showed as much concern for Egypt and Assyria, Israel's enemies, as for Israel itself (Is. 19:19–25).

Great leaders are great not just because they care for their own people – everyone except a self-hater does that – but because they care for humanity. That is what gives their devotion to their own people its dignity and moral strength.

To be an agent of hope, to love the people you lead, and to widen their horizons to embrace humanity as a whole – that is the kind of leadership that gives people the ability to recover from crisis and move on. It is what made Moses, Isaiah, and Jeremiah three of the greatest leaders of all time.

Deuteronomy
דברים

Devarim

The Leader as Teacher

I t was one of the great moments of personal transformation, and it changed not only Moses but our very conception of leadership itself.

By the end of the book of Numbers, Moses' career as a leader seemed to have come to its end. He had appointed his successor, Joshua, and it would be Joshua, not Moses, who would lead the people across the Jordan into the Promised Land. Moses seemed to have achieved everything he was destined to achieve. For him there would be no more battles to fight, no more miracles to perform, no more prayers to say on behalf of the people.

It is what Moses did next that bears the mark of greatness. For the last month of his life he assembled the people and delivered the series of addresses we know as the book of Deuteronomy or *Devarim*, literally "words." In them, he reviewed the people's past and foresaw their future. He gave them laws. Some he had given them before but in a different form. Others were new; he had waited to announce them until the people were about to enter the land. Linking all these details of law and history into a single overarching vision, he taught the people to see themselves as an *am kadosh*, a holy people, the only people whose sovereign and lawgiver was God Himself.

If someone who knew nothing about Judaism and the Jewish people were to ask you for a single book that would explain them both – who Jews are and why they do what they do – the best answer would be Deuteronomy. No other book so encapsulates and dramatises all the key elements of Judaism as a faith and way of life.

In a much-watched TED talk, and a book with the same name,[1] Simon Sinek says that the transformative leaders are those who "Start with Why." More poetically, Antoine de Saint-Exupery reputedly said, "If you want to build a ship, don't drum up people together to collect wood and don't assign them tasks and work, but rather *teach them to long for the endless immensity of the sea.*"

In Deuteronomy, Moses gives the people their "why." They are God's people, the nation on whom He has set His love, the people He rescued from slavery and gave, in the form of the commandments, the constitution of liberty. They may be small but they are unique. They are the people who, in themselves, testify to something beyond themselves. They are the people whose fate will defy the normal laws of history. Other nations, says Moses, will recognise the miraculous nature of the Jewish story – and so, from Blaise Pascal to Nikolai Berdyaev and beyond, they did.

In the last month of his life Moses ceased to be the liberator, the miracle-worker, and redeemer, and became instead *Moshe Rabbenu*, "Moses, our teacher." He was the first example in history of a leadership type in which Jews have excelled: the leader as teacher.

Moses surely knew that some of his greatest achievements would not last forever. The people he had rescued would one day suffer exile and persecution again. The next time, though, they would not have a Moses to do miracles. So he planted a vision in their minds, hope in their hearts, a discipline in their deeds, and a strength in their souls that would never fade. When leaders become educators they change lives.

1. Simon Sinek, *Start with Why: How Great Leaders Inspire Everyone to Take Action* (New York: Portfolio, 2009). The lecture can be seen at http://www.youtube.com/watch?v=qpoHIF3SfI4.

In a powerful essay titled "Who Is Fit to Lead the Jewish People?" Rabbi Joseph Soloveitchik contrasts the Jewish attitude to kings and teachers as leadership types.[2] The Torah places severe limits on the power of kings. They must not multiply gold, or wives, or horses. A king is commanded "not to consider himself better than his fellow Israelites nor turn from the law to the right or to the left" (Deut. 17:20).

A king was only to be appointed at the request of the people. According to Ibn Ezra, the appointment of a king was permission, not an obligation. Abrabanel held that it was a concession to human frailty. Rabbenu Baḥya regarded the existence of a king as a punishment, not a reward.[3] In short, Judaism is at best ambivalent about monarchy – that is to say, about leadership as power.

On the other hand, its regard for teachers is almost unlimited. "Let the fear of your teacher be as the fear of Heaven," says the Talmud (Pesaḥim 108b). Respect and reverence for your teacher should be greater even than respect and reverence for your parents, rules the Rambam, because parents bring you into this world, while teachers give you entrance to the World to Come.[4]

When someone exercises power over us, he diminishes us, but when someone teaches us, he helps us grow. That is why Judaism, with its acute concern for human dignity, favours leadership as education over leadership as power. And it began with Moses, at the end of his life.

For twenty-two years, as a Chief Rabbi, I have carried with me the following quotation from one of the greatest leaders of the Zionist movement, Israel's first prime minister, David Ben-Gurion. Although he was a secular Jew, he was enough of a historian and Bible scholar to understand this dimension of leadership, and said so in eloquent words:

2. Abraham R. Besdin, *Reflections of the Rav* (Jerusalem: World Zionist Organisation, 1979), 127–139.
3. In their commentaries to Deuteronomy 17:15. Rabbenu Baḥya's point is that the people should in principle have needed no other king than God Himself. In support of his view he quotes Hosea: "They set up kings without My consent; they choose princes without My approval" (8:4); and "So in My anger I gave you a king, and in My wrath I took him away" (13:11).
4. *Mishneh Torah, Hilkhot Talmud Torah* 5:1.

Whether you hold humble office in a municipality or in a small union or high office in a national government, the principles are the same: you must know what you want to achieve, be certain of your aims, and have these goals constantly in mind. You must fix your priorities. You must educate your party, and must educate the wider public. You must have confidence in your people – often greater than they have in themselves, for the true political leader knows instinctively the measure of man's capacities and can rouse him to exert them in times of crisis. You must know when to fight your political opponents, and when to mark time. You must never compromise on matters of principle. You must always be conscious of the element of timing, and this demands a constant awareness of what is going on around you – in your region if you are a local leader, in your country and in the world if you are a national leader. And since the world never stops for a moment, and the pattern of power changes its elements like the movement of a kaleidoscope, you must constantly reassess chosen policies towards the achievement of your aims. A political leader must spend a lot of time thinking. And he must spend a lot of time educating the public, and educating them anew.[5]

The poet Shelley once said that "poets are the unacknowledged legislators of the world."[6] Whether this is true or false, I do not know, but this I know: that there is all the difference between giving people what they want and teaching them what to want.

Teachers are the unacknowledged builders of the future, and if a leader seeks to make lasting change, he or she must follow in the footsteps of Moses and become an educator. The leader as teacher – using influence rather than power, spiritual and intellectual authority rather than coercive force – was one of the greatest contributions Judaism

5. Moshe Pearlman, *Ben Gurion Looks Back in Talks with Moshe Pearlman* (London: Weidenfeld and Nicolson, 1965), 52. I owe this quotation to Jonathan (now Lord) Kestenbaum, executive director of the Office of the Chief Rabbi, 1991–1996.
6. Percy Bysshe Shelley, *A Defence of Poetry: An Essay* (ReadHowYouWant, 2006), 53.

ever made to the moral horizons of humankind. This can be seen most clearly in the book of Deuteronomy, when Moses, for the last month of his life, summoned the next generation and taught it laws and lessons that would survive, and inspire, as long as there are human beings on earth.

The Fewest of All Peoples

Buried inconspicuously in *Parashat Va'ethanan* is a short sentence with explosive potential, causing us to think again about the nature of Jewish history and the Jewish task in the present.

Moses has been reminding the new generation, the children of those who left Egypt, of the extraordinary story of which they are the heirs:

> Has anything so great as this ever happened, or has anything like it ever been heard of? Has any other people heard the voice of God speaking out of fire, as you have, and lived? (Deut. 4:32–33)

The Israelites have not yet crossed the Jordan. They have not yet begun their life as a sovereign nation in their own land. Yet Moses is sure, with a certainty that can only be prophetic, that they are a people like no other. What has happened to them is unique. They were and are a nation summoned to greatness.

Moses reminds them of the great Revelation at Mount Sinai. He recalls the Ten Commandments. He delivers the most famous of all summaries of the Jewish faith: "Listen, Israel: The Lord our God, the Lord is one" (Deut. 6:4). He issues the most majestic of all commands: "Love the Lord your God with all your heart and with all your soul and with all your strength" (6:5). Twice he tells the people to teach these things to their children. He gives them their eternal mission statement as a nation: "You are a people holy to the Lord your God. The Lord your God has chosen you out of all the peoples on the face of the earth to be His people, His treasured possession" (7:6). Then he says: "The Lord did not set His affection on you and choose you because you were more numerous than other peoples, for you are the fewest of all peoples" (7:7).

The fewest of all peoples? What has happened to all the promises of Genesis, that Abraham's children would be numerous, uncountable, as many as the stars of the sky, the dust of the earth, and the grains of sand on a seashore? What of Moses' own statement at the beginning of Deuteronomy: "The Lord your God has increased your numbers so that today you are as numerous as the stars in the sky" (Deut. 1:10)?

The simple answer is this: the Israelites were indeed numerous *compared to what they once were.* Moses himself puts it this way in the next *parasha*: "Your ancestors who went down into Egypt were seventy in all, and now the Lord your God has made you as numerous as the stars in the sky" (Deut. 10:22). They were once a single family – Abraham, Sarah, and their descendants; now they have become a nation of twelve tribes.

But – and this is Moses' point here – compared to other nations, they were still small. "When the Lord your God brings you into the land you are entering to possess and drives out before you many nations – the Hittites, Girgashites, Amorites, Canaanites, Perizzites, Hivites, and Jebusites, seven nations *larger and stronger than you...*" (Deut. 7:1). In other words, not only were the Israelites smaller than the great empires of the ancient world. They were smaller even than the other nations in the region. Compared to their origins they had grown, but compared to their neighbours they remained tiny.

Moses then tells them what this means: "You may say to yourselves, '*These nations are stronger than we are.* How can we drive them out?' But do not be afraid of them; remember well what the Lord your God did to Pharaoh and to all Egypt" (Deut. 7:17–18).

Israel will be the smallest of the nations for a reason that goes to the very heart of its existence as a nation. It will show the world that *a people does not have to be large in order to be great*. It does not have to be numerous to defeat its enemies. Israel's unique history will show that, in the words of the prophet Zechariah (4:6), "'Not by might nor by power, but by My spirit,' says the Lord Almighty."

In itself, Israel would be witness to something greater than itself. As former Marxist philosopher Nicolai Berdyaev put it:

> I remember how the materialist interpretation of history, when I attempted in my youth to verify it by applying it to the destinies of peoples, broke down in the case of the Jews, where destiny seemed absolutely inexplicable from the materialistic stand-point.... Its survival is a mysterious and wonderful phenomenon demonstrating that the life of this people is governed by a special predetermination, transcending the processes of adaptation expounded by the materialistic interpretation of history. The survival of the Jews, their resistance to destruction, their endurance under absolutely peculiar conditions and the fateful role played by them in history: all these point to the particular and mysterious foundations of their destiny.[1]

Moses' statement has immense implications for Jewish identity. One central proposition implicit throughout this book is that Jews have had an influence out of all proportion to their numbers because *we are all called on to be leaders*, to take responsibility, to contribute, to make a difference to the lives of others, to bring the Divine Presence into the world. Precisely because we are small, we are each summoned to greatness.

S. Y. Agnon, the great Hebrew writer, composed a prayer to accompany the Mourner's Kaddish. He noted that the Children of Israel have always been few in number compared to other nations. He then said that when a king rules over a large population, he does not notice when one dies, for there are others to take his or her place.

---

1. Nicolai Berdyaev, *The Meaning of History* (Piscataway, N.J.: Transaction Publishers, 2005), 86.

But our King, the King of kings, the Holy One, Blessed Be He...
chose us, and not because we are a large nation, for we are one
of the smallest of nations. We are few, and owing to the love with
which He loves us, each one of us is, for Him, an entire legion. He
does not have many replacements for us. If one of us is missing,
Heaven forfend, then the King's forces are diminished, with the
consequence that His kingdom is weakened, as it were. One of
His legions is gone and His greatness is lessened. For this reason
it is our custom to recite the Kaddish when a Jew dies.[2]

Margaret Mead once said: "Never doubt that a small group of
thoughtful, committed citizens can change the world. Indeed, it is the
only thing that ever has." Gandhi said: "A small body of determined spirits fired by an unquenchable faith in their mission can alter the course
of history."[3] That must be our faith as Jews. We may be the fewest of all
peoples, but when we heed God's call, we have the ability, proven many
times in our past, to mend and transform the world.

2. Quoted in Leon Wieseltier, *Kaddish* (New York: Knopf, 1998), 22–23.
3. *Harijan*, November 19, 1938.

Ekev

To Lead Is to Listen

I f only you would listen to these laws…" (Deut. 7:12). These words with which *Parashat Ekev* begins contain a verb that is a fundamental motif of the book of Deuteronomy. The verb is SH-M-A. It occurred in the previous *parasha* in the most famous line of the whole of Judaism, *Shema Yisrael*. It occurs later in *Parashat Ekev* in the second paragraph of the *Shema*, "It shall be if you surely listen [*shamo'a tishme'u*]" (Deut. 11:13). It appears no less than ninety-two times in Deuteronomy as a whole.

We often miss the significance of this word because of what I call *the fallacy of translatability*: the assumption that one language is fully translatable into another. We hear a word translated from one language to another and assume that it has the same meaning in both. But often it does not. Languages are only partially translatable into one another.[1] The key terms of one civilisation are often not fully

---

1. Robert Frost said: "Poetry is what gets lost in translation." Cervantes compared translation to the other side of a tapestry. At best, we see a rough outline of the pattern we know exists on the other side, but it lacks definition and is full of loose threads.

reproducible in another. The Greek word *megalopsychos*, for example, Aristotle's "great-souled man" who is great and knows he is, who carries himself with aristocratic pride, is untranslatable into a moral system like Judaism in which humility is a virtue. The English word "tact" has no precise equivalent in Hebrew. And so on.

This is particularly so in the case of the Hebrew verb SH-M-A. Listen, for example, to the way the opening words of *Parashat Ekev* have been translated into English:

If you *hearken* to these precepts...
If you *completely obey* these laws...
If you *pay attention to* these laws...
If you *heed* these ordinances...
Because you *hear* these judgements...

There is no single English word that means to hear, to listen, to heed, to pay attention to, and to obey. SH-M-A also means "to understand," as in the story of the Tower of Babel, when God says, "Come, let us go down and confuse their language so they will not understand [*yishme'u*] each other" (Gen. 11:7).

As I have argued elsewhere, one of the most striking facts about the Torah is that, although it contains 613 commands, it does not contain a word that means "to obey." When such a word was needed in modern Hebrew, the verb *letzayet* was borrowed from Aramaic. The verb used by the Torah in place of "to obey" is SH-M-A. This is of the highest possible significance. It means that *blind obedience is not a virtue in Judaism.* God wants us to understand the laws He has commanded us. He wants us to reflect on why this law, not that. He wants us to listen, to reflect, to seek to understand, to internalise, and to respond. He wants us to become *a listening people.*

Ancient Greece was a visual culture, a culture of art, architecture, theatre, and spectacle. For the Greeks generally, and Plato specifically, knowing was a form of *seeing.* Judaism, as Freud pointed out in *Moses and Monotheism,*[2] is a non-visual culture. We worship a God who cannot be

2. Vintage, 1955.

seen; making sacred images, icons, is absolutely forbidden. In Judaism we do not see God; we hear God. Knowing is a form of *listening*. Ironically, Freud himself, deeply ambivalent though he was about Judaism, invented the *listening cure* in psychoanalysis: listening as therapy.[3]

It follows that in Judaism, listening is a deeply spiritual act. To listen to God is to be open to God. That is what Moses is saying throughout Deuteronomy: "If only you would listen." So it is with leadership – indeed with all forms of interpersonal relationship. Often the greatest gift we can give someone is to listen to them.

Viktor Frankl, who survived Auschwitz and went on to create a new form of psychotherapy based on "man's search for meaning," once told the story of a patient of his who phoned him in the middle of the night to tell him, calmly, that she was about to commit suicide. He kept her on the phone for two hours, giving her every conceivable reason to live. Eventually she said that she had changed her mind and would not her life. When he next saw the woman he asked her which of his many reasons had persuaded her to change her mind. "None," she replied. "Why then did you decide not to commit suicide?" he asked. She replied that the fact that someone was prepared to listen to her for two hours in the middle of the night convinced her that life was worth living after all.[4]

As Chief Rabbi, I was involved in resolving a number of highly intractable *aguna* cases, situations in which a husband was unwilling to give his wife a *get* so that she could remarry. We resolved all these cases not by using legal devices but by the simple act of listening: deep listening, in which we were able to convince both sides that we had heard their pain and their sense of injustice. This took many hours of total concentration and a principled absence of judgement and direction. Eventually our listening absorbed the acrimony and the couple was able to resolve its differences together. Listening is intensely therapeutic.

3. Anna O. (Bertha Pappenheim) famously described Freudian psychoanalysis as "the talking cure," but it is in fact a listening cure. Only through the active listening of the analyst can there be the therapeutic or cathartic talking of the patient.
4. Anna Redsand, *Viktor Frankl: A Life Worth Living* (New York: Clarion Books, 2006), 113–14.

Before I became Chief Rabbi I was head of our rabbinical training seminary, Jews' College. There in the 1980s we ran one of the most advanced practical rabbinics programmes ever devised. It included a three-year programme in counselling. The professionals we recruited to run the course told us that they had one precondition. We had to agree to take all the participants away to an enclosed location for two days. Only those who were willing to do this would be admitted to the course. We did not know in advance what the counsellors were planning to do, but we soon discovered. They planned to teach us the method pioneered by Carl Rogers, known as non-directive or person-centred therapy. This involves active listening and reflective questioning, but no guidance on the part of the therapist.

As the nature of the method became clear, the rabbis began to object. It seemed to oppose everything they stood for. To be a rabbi is to teach, to direct, to tell people what to do. The tension between the counsellors and the rabbis grew almost to the point of crisis, so much so that we had to stop the course for an hour while we sought some way of reconciling what the counsellors were doing with what the Torah seemed to be saying. That is when we began to reflect, for the first time as a group, on the spiritual dimension of listening, of *Shema Yisrael*.

The deep truth behind person-centred therapy is that listening is the key virtue of the religious life. That is what Moses was saying throughout Deuteronomy. If we want God to listen to us, we have to be prepared to listen to Him. And if we learn to listen to Him, then we eventually learn to listen to our fellow humans: the silent cry of the lonely, the poor, the weak, the vulnerable, the people in existential pain.

When God appeared to King Solomon in a dream and asked him what he would like to be given, Solomon replied: *lev shome'a*, literally "a listening heart" to judge the people (1 Kings 3:9). The choice of words is significant. Solomon's wisdom lay, at least in part, in his ability to listen, to hear the emotion behind the words, to sense what was being left unsaid as well as what was said. It is common to find leaders who speak; it is very rare to find leaders who listen. But listening often makes the difference.

Listening matters in a moral environment as insistent on human dignity as Judaism. The very act of listening is a form of respect. The royal family in Britain is known always to arrive on time and depart on time. I will never forget the occasion – her aides told me that they had never witnessed it before – when the queen stayed for two hours longer than her scheduled departure time. The day was January 27, 2005; the occasion, the sixtieth anniversary of the liberation of Auschwitz. The queen had invited survivors to a reception at St James's Palace. Each had a story to tell, and the queen took the time to listen to every one of them. One after another came up to me and said, "Sixty years ago I did not know whether tomorrow I would be alive, and here I am talking to the queen." That act of listening was one of the most gracious royal acts I have ever witnessed. Listening is a profound affirmation of the humanity of the Other.

In the encounter at the burning bush, when God summoned Moses to be a leader, Moses replied, "I am not a man of words, not yesterday, not the day before, not from the first time You spoke to Your servant. I am slow of speech and tongue" (Ex. 4:10). Why would God choose a man who found it hard to speak to lead the Jewish people? *Perhaps because one who cannot speak learns how to listen.* A leader is one who knows how to listen: to the unspoken cry of others and to the still, small voice of God.

Re'eh

Defining Reality

One of the gifts of great leaders, and one from which each of us can learn, is that they *frame reality for the group*. They define its state. They specify its aims. They articulate its choices. They tell us where we are and where we are going in a way no satellite navigation system could. They show us the map and the destination, and help us see why we should choose this route and not that. That is one of their most magisterial roles, and no one did it more powerfully than Moses in the book of Deuteronomy.

Here is how he does it at the beginning of *Parashat Re'eh*:

> See, I am setting before you today the blessing and the curse – the blessing if you obey the commands of the Lord your God that I am giving you today; the curse if you disobey the commands of the Lord your God and turn from the way that I command you today by following other gods, which you have not known. (Deut. 11:26–28)

Here, in even more powerful words, is how he puts it later in the book:

See, I have set before you today life and good, death and evil....
I call heaven and earth as witnesses today against you, that I
have set before you life and death, the blessing and the curse;
therefore choose life, that you and your children may live.
(Deut. 30:15, 19)

What Moses is doing here is *defining reality* for the next generation and for all generations. He is doing so as a preface to what is about to follow in the next chapters, namely a systematic restatement of Jewish law covering all aspects of life for the new nation in its land.

Moses does not want the people to lose the big picture by being overwhelmed by the details. Jewish law with its 613 commands *is* detailed. It aims at the sanctification of all aspects of life, from daily ritual to the very structure of society and its institutions. Its aim is to shape a social world in which we turn even seemingly secular occasions into encounters with the Divine Presence. Despite the details, says Moses, the choice I set before you is really quite simple.

We, he tells the next generation, are unique. We are a small nation. We have not the numbers, the wealth, nor the sophisticated weaponry of the great empires. We are smaller even than many of our neighbouring nations. As of now we do not even have a land. But we are different, and that difference defines, once and for all, who we are and why. God has chosen to make us His stake in history. He set us free from slavery and took us as His own covenantal partner.

This is not because of our merits. "It is not because of your righteousness or your integrity that you are going in to take possession of their land" (Deut. 9:5). We are not more righteous than others, says Moses. It is because our ancestors – Abraham, Isaac, Jacob, Sarah, Rebecca, Rachel, and Leah – were the first people to heed the call of the one God and follow Him, worshipping not nature but the Creator of nature, not power but justice and compassion, not hierarchy but a society of equal dignity that includes within its ambit of concern the widow, the orphan, and the stranger.

Do not think, says Moses, that we can survive as a nation among nations, worshipping what they worship and living as they live. If we do, we will be subject to the universal law that has governed the fate of nations from the dawn of civilisation to today. Nations are born, they grow, they flourish; they become complacent, then corrupt, then divided, then defeated, then they die, to be remembered only in history books and museums. In the case of Israel, small and intensely vulnerable, that fate will happen sooner rather than later. That is what Moses calls "the curse."

The alternative is simple – even though it is demanding and detailed. It means taking God as our sovereign, judge of our deeds, framer of our laws, author of our liberty, defender of our destiny, object of our worship and our love. If we predicate our existence on something – some One – vastly greater than ourselves then we will be lifted higher than we could reach by ourselves. But that demands total loyalty to God and His law. That is the only way we will avoid decay, decline, and defeat.

There is nothing puritanical about this vision. Two of the key-words of Deuteronomy are *love* and *joy*. The word "love" (the root A-H-V) appears twice in Exodus, twice in Leviticus, not at all in Numbers, and twenty-three times in Deuteronomy. The word "joy" (root S-M-Ḥ) appears only once in Genesis, once in Exodus, once in Leviticus, once in Numbers, and twelve times in Deuteronomy. Moses does not hide the fact, though, that life under the covenant will be demanding. Neither love nor joy can be found in a social setting that does not have codes of self-restraint and commitment to the common good.

Moses knows that people often think and act in short-term ways, preferring today's pleasure to tomorrow's happiness, personal advantage to the good of society as a whole. They do foolish things, individually and collectively. So throughout Deuteronomy he insists time and again that the road to long-term flourishing – the "good," the "blessing," life itself – consists in making one simple choice: accept God as your sovereign, do His will, and blessings will follow. If not, sooner or later you will be conquered and dispersed and you will suffer more than you can imagine. Thus Moses defines reality for the Israelites of his time and all time.

What has this to do with leadership? The answer is that the meaning of events is never self-evident. It is always subject to interpretation. Sometimes, out of folly or fear or failure of imagination, leaders get it wrong. Neville Chamberlain defined the challenge of the rise to power of Nazi Germany as the search for "peace for our time." It took a Churchill to realise that this was wrong and that the real challenge was the defence of liberty against tyranny.

In Lincoln's day there were any number of people for and against slavery but it took Lincoln to define the abolition of slavery as the necessary step to the preservation of the union. It was that larger vision that allowed him to say, in the Second Inaugural, "With malice towards none, with charity for all, with firmness in the right as God gives us to see the right, let us strive on to finish the work we are in, to bind up the nation's wounds."[1] He allowed neither abolition itself, nor the end of the Civil War, to be seen as a victory for one side over the other but instead defined it as a victory for the nation as a whole.

I explained in my book on religion and science, *The Great Partnership*,[2] that there is a difference between the *cause* of something and its *meaning*. The search for causes is the task of *explanation*. The search for meaning is the work of *interpretation*. Science can explain but it cannot interpret. Were the ten plagues in Egypt a natural sequence of events, or divine punishment, or both? There is no scientific experiment that can resolve this question. Was the division of the Red Sea a divine intervention in history or a freak easterly wind exposing a submerged and ancient river bank? Was the Exodus an act of divine liberation or a series of lucky coincidences that allowed a group of fugitive slaves to escape? When all the causal explanations have been given, the quality of miracle – an epoch-changing event in which we see the hand of God – remains. Culture is not nature. There are causes in nature, but only in culture are there meanings. Homo sapiens is uniquely the culture-creating, meaning-seeking animal, and this affects all we do.

Viktor Frankl used to emphasise that our lives are determined not by what happens to us but by how we respond to what happens to us – and how we respond depends on how we interpret events. Is this disaster the end of my world or is it life calling on me to exercise heroic

1. Abraham Lincoln, Second Inaugural Address (United States Capitol, March 4, 1865).
2. *The Great Partnership: Science, Religion, and the Search for Meaning* (New York: Schocken Books, 2011).

strength so that I can survive and help others to survive? The same circumstances may be interpreted differently by two people, leading one to despair, the other to heroic endurance. The facts may be the same but the meanings are diametrically different. How we interpret the world affects how we respond to the world, and it is our responses that shape our lives, individually and collectively. That is why, in the famous words of Max De Pree, "The first responsibility of a leader is to define reality."[3]

Within every family, every community, and every organisation, there are trials, tests, and tribulations. Do these lead to arguments, blame, and recrimination? Or does the group see them providentially, as a route to some future good (a "descent that leads to an ascent" as the Lubavitcher Rebbe always used to say)? Does it work together to meet the challenge? Much, perhaps all, will depend on how the group defines its reality. This, in turn, will depend on the leadership or absence of leadership that it has had until now. Strong families and communities have a clear sense of what their ideals are, and they are not blown off course by the winds of change.

No one did this more powerfully than Moses in the way he monumentally framed the choice: between good and bad, life and death, the blessing and the curse, following God on the one hand and choosing the values of neighbouring civilisations on the other. That clarity is why the Hittites, Canaanites, Perizzites, and Jebusites are no more while the people of Israel still lives, despite an unparalleled history of circumstantial change.

Who are we? Where are we? What are we trying to achieve and what kind of people do we aspire to be? These are the questions leaders help the group ask and answer, and when a group does so together it is blessed with exceptional resilience and strength.

3. Max De Pree, *Leadership Is an Art* (New York: Doubleday, 1989), 11.

Shofetim

Learning and Leadership

P *arashat Shofetim* is the classic source of the three types of leadership in Judaism, called by the sages the "three crowns" – priesthood, kingship, and Torah[1] – which we discussed at length in our study of *Parashat Tetzaveh*. This is the first statement in history of the principle, set out in the eighteenth century by Montesquieu in *The Spirit of Laws*, and later made fundamental to the American constitution, of "the separation of powers."[2]

1. Mishna Avot 4:13; *Mishneh Torah, Hilkhot Talmud Torah* 3:1.
2. Montesquieu's division, followed in most Western democracies, is between legislature, executive, and judiciary. As we saw in our discussion of *Parashat Tetzaveh*, in Judaism, primary legislation comes from God. Kings and the sages had the power to introduce only secondary legislation, to secure order and "make a fence around the law." Hence in Judaism the king was the executive; the priesthood in biblical times was the judiciary. The "crown of Torah" worn by the prophets was a unique institution: a divinely sanctioned form of social criticism – a task assumed in the modern age, not always successfully, by public intellectuals. There is today a shortage of prophets. Perhaps there always was.

Power, in the human arena, is to be divided and distributed, not concentrated in a single person or office. In biblical Israel, there were kings, priests, and prophets. Kings had secular or governmental power. Priests were the leaders in the religious domain, presiding over the service in the Temple and other rites, and giving rulings on matters to do with holiness and purity. Prophets were mandated by God to be critical of the corruptions of power and to recall the people to their religious vocation whenever they drifted from it.

This *parasha* deals with all three roles. Undoubtedly, though, the most attention-catching is the section on kings, for many reasons. First, this is the only command in the Torah to carry with it the explanation that this is what other people do: "When you enter the land the Lord your God is giving you and have taken possession of it and settled in it, and you say, 'Let us set a king over us like all the nations around us...'" (Deut. 17:14). Normally, in the Torah, the Israelites are commanded to be different. The fact that this command is an exception was enough to signal to commentators throughout the ages that there is a certain ambivalence about the idea of monarchy altogether.

Second, the passage is strikingly negative. It tells us what a king must not do, rather than what he should do. He should not "acquire great numbers of horses," or "take many wives," or "accumulate large amounts of silver and gold" (Deut. 17:16–17). These are the temptations of power, and as we know from the rest of Tanakh, even the greatest – King Solomon himself – was vulnerable to them.

Third, consistent with the fundamental Judaic idea that leadership is service, not dominion or power or status or superiority, the king is commanded to be humble: he must constantly read the Torah "so that he may learn to revere the Lord his God... and not consider himself better than his fellow Israelites" (Deut. 17:19–20). It is not easy to be humble when everyone is bowing down before you and when you have the power of life and death over your subjects.

Hence the extreme variation among the commentators as to whether monarchy is a good institution or a dangerous one. The Rambam holds that the appointment of a king is an obligation, Ibn Ezra that it is a consent, Abrabanel that it is a concession, and Rabbenu Baḥya that it is a punishment – an interpretation quoted, as it happens, by

John Milton at one of the most volatile (and anti-monarchical) periods of English history.[3]

There is, though, one positive and exceptionally important dimension of royalty. The king is commanded to study constantly: "and he is to read it all the days of his life" (Deut. 17:19).

Later, in the book that bears his name, Joshua – Moses' successor – is commanded in very similar terms:

> Keep this Book of the Law always on your lips; meditate on it day and night, so that you may be careful to do everything written in it. Then you will be prosperous and successful. (Josh. 1:8)

Leaders learn. That is the principle at stake here. Yes, they have advisers, elders, counsellors, an inner court of sages and literati. And yes, biblical kings had prophets – Samuel to Saul, Nathan to David, Isaiah to Hezekiah and so on – to bring them the word of the Lord. But those on whom the destiny of the nation turns may not delegate away the task of thinking, reading, studying, and remembering. They are not entitled to say: I have affairs of state to worry about. I have no time for books. Leaders must be scholars, *Benei Torah*, "Children of the Book," if they are to direct and lead the People of the Book.

The great statesmen of modern times understood this, at least in secular terms. Gladstone, four times prime minister of Britain, had a library of thirty-two thousand books. We know – because he made a note in his diary every time he finished reading a book – that he read twenty-two thousand of them. Assuming he did so over the course of eighty years (he lived to be eighty-eight), this meant that he read on average two hundred and seventy-five books a year, or more than five each week for a lifetime. He also wrote many books on a wide variety of topics, from politics to religion to Greek literature, and his scholarship was often quite impressive. For example, he was, according to Guy

---

3. See Eric Nelson, *The Hebrew Republic* (Boston: Harvard University Press, 2010), 41–42.

Deutscher in *Through the Language Glass*,[4] the first person to realise that the ancient Greeks did not have a sense of colour and that Homer's famous phrase "the wine-dark sea" referred to texture rather than colour.

Visit David Ben-Gurion's house in Tel Aviv and you will see that, while the ground floor is spartan to the point of austerity, the first floor is a single vast library of papers, periodicals, and twenty thousand books. He had another four thousand or so in Sde Boker. Like Gladstone, Ben-Gurion was a voracious reader as well as a prolific author. Disraeli was a best-selling novelist before he entered politics. Winston Churchill wrote almost fifty books and won the Nobel Prize for Literature. Reading and writing are what separate the statesman from the mere politician.

The two greatest kings of early Israel, David and Solomon, were both authors, David of Psalms, Solomon (according to tradition) of The Song of Songs, Proverbs, and Ecclesiastes. The key biblical word associated with kings is *ḥokhma*, "wisdom." Solomon in particular was known for his wisdom:

> When all Israel heard the verdict the king had given, they held the king in awe, because they saw that he had wisdom from God to administer justice. (1 Kings 3:12)

> Solomon's wisdom was greater than the wisdom of all the people of the East, and greater than all the wisdom of Egypt.... From all nations people came to listen to Solomon's wisdom, sent by all the kings of the world, who had heard of his wisdom. (1 Kings 5:10–14)

> When the queen of Sheba saw all the wisdom of Solomon...she was overwhelmed. She said to the king, "The report I heard in my own country about your achievements and your wisdom is true. But I did not believe these things until I came and saw with my own eyes. Indeed, not even half was told me; in wisdom and wealth you have far exceeded the report I heard...." The whole

---

4. *Through the Language Glass: Why the World Looks Different in Other Languages* (New York: Metropolitan Books/Henry Holt and Co., 2010).

world sought an audience with Solomon to hear the wisdom God
had put in his heart. (1 Kings 10:4–24)

We should note that *ḥokhma*, wisdom, means something slightly
different from Torah, which is more commonly associated with priests
and prophets than kings. *Ḥokhma* includes worldly wisdom, which is
human and universal rather than a special heritage of Jews and Judaism.
A midrash states, "If someone says to you, 'There is wisdom among the
nations of the world,' believe it. If they say, 'There is Torah among the
nations of the world,' do not believe it."[5] Broadly speaking, in contemporary terms *ḥokhma* refers to the sciences and humanities – to whatever allows us to see the universe as the work of God and the human
person as the image of God. Torah is the specific moral and spiritual
heritage of Israel.

The case of Solomon is particularly poignant because, for all
his wisdom, he was not able to avoid the three temptations set out in
this *parasha*: he did acquire great numbers of horses, he did take many
wives, and he did accumulate great wealth. Wisdom without Torah is
not enough to save a leader from the corruptions of power.

Though few of us are destined to be kings, presidents, or prime
ministers, there is a general principle at stake. Leaders learn. They read.
They study. They take time to familiarise themselves with the world of
ideas. Only thus do they gain the perspective to be able to see further
and clearer than others. To be a Jewish leader means spending time to
study both Torah and *ḥokhma*: *ḥokhma* to understand the world as it is,
Torah to understand the world as it ought to be.

Leaders should never stop learning. That is how they grow and
teach others to grow with them.

5. Lamentations Rabba, 2:13.

Ki Tetzeh

Against Hate

Ki Tetzeh contains more laws than any other *parasha* in the Torah, and it is possible to be overwhelmed by this *embarras de richesses* of detail. One verse, however, stands out by its sheer counter-intuitiveness:

> Do not despise an Edomite, because he is your brother. Do not despise the Egyptian, because you were a stranger in his land. (Deut. 23:8)

These are very unexpected commands. Understanding them will teach us an important lesson about leadership.

First, a general point. Jews have been subjected to racism more and longer than any other nation on earth. Therefore we should be doubly careful never to be guilty of it ourselves. We believe that God created each of us, regardless of colour, class, culture, or creed, in His image. If we look down on other people because of their race, then we are demeaning God's image and failing to treat others with *kavod habriyot*, human dignity.

If we think less of a person because of the colour of his or her skin, we are repeating the sin of Aaron and Miriam – "Miriam and Aaron spoke against Moses because of the Cushite woman whom he had married, for he had married a Cushite woman" (Num. 12:1). There are midrashic interpretations that read this passage differently but the plain sense is that they looked down on Moses' wife because, like Cushite women generally, she had dark skin, making this one of the first recorded instances of colour prejudice. For this sin Miriam was struck with leprosy.

Instead we should remember the lovely line from Song of Songs: "I am black but beautiful, O daughters of Jerusalem, like the tents of Kedar, like the curtains of Solomon. Do not stare at me because I am dark, because the sun has looked upon me" (Song. 1:5).

Jews cannot complain that others have racist attitudes towards them if they hold racist attitudes towards others. "First correct yourself; then [seek to] correct others," says the Talmud (Bava Metzia 107b). The Tanakh contains negative evaluations of some other nations, but always and only because of their moral failures, never because of ethnicity or skin colour.

Now to Moses' two commands against hate,[1] both of which are surprising. "Do not despise the Egyptian, because you were a stranger in his land." This is extraordinary. The Egyptians enslaved the Israelites, planned a programme against them of slow genocide, and then refused to let them go despite the plagues that were devastating the land. Are these reasons not to hate?

True. But the Egyptians had initially provided a refuge for the Israelites at a time of famine. They had honoured Joseph and made him second-in-command. The evils they committed against the Israelites under "a new king who did not know of Joseph" (Ex. 1:8) were at the instigation of Pharaoh, not the people as a whole. Besides which, it was the daughter of that same Pharaoh who had rescued Moses and adopted him.

---

1. Whenever I refer, here and elsewhere, to "Moses' commands," I mean, of course, to imply that these were given by divine instruction and revelation. This, in a deep sense, is why God chose Moses, a man who said repeatedly of himself that he was not a man of words. The words he spoke were those of God. That, and that alone, is what gives them timeless authority for the people of the covenant.

The Torah makes a clear distinction between the Egyptians and the Amalekites. The latter were destined to be perennial enemies of Israel, but not the former. In a later age Isaiah would make a remarkable prophecy – that a day would come when the Egyptians would suffer their own oppression. They would cry out to God, who would rescue them just as he had rescued the Israelites: "When they cry out to the Lord because of their oppressors, He will send them a saviour and defender, and he will rescue them. So the Lord will make Himself known to the Egyptians, and on that day they will acknowledge the Lord" (Is. 19:20–21).

The wisdom of Moses' command not to despise Egyptians still shines through today. If the people had continued to hate their erstwhile oppressors, Moses would have taken the Israelites out of Egypt but would have failed to take Egypt out of the Israelites. They would still be slaves, not physically but psychologically. They would be slaves to the past, held captive by the chains of resentment, unable to build the future. *To be free, you have to let go of hate.* That is a difficult truth but a necessary one.

No less surprising is Moses' insistence: "Do not despise an Edomite, because he is your brother." Edom was, of course, the other name of Esau. There was a time when Esau hated Jacob and vowed to kill him. Besides which, before the twins were born, Rebecca received an oracle telling her, "Two nations are in your womb, and two peoples from within you will be separated; one people will be stronger than the other, and the elder will serve the younger" (Gen. 25:23). Whatever these words mean, they seem to imply that there will be eternal conflict between the two brothers and their descendants.

At a much later age, during the Second Temple period, the prophet Malachi said: "'Was not Esau Jacob's brother?' declares the Lord. 'Yet I have loved Jacob, but Esau I have hated'" (Mal. 1:2–3). Centuries later still, R. Shimon b. Yoḥai said, "It is a halakha [rule, law, inescapable truth] that Esau hates Jacob."[2] Why then does Moses tell us not to despise Esau's descendants?

The answer is simple. *Esau may hate Jacob. It does not follow that Jacob should hate Esau.* To answer hate with hate is to be dragged down

---

2. *Sifrei*, Numbers, *Behaalotekha*, 69.

to the level of your opponent. When, in the course of a television programme, I asked Judea Pearl, father of the murdered journalist Daniel Pearl, why he was working for reconciliation between Jews and Muslims, he replied with heartbreaking lucidity, "Hate killed my son. Therefore I am determined to fight hate." As Martin Luther King Jr. wrote, "Darkness cannot drive out darkness; only light can do that. Hate cannot drive out hate; only love can do that."[3] Or as Ecclesiastes said, there is "a time to love and a time to hate, a time for war and a time for peace" (Eccl. 3:8).

It was none other than R. Shimon b. Yoḥai who said that when Esau met Jacob for the last time, he kissed and embraced him "with a full heart."[4] Hate, especially between brothers, is not eternal and inexorable. Always be ready, Moses seems to imply, for reconciliation between enemies.

Contemporary Game Theory – the study of decision making – suggests the same. Martin Nowak's strategy, "Generous Tit-for-Tat," is a winning approach to the scenario known as the Iterated Prisoner's Dilemma, an example created for the study of cooperation of two individuals. Tit-for-Tat says: start by being nice to your opponent, then do to him what he does to you (in Hebrew, *midda keneged midda*). Generous Tit-for-Tat says, do not always do to him what he does to you or you may find yourself locked into a mutually destructive cycle of retaliation. Every so often, ignore (i.e., forgive) your opponent's last harmful move. That, roughly speaking, is what the sages meant when they said that God originally created the world under the attribute of strict justice but saw that it could not survive. Therefore He built into it the principle of compassion (see Rashi to Gen. 1:1, s.v. *bara*).

Moses' two commands against hate are testimony to his greatness as a leader. It is the easiest thing in the world to become a leader by mobilising the forces of hate. That is what Radovan Karadzic and Slobodan Milosevic did in the former Yugoslavia, and it led to mass murder and ethnic cleansing. It is what the state-controlled media did – describing Tutsis as *inyenzi*, "cockroaches" – before the 1994 genocide in Rwanda. It is what dozens of preachers of hate are doing today, often using the

3. *Strength to Love* (Minneapolis, Minn.: Fortress Press, 1977), 53.
4. *Sifrei*, Numbers, *Behaalotekha*, 69.

Internet to communicate paranoia and incite acts of terror. Finally, this was the technique mastered by Hitler as a prelude to the worst-ever crime of man against man. The language of hate is capable of creating enmity between people of different faiths and ethnicities who have lived peaceably together for centuries. It has consistently been the most destructive force in history, and yet knowledge of the Holocaust has not put an end to it, even in Europe. It is the unmistakable mark of toxic leadership.

In his classic work, *Leadership*, James MacGregor Burns distinguishes between transactional and transformational leaders. The former address people's interests. The latter attempt to raise their sights. "Transforming leadership is elevating. It is moral but not moralistic. Leaders engage with followers, but from higher levels of morality; in the enmeshing of goals and values both leaders and followers are raised to more principled levels of judgement."[5]

Leadership at its highest transforms those who exercise it and those who are influenced by it. The great leaders make people better, kinder, nobler than they would otherwise be. That was the achievement of Washington, Lincoln, Churchill, Gandhi, and Mandela. The paradigm case was Moses, the man who had more lasting influence than any other leader in history. He did it by teaching the Israelites not to hate. A good leader knows: hate the sin but not the sinner. Do not forget the past but do not be held captive by it. Be willing to fight your enemies but never allow yourself to be defined by them or become like them. Learn to love and forgive. Acknowledge the evil men do, but stay focused on the good that is in our power to do. Only thus do we raise the moral sights of humankind and help redeem the world we share.

5. James MacGregor Burns, *Leadership* (New York: Harper Perennial, 2010), 455.

Ki Tavo

A Nation of Storytellers

Howard Gardner, professor of education and psychology at Harvard University, is one of the great minds of our time. He is best known for his theory of "multiple intelligences," the idea that there is not one thing that can be measured and defined as intelligence but many different facets – one dimension of the dignity of difference. He has also written many books on leadership and creativity, including one in particular, *Leading Minds*, that is important in understanding *Parashat Ki Tavo*.[1]

Gardner's argument is that what makes a leader is *the ability to tell a particular kind of story* – one that explains ourselves to ourselves and gives power and resonance to a collective vision. So Churchill told the story of Britain's indomitable courage in the fight for freedom. Gandhi spoke about the dignity of India and non-violent protest. Margaret Thatcher talked about the importance of the individual against an ever-encroaching state. Martin Luther King Jr. told of how a great nation

---

1. Howard Gardner in collaboration with Emma Laskin, *Leading Minds: An Anatomy of Leadership* (New York: Basic Books, 2011).

is colour-blind. Stories give the group a shared identity and sense of purpose.

Philosopher Alasdair MacIntyre has also emphasised the importance of narrative to the moral life. "Man," he writes, "is in his actions and practice as well as in his fictions, essentially a story-telling animal."[2] It is through narrative that we begin to learn who we are and how we are called on to behave. "Deprive children of stories and you leave them unscripted, anxious stutterers in their actions as in their words."[3] To know who we are is in large part to understand the story or stories that we are a part of.

The great questions – "Who are we?" "Why are we here?" "What is our task?" – are best answered by telling a story. As Barbara Hardy put it: "We dream in narrative, daydream in narrative, remember, anticipate, hope, despair, believe, doubt, plan, revise, criticise, construct, gossip, learn, hate, and love by narrative."[4] This is fundamental to understanding why Torah is the kind of book it is: not a theological treatise or a metaphysical system but a series of interlinked stories extended over time, from Abraham and Sarah's journey from Mesopotamia to Moses' and the Israelites' wanderings in the desert. Judaism is less about *truth as system* than about *truth as story*. And we are part of that story. That is what it is to be a Jew.

A large part of what Moses is doing in the book of Deuteronomy is retelling that story to the next generation, reminding them of what God did for their parents and of some of the mistakes their parents made. Moses, as well as being the great liberator, is the supreme storyteller. Yet what he does in *Parashat Ki Tavo* extends way beyond this.

He tells the people that when they enter, conquer, and settle the land, they must bring the first ripened fruits to the central Sanctuary, the Temple, as a way of giving thanks to God. A mishna in Bikkurim (3:3) describes the joyous scene as people converged on Jerusalem from across the country, bringing their first fruits to the accompaniment of music and celebration. Merely bringing the fruits, though, was not enough. Each

---

2. Alasdair MacIntyre, *After Virtue* (Notre Dame, Ind.: University of Notre Dame Press, 1981), 216.
3. Ibid.
4. Barbara Hardy, "An Approach Through Narrative," *Novel: A Forum on Fiction* 2 (Durham, N.C.: Duke University Press, 1968), 5.

person had to make a declaration. That declaration became one of the best-known passages in the Torah because, though it was originally said on Shavuot, the Festival of First Fruits, in post-biblical times it became a central element of the Haggada on Seder night:

> My father was a wandering Aramean, and he went down into Egypt and lived there, few in number, there becoming a great nation, powerful and numerous. But the Egyptians ill-treated us and made us suffer, subjecting us to harsh labour. Then we cried out to the Lord, the God of our ancestors, and the Lord heard our voice and saw our misery, toil, and oppression. So the Lord brought us out of Egypt with a mighty hand and an outstretched arm, with great terror and with signs and wonders. (Deut. 26:5–8)

Here for the first time, *the retelling of the nation's history becomes an obligation for every citizen of the nation.* In this act, known as *vidui bikkurim,* "the confession made over first fruits," Jews were commanded, as it were, to become a nation of storytellers.

This is a remarkable development. Yosef Hayim Yerushalmi tells us that "only in Israel and nowhere else is the injunction to remember felt as a religious imperative to an entire people."[5] Time and again throughout Deuteronomy comes the command to remember: "Remember that you were a slave in Egypt" (5:14; 15:15; 16:12; 24:18; 24:22); "Remember what Amalek did to you" (25:17); "Remember what God did to Miriam" (24:9); "Remember the days of old; consider the generations long past. Ask your father and he will tell you, your elders, and they will explain to you" (32:7).

The *vidui bikkurim* is more than this. It is, compressed into the shortest possible space, the entire history of the nation in summary form. In a few short sentences we have here

the patriarchal origins in Mesopotamia, the emergence of the Hebrew nation in the midst of history rather than in mythic

---

5. Yosef Hayim Yerushalmi, *Zakhor: Jewish History and Jewish Memory* (New York: Schocken Books, 1989), 9.

prehistory, slavery in Egypt and liberation therefrom, the climactic acquisition of the land of Israel, and throughout – the acknowledgement of God as lord of history.[6]

We should note here an important nuance. Jews were the first people to find God in history. They were the first to think in historical terms – of time as an arena of change as opposed to cyclical time in which the seasons rotate, people are born and die, but nothing really changes. Jews were the first people to write history – many centuries before Herodotus and Thucydides, often wrongly described as the first historians. Yet biblical Hebrew has no word that means "history" (the closest equivalent is *divrei hayamim*, "chronicles"). Instead it uses the root *zakhor*, meaning "remember."

There is a fundamental difference between history and memory. History is "his story,"[7] an account of events that happened sometime else to someone else. Memory is "my story." It is the past internalised and made part of my identity. That is what the mishna in Pesaḥim means when it says, "Each person must see himself as if he went out of Egypt" (10:5).

Throughout Deuteronomy, Moses warns the people – no less than fourteen times – *not to forget*. If they forget the past they will lose their identity and sense of direction and disaster will follow. Moreover, not only are the people commanded to remember, they are also commanded to pass that memory down to their children.

This entire phenomenon represents a remarkable cluster of ideas: about identity as a matter of collective memory, about the ritual retelling of the nation's story, and above all, about the fact that *every one of us is a guardian of that story and memory*. It is not the leader alone, or some elite, who are trained to recall the past, but every one of us. This too is an aspect of the devolution and democratisation of leadership that we find throughout Judaism as a way of life. The great leaders tell the story of the group, but the greatest of leaders, Moses, taught the group to become a nation of storytellers.

6. Ibid., 12.
7. This is a simple reminder, not an etymology. *Historia* is a Greek word meaning inquiry. The same word comes to mean, in Latin, a narrative of past events.

You can still see the power of this idea today. As I point out in my book *The Home We Build Together*,[8] if you visit the presidential memorials in Washington, you see that each carries an inscription taken from their words: Jefferson's "We hold these truths to be self-evident" in the Declaration of Independence; Roosevelt's "The only thing we have to fear, is fear itself";[9] Lincoln's Gettysburg Address[10] and Second Inaugural Address, "With malice towards none; with charity for all."[11] Each memorial tells a story.

London has no equivalent. It contains many memorials and statues, each with a brief inscription stating who it represents, but there are no speeches or quotations. There is no story. Even the memorial to Churchill, whose speeches rivalled Lincoln's in power, carries only one word: "Churchill."

America has a national story because it is a society based on the idea of covenant. Narrative is at the heart of covenantal politics because it locates national identity in a set of historic events. The memory of those events evokes the values for which those who came before us fought and of which we are the guardians.

A covenantal narrative is always inclusive, the property of all its citizens, newcomers as well as the native-born. It says to everyone, regardless of class or creed: this is who we are. It creates a sense of common identity that transcends other identities. That is why, for example, Martin Luther King Jr. was able to use it to such effect in some of his greatest speeches. He was telling his fellow African-Americans to see themselves as an equal part of the nation. At the same time, he was telling white Americans to honour their commitment to the Declaration of Independence and its statement that "all men are created equal."

England does not have the same kind of national narrative because it is based not on covenant but on hierarchy and tradition. England, writes Roger Scruton, "was not a nation or a creed or a language

8. Jonathan Sacks, *The Home We Build Together: Recreating Society* (London: Bloomsbury Academic, 2009).
9. First Inaugural Address (United States Capitol, March 4, 1933).
10. November 19, 1863.
11. United States Capitol, March 4, 1865.

or a state but a home. Things at home don't need an explanation. They are there because they are there."[12] England, historically, was a class-based society in which there were ruling elites who governed on behalf of the nation as a whole. America, founded by Puritans who saw themselves as a new Israel bound by covenant, was not a society of rulers and ruled, but rather one of collective responsibility. Hence the phrase, central to American politics but never used in English politics: "We the people."

By making the Israelites a nation of storytellers, Moses helped turn them into a people bound by collective responsibility – to one another, to the past and future, and to God. By framing a narrative that successive generations would make their own and teach to their children, Moses turned Jews into a nation of leaders.

12. Roger Scruton, *England: An Elegy* (London; New York: Continuum, 2006), 16.

Nitzavim

Defeating Death

Only now, reaching *parashot Nitzavim* and *Vayelekh,* can we begin to get a sense of the vast, world-changing project at the heart of the divine-human encounter that took place in the lifetime of Moses and the birth of the Jews/Hebrews/Israel as a nation.

To understand it, recall the famous remark of Sherlock Holmes. "I draw your attention," he said to Dr Watson, "to the curious incident of the dog at night." "But the dog did nothing at night," said Watson. "That," said Holmes, "is the curious incident."[1] Sometimes, to know what a book is about you need to focus on what it does *not* say, not just on what it does.

What is missing from the Torah, almost inexplicably so given the background against which it is set, is a *fixation with death.* The ancient Egyptians were obsessed with death. Their monumental buildings were an attempt to defy death. The pyramids were giant mausoleums. More precisely, they were portals through which the soul of a deceased pharaoh could ascend to heaven and join the immortals. The most famous

1. Arthur Conan Doyle, "The Adventure of Silver Blaze."

Egyptian text that has come down to us is *The Book of the Dead*. For the Egyptians, only the afterlife was real; life was a preparation for death.

There is nothing of this in the Torah, at least not explicitly. Jews believed in *Olam HaBa*, the World to Come, life after death. They believed in *teḥiyat hametim*, the resurrection of the dead.[2] There are six references to it in the second paragraph of the *Amida* alone. But not only are these ideas almost completely absent from Tanakh, they are absent at the very points where we would expect them.

The book of Ecclesiastes is an extended lament of human mortality. *Havel havalim... hakol havel*: everything is worthless because life is a mere fleeting breath (1:2). Why did the author of Ecclesiastes not mention the World to Come and life after death? Another example: the book of Job is a sustained protest against the apparent injustices of the world. Why did no one answer Job, "You and other innocent people who suffer will be rewarded in the afterlife"? We believe in the afterlife. Why then is it not mentioned – merely hinted at – in the Torah? That is the curious incident.

The simple answer is that obsession with death ultimately devalues life. Why fight against the evils and injustices of the world if this life is only a preparation for the World to Come? Ernest Becker in his classic *The Denial of Death*[3] argues that fear of our own mortality has been one of the driving forces of civilisation. It is what led the ancient world to enslave the masses, turning them into giant labour forces to build monumental buildings that would stand as long as time itself. It led to the ancient cult of the hero, the man who becomes immortal through daring deeds on the field of battle. We fear death; we have a love-hate relationship with it. Freud called this Thanatos, the death instinct, and said it was one of the two driving forces of life, the other being Eros.

Judaism is a sustained protest against this worldview. That is why "no one knows where Moses is buried" (Deut. 34:6), so that his tomb

2. The Mishna, Sanhedrin 10:1, says that believing that the resurrection of the dead is stated in the Torah is a fundamental part of Jewish faith. However, according to any interpretation, the statement is implicit, not explicit.
3. New York: Free Press, 1973.

should never become a place of pilgrimage and worship. That is why in place of a pyramid or a temple such as Ramses II built at Abu Simbel, all the Israelites had for almost five centuries until the days of Solomon was the *Mishkan*, a portable sanctuary, more like a tent than a temple. That is the reason that in Judaism, death defiles; it is why the rite of the Red Heifer was necessary to purify people from contact with death. That is why the holier you are – if you are a priest, more so if you are the high priest – the less you can be in contact with or under the same roof as a dead person. God is not in death but in life.

Only against this Egyptian background can we fully sense the drama behind words that have become so familiar to us that we are no longer surprised by them, the great words in which Moses frames the choice for all time: "See, I have set before you today life and good, death and evil.... I call heaven and earth as witnesses today against you, that I have set before you life and death, the blessing and the curse; therefore choose life, that you and your children may live" (Deut. 30:15, 19).

Life is good; death is bad. Life is a blessing; death is a curse. These are truisms for us. Why even mention them? Because they were not common ideas in the ancient world. They were revolutionary. They still are.

How then do you defeat death? Yes, there is an afterlife. Yes, there is *teḥiyat hametim*, resurrection. But Moses does not focus on these obvious ideas. He tells us something different altogether. You achieve immortality by being part of a covenant – a covenant with eternity itself, that is to say, a covenant with God.

When you live your life within a covenant, something extraordinary happens. Your parents and grandparents live on in you. You live on in your children and grandchildren. They are part of your life. You are part of theirs. That is what Moses meant when he said, near the beginning of this *parasha*: "It is not with you alone that I am making this covenant and oath, but with whoever stands with us here today before the Lord our God *as well as those not with us here today*" (Deut. 29:13–14). In Moses' day that last phrase meant "your children not yet born." He did not need to include "your parents, no longer alive" because their parents had themselves made a covenant with God forty years before at Mount Sinai. But what Moses meant in a larger sense was that when we renew the covenant, when we dedicate our lives to the faith and way of life of our ancestors, they become immortal in us, as we become immortal in our children.

It is precisely because Judaism focuses on this world, not the next, that it is the most child-centred of all the great religions. They are our immortality. That is what Rachel meant when she said, "Give me children, or else I am like one dead" (Gen. 30:1). It is what Abraham meant when he said, "Lord, God, what will you give me if I remain childless?" (Gen. 15:2). We are not all destined to have children. The rabbis said that the good we do constitutes our *toledot*, our posterity (Rashi to Gen. 6:9). But by honouring the memory of our parents and bringing up children to continue the Jewish story, we achieve the one form of immortality that lies this side of the grave, in this world that God pronounced good.

Now consider the two last commands in the Torah, set out in *Parashat Vayelekh*, the ones Moses gave at the very end of his life. One is *hak'hel*, the command that the king summon the nation to an assembly every seven years: "At the end of every seven years … assemble the people – men, women, and children and the stranger living in your towns – so that they can listen and learn to fear the Lord your God and follow carefully all the words of this law" (Deut. 31:12).

The meaning of this command is simple. Moses is saying: it is not enough that your parents made a covenant with God at Mount Sinai or that you yourselves renewed it with me here on the plains of Moab. The covenant must be perpetually renewed, every seven years, so that it never becomes history. It always remains memory. It never becomes old because every seven years it becomes new again.

And the last command? "Now write down this song and teach it to the Israelites and make them sing it, so that it may be a witness for Me against them" (Deut. 31:19). This, according to tradition, is the command to write (at least part of) a *sefer Torah*. As Maimonides puts it: "Even if your ancestors have left you a *sefer Torah*, nonetheless you are commanded to write one for yourself."[4]

---

4. *Mishneh Torah, Hilkhot Tefillin, Mezuza, VeSefer Torah* 7:1.

What Moses is saying in this, his last charge to the people he had led for forty years, is: it is not sufficient to say, "Our ancestors received the Torah from Moses," or "Our ancestors received the Torah from God." You have to take it and make it new in every generation. You must make the Torah not just your parents' or grandparents' faith, but your own. If you write it, it will write you. The eternal word of the eternal God is your share in eternity.

We now sense the full force of the drama of these last days of Moses' life. Moses knew he was about to die, knew he would not cross the Jordan and enter the land he had spent his entire life leading the people towards. Moses, confronting his own mortality, asks us in every generation to confront ours.

Our faith – Moses is telling us – is not like that of the Egyptians, the Greeks, the Romans, or virtually every other civilisation known to history. We do not find God in a realm beyond life – in heaven or after death, in mystic disengagement from the world or in philosophical contemplation. We find God in life. We find God in love and joy (the keywords of Deuteronomy). To find God, he says in *Parashat Nitzavim*, you do not have to climb to heaven or cross the sea (Deut. 30:12–13). God is here. God is now. God is life.

And that life, though it will end one day, in truth does not end. For if you keep the covenant, then your ancestors will live in you, and you will live on in your children (or your disciples or the recipients of your kindness). Every seven years the covenant will become new again. Every generation will write its own *sefer Torah*. The gate to eternity is not death: it is life lived in a covenant endlessly renewed, in words engraved on our hearts and the hearts of our children.

And so Moses, the greatest leader we ever had, became immortal. Not by living forever. Not by building a tomb and temple to his glory. We do not even know where he is buried. The only physical structure he left us was portable because life itself is a journey. He did not even become immortal the way Aaron did, by seeing his children become his successors. He became immortal by making us his disciples. And in one of their first recorded utterances, the rabbis said likewise: "Raise up many disciples" (Mishna Avot 1:1).

To be a leader, you do not need a crown or robes of office. All you need to do is to write your chapter in the story, do deeds that heal some of the pain of this world, and act so that others become a little better for having known you. Live so that, through you, our ancient covenant with God is renewed in the only way that matters: in life. Moses' last testament to us at the very end of his days, when his mind might so easily have turned to death, was: choose life.

Vayelekh

Consensus or Command?

What do you say to your successor? What advice do you give him? *Parashat Vayelekh* is the place to look for the answer, because it is here that Moses finally hands the reins over to Joshua, and he and God both give him a blessing for the future – but they give different blessings.

Listen to them and they sound almost the same. Moses says, "Be strong and of good courage, for you will come [*tavo*] with this people into the land" (Deut. 31:7). God says, "Be strong and of good courage, for you will bring [*tavi*] the Israelites into the land" (31:23). *Tavo* or *tavi*, "come with" or "bring." The words sound and seem similar. But the difference as understood by the sages was total.

Here is how Rashi puts it:

> Moses said to Joshua, "Make sure that the elders of the generation are with you. Always act according to their opinion and advice." However, the Holy One, Blessed Be He, said to Joshua, "For you will *bring* the Israelites into the land I promised them" – meaning, "Bring them even against their will. It all depends on

you. If necessary, take a stick and beat them over the head. There is only one leader for a generation, not two." (Rashi to Deut. 31:7)

These are the two extremes of leadership: consensus or command. Moses advises Joshua to pursue a policy of consultation and conciliation. What he is saying in effect is, "You don't need to follow the people. You are the leader, not they. But you do need to work with the elders. They too are leaders. They constitute, in effect, your team. They need to feel that they are part of the decision-making process. They will not expect you always to agree with them. Often they will not agree with one another. But they do need to feel consulted.

"If they sense that you are not interested in their opinions, if the impression they have of you is of a person determined to do things his way regardless of everyone else because you know better, they will attempt to sabotage you. They will do you harm. They may not succeed. You may survive. But you will be injured. You will limp. Your standing among the people will be diminished. They will say: how can we respect one who is not respected by the elders?

"I speak from experience. The Korah rebellion was serious. It was not just Korah; it was also the Reubenites and other leaders from the various tribes. And though the rebellion was cut short in the most dramatic way possible, we were all diminished and nothing was quite the same ever again. So: make sure that the elders of the generation are with you. If they are, you will succeed."

God, according to the sages, takes the opposite approach. "The time has come to leave the wilderness, cross the Jordan, conquer the land, and build the kind of society that honours the human beings I made in My image instead of enslaving and exploiting them. Don't look for consensus. You will never find it. People's interests are different. Their perspectives are not the same. Politics is an arena of conflict. I did not want it to be that way, but having given humanity the gift of freedom, I cannot take it back and impose My will by force. So you must show the people the way.

"Lead from the front. Be clear. Be consistent. Be strong. The last person who gave the people what they wanted was Aaron, and what they wanted was a Golden Calf. That was nearly the end of the Jewish people. Consensus, in politics or business or even in pursuit of truth, is not leadership but the abdication of leadership. I chose you to be Moses' successor because I believe in you. Therefore, believe in yourself. Tell the people what they must do, and tell them why.

"Be respectful of them. By all means, listen to them. But at the end of the day the responsibility is yours. Leaders lead. They do not follow. And believe Me, though they may criticise you now they will eventually admire you. People want their leaders to know the way, go the way, and show the way. They want them to be decisive. Always treat people with the utmost courtesy and respect. But if they do not behave towards you as you do towards them, if they oppose and try to frustrate what you are doing, there may be no choice but to take a stick and hit them on the head. There is only one leader in a generation. If everyone is empowered, there is no music, only noise; no achievement, only an endless committee meeting at which everyone speaks and no one listens."

Those were, then and now, the two great options. But notice something odd: the person urging consensus is Moses. But Moses never acted by consensus. This is the man who almost had to drag the people out of Egypt, through the sea, and across a howling desert, the man who did things of his own initiative without even asking God. This is the man who broke the tablets of stone hewn and engraved by God Himself. When did Moses ever lead by consensus? To be sure he had seventy elders, princes of tribes, and a devolved structure of administration with heads of thousands, hundreds, fifties, and tens, but though they helped him, they did not advise him nor did he seek their advice. What suddenly turned Moses into a peacenik, a lead-by-consensus man?

That is one problem. The other is the advice given by God Himself: lead from the front, even against their will. But that is not how God acted, as understood by the sages. This is what they said on the words immediately prior to the creation of humanity, "Let us make man in our image" (Gen. 1:26):

> Let us make man: From here we learn the humility of the Holy One, Blessed Be He. Since man was created in the likeness of the angels, and they would envy him, He consulted them....

Even though they [the angels] did not assist Him in His creation, and there is an opportunity for the heretics to rebel [to misconstrue the plural "us" as a basis for their heresies], Scripture did not hesitate to teach proper conduct and the trait of humility, that a great person should consult with and receive permission from a smaller one.[1]

The sages, puzzled by the plural, "Let *us* make man," interpret it to mean that God consulted with the angels. Despite the fact that the use of the word "us" is dangerous – it can be read as compromising the pure monotheism of Judaism – nonetheless the principle of consultation is so important that the Torah takes the risk of being open to misinterpretation. God consults, according to the sages. "God does not act tyrannically towards His creatures" (Avoda Zara 3a).

To be sure, the sages say that at Sinai, God suspended the mountain above the Israelites and said, "If you say no, this will be your grave" (Shabbat 88a). But this is not the plain sense of the verse. To the contrary, before He gave the Torah to Israel He commanded Moses to explain to the people what was being proposed (Ex. 19:4–6). And it was only when the people – "*all* the people *together*" (19:8) responded "*with one voice*" (24:3) – that the covenant was made. That is the biblical basis for the idea, in the American Declaration of Independence, that governments gain their authority from "the consent of the governed." The very act of giving humans freedom means that God never forces us against our will. As Eisenhower once said, "You do not lead by hitting people over the head – that's assault, not leadership." So why is God here, as it were, speaking out of character?

The answer, it seems to me, is this: Both God and Moses want Joshua to know that true leadership cannot be a one-sided affair, be it the pursuit of consensus or command-and-control. It must be a deft balance of both. They want Joshua to hear this in the most striking way, so each says what they are least expected to say.

Moses, whom everyone associates with strong, decisive leadership, in effect tells Joshua, "Don't forget to strive for consensus. Your

1. Rashi to Genesis 1:27; Genesis Rabba, 8.

task is not what mine was. I had to take people out of slavery. You have to lead them into a land of freedom. Freedom means taking people seriously. The leadership of a free people involves listening, respecting, and striving for consensus wherever possible."

God, who gave humans their freedom and never imposed Himself on people against their will, says, "Joshua, I am God; you are not. I have to respect people's freedom. I have to let them go the way they are determined to go, even if it is wrong and self-destructive. But you are a human among humans and it is your task to show them the way that leads to justice, compassion, and good society. If the people do not agree with you, you have to teach them, persuade them, but ultimately you have to lead them, because if everyone does what is right in his or her own eyes, that is not freedom, but chaos."

In short, leadership is not simple. It is complex because it involves people and people are complex. You have to listen, and you have to lead. You have to strive for consensus but ultimately, if there is none, you must take the risk of deciding. Had they waited for consensus, Lincoln would never have ended slavery, Roosevelt and Churchill would never have led the free world to victory, and David Ben-Gurion would never have proclaimed the State of Israel.

It is not the job of leaders to give people what they want. It is the job of leaders to teach people what they ought to want. But at the same time, they must involve people in the decision-making process. Key figures and constituencies must feel that they were consulted. Collaborative, consultative, listening leadership is essential in a free society. Otherwise, there is autocracy tempered by assassination.[2]

Leaders must be teachers but also learners. They must be visionaries and yet have time for the details. They must push people – but never too far, never too fast, or they will fail. They must speak to the better angels of our nature, teaching us to love, not hate; to forgive, not seek revenge. They must always prefer the peaceful solution to the one that involves taking a stick and hitting people on the head, even though they are prepared to do so if there is no alternative. Leaders must be capable

2. A phrase attributed to Voltaire but actually from German diplomat Georg Herbert zu Munster (1820–1902).

of more than one style of leadership. Otherwise, as Abraham Maslow said, when one only has a hammer, it becomes tempting "to treat everything as if it were a nail."[3]

Considering the effort, energy, stress, and pain, why anyone should seek to be a leader would remain a mystery, were it not for this luminous truth: that there is no better way to flood life with meaning than to have lifted others and helped them to a greatness they never knew they had; to have, together with others, righted some of the wrongs of this injured earth and its creatures; to have acted rather than waited for others to act; and to have brought others with you, for the greatest leader on earth or in heaven cannot lead alone.

These are what make leadership the greatest privilege by which any of us can be blessed. As Moses said to Joshua, "Happy are you to have merited leading the children of God" (Rashi to Num. 27:18). The crown of leadership is invisible, yet you know who is wearing it and who is not. It is there, in front of you, waiting for you to put it on.[4] Wear it with pride and may all you do be blessed.

---

3. *The Psychology of Science: A Reconnaissance* (New York: Harper & Row, 1966), 15–16.
4. *Mishneh Torah, Hilkhot Talmud Torah* 3:1.

Haazinu

A Leader's Call to Responsibility

When words take wing, they modulate into song. That is what they do here in *Parashat Haazinu* as Moses, with the Angel of Death already in sight, prepares to take leave of this life. Never before has he spoken with such passion. His language is vivid, even violent. He wants his final words never to be forgotten. In a sense he has been articulating this truth for forty years, but never before with such emotion. This is what he says:

> Give ear, O heavens, that I may speak,
> Earth, hear the sayings of my mouth....
> The Rock, His acts are perfect,
> For all His ways are just.
> A faithful God without wrong,
> Right and straight is He.
> He is not corrupt; the defect is in His children,
> A warped and twisted generation.

Is this the way you repay God,
Ungrateful, unwise people?
Is He not your father, your master?
He made you and established you. (Deut. 32:1–6)

Do not blame God when things go wrong. That is what Moses feels so passionately. Do not believe, he says, that God is there to serve us. We are here to serve Him and through Him be a blessing to the world. God is straight; it is we who are complex and self-deceiving. God is not there to relieve us of responsibility. It is God who is calling us to responsibility.

With these words, Moses brings to closure the drama that began in the beginning with Adam and Eve in the Garden of Eden. When they sinned, Adam blamed the woman, the woman blamed the serpent. So it was in the beginning and so it still is in the twenty-first century.

The story of humanity has been, for the most part, a flight from responsibility. The culprits change. Only the sense of victimhood remains. It wasn't us. It was the politicians. Or the media. Or the bankers. Or our genes. Or our parents. Or the system – be it capitalism, communism, or anything in between. Most of all, it is the fault of the others, the ones not like us, infidels, sons of Satan, children of darkness, the unredeemed. The perpetrators of the greatest crime against humanity in all of history were convinced it wasn't them. They were "only obeying orders." When all else fails, blame God. And if you do not believe in God, blame the people who do. To be human is to seek to escape from responsibility.

That is what makes Judaism different. It is what made some people admire Jews and others hate them. For Judaism is God's call to human responsibility. From this call you cannot hide, as Adam and Eve discovered when they tried, and you cannot escape, as Jonah learnt in the belly of a fish.

What Moses was saying in his great farewell song can be paraphrased thus: "Beloved people, I have led you for forty years, and my time is coming to an end. For the last month, since I began these speeches, these *devarim*, I have tried to tell you the most important things about your past and future. I beg you not to forget them.

"Your parents were slaves. God brought them and you to freedom. But that was negative freedom, *hofesh*. It meant that there was no one to order you about. That kind of freedom is not inconsequential, for its absence tastes like unleavened bread and bitter herbs. Eat them once a year so you never forget where you came from and who brought you out.

"But don't think that *hofesh* alone can sustain a free society. When everyone is free to do what they like, the result is anarchy, not freedom. A free society requires *herut*, the positive freedom that only comes when people internalise the habits of self-restraint – so that my freedom is not bought at the expense of yours, nor yours at the cost of mine.

"That is why I have taught you all these laws, judgements, and statutes. None of them is arbitrary. None of them exists because God likes giving laws. God gave laws to the very structures of matter – laws that generated a vast, wondrous, almost unfathomable universe. If God were only interested in giving laws, He would have confined Himself to the things that obey those laws, namely matter without mind and life forms that know not liberty.

"The laws God gave me and I gave you exist not for God's sake but for ours. God gave us freedom – the most rare, precious, unfathomable thing of all other than life itself. But with freedom comes responsibility. That means that we must take the risk of action. God gave us the land but we must conquer it. God gave us the fields but we must plough, sow, and reap them. God gave us bodies but we must tend and heal them. God is our father; He made us and established us. But parents cannot live their children's lives. They can only show them by instruction and love how to live.

"So when things go wrong, don't blame God. He is not corrupt; we are. He is straight; it is we who are sometimes warped and twisted."

That is the Torah's ethic of responsibility. No higher estimate has ever been given of the human condition. No higher vocation was ever entrusted to mortal creatures of flesh and blood.

Judaism does not see human beings, as some religions do, as irretrievably corrupt, stained by original sin, incapable of good without God's grace. That is a form of faith, but it is not ours. Nor do we see religion as a matter of blind submission to God's will. That too is a form of faith, but not ours.

We do not see human beings, as the pagans did, as the playthings of capricious gods. Nor do we see them, as some scientists do, as mere matter, a gene's way of producing another gene, a collection of chemicals driven by electrical impulses in the brain, without any special dignity or sanctity, temporary residents in a universe devoid of meaning that came into existence for no reason and will one day, equally for no reason, cease to be.

We believe that we are God's image, free as He is free, creative as He is creative. We exist on an infinitely smaller and more limited scale, to be sure, but still we are the one point in all the echoing expanse of space where the universe becomes conscious of itself, the one life form capable of shaping its own destiny: choosing, therefore free, therefore responsible.

Which means: *thou shalt not see thyself as a victim.* Do not believe as the Greeks did that fate is blind and inexorable; that our fate, once disclosed by the Delphic oracle, has already been sealed before we were born; that like Laius and Oedipus we are fated, however hard we try to escape the bonds of fate. That is a tragic view of the human condition. To some extent it was shared in different ways by Spinoza, Marx, and Freud, the great triumvirate of Jews-by-descent who rejected Judaism and all its works.

Instead, like Viktor Frankl, survivor of Auschwitz, and Aaron T. Beck, co-founder of cognitive behavioural therapy, believe that we are not defined by what happens to us but rather by how we respond to what happens to us. That itself is determined by how we interpret what happens to us. If we change the way we think – which we can, because of the plasticity of the brain – then we can change the way we feel and the way we act. Fate is never final. There may be such a thing as an evil decree, but penitence, prayer, and charity can avert it. And what we cannot do alone we can do together, for we believe "it is not good for man to be alone" (Gen. 2:18).

So Jews developed a morality of guilt in place of what the Greeks had, a morality of shame. A morality of guilt makes a sharp distinction between the person and the act, between the sinner and the sin. Because we are not wholly defined by what we do, there is a core within us that remains intact – "My God, the soul You gave me is pure" – so that whatever wrong we may have done, we can repent and be forgiven. That creates a language of hope, the only force strong enough to defeat a culture of despair.

It is that power of hope, born whenever God's love and forgiveness gives rise to human freedom and responsibility, that has made Judaism the moral force it has always been to those whose minds and hearts are open. But that hope, says Moses with a passion that still sears us whenever we read it afresh, does not just happen. It has to be worked for and won. The only way it is achieved is by *not blaming God*. He is not corrupt. The defect is in us, His children. If we seek a better world, we must make it. God teaches us, inspires us, forgives us when we fail, and lifts us when we fall, but we must make this world. It is not what God does for us that transforms us; it is what we do for God.

The first humans lost paradise when they sought to hide from responsibility. We will only ever regain it if we accept responsibility and become a nation of leaders, each respecting and making space for those not like us. People do not like people who remind them of their responsibility. That is one of the reasons (not the only one, to be sure) for Judaeophobia through the ages. But we are not defined by those who do not like us. To be a Jew is to be defined by the One who loves us.

The deepest mystery of all is not our faith in God but God's faith in us. May that faith sustain us as we heed the call to responsibility and take the risk of healing some of the needless wounds of an injured but still wondrous world.

Vezot Haberakha

Staying Young

M

oses did not fade. That is the accolade the Torah gives him at the end of his long and eventful life: "Moses was 120 years old when he died, yet his eyes were undimmed and his natural energy unabated" (Deut. 34:7).

Somehow Moses defied the law of entropy that states that all systems lose energy over time. The law also applies to people, especially leaders. The kind of leadership Moses undertook – adaptive, getting people to change, persuading them to cease to think and feel like slaves and instead embrace the responsibilities of freedom – is stressful and exhausting. There were times when Moses came close to burnout and despair. What then was the secret of the undiminished energy of his last years?

The Torah suggests the answer in the very words in which it describes the phenomenon. I used to think that "his eyes were undimmed" and "his natural energy unabated" were simply two descriptions, until it dawned on me that the first was an explanation of the second. Why was his energy unabated? Because his eyes were undimmed. He never lost the vision and high ideals of his youth. He was as passionate at the end as he was at the beginning. His commitment to justice, compassion, liberty, and responsibility was unyielding, despite the many disappointments of his forty years as a leader. The moral is clear: if you want to stay young, never compromise your ideals.

I still remember, as clearly as if it happened yesterday, a bruising experience I had almost forty years ago as I was starting my studies to become a rabbi. Whenever a congregation needed someone to give a sermon or take a service – their own rabbi was ill, or taking a holiday – I volunteered. It was often arduous and thankless work. It meant being away from home on Shabbat, preaching to a three-quarters empty synagogue, and more often than not, being taken for granted. I once voiced a complaint to the rabbi of one of these communities whose place I had temporarily taken. "So," he said, "you are an idealist, are you? Well, let's see where that gets you."

I felt sorry for this sad and embittered man. Perhaps fate had been unkind to him. I never knew why he replied as he did. But somewhere along the road he had accepted defeat. He still went through the motions, but his heart was no longer in what he was doing. Idealism seemed to him an illusion of youth, destined to be shipwrecked on the hard rocks of reality.

My own view was and is that without passion you cannot be a transformative leader. Unless you yourself are inspired you cannot inspire others. Moses never lost the vision of his first encounter with God at the bush that burned but was not consumed. That is how I see Moses: as the man who burned but was not consumed. So long as that vision stayed with him, as it did until the end of his life, he remained full of energy. You feel that in the sustained power of the book of Deuteronomy, the greatest sequence of speeches in Tanakh.

Ideals are what keep the human spirit alive. They did so under some of the most repressive regimes in history such as Stalinist Russia and Communist China. Whenever they catch fire in the human heart, they have the power to energise resistance.

So the rule is: never compromise on your ideals. If you find one way blocked, seek another way. If you find that one approach fails, there may be another. If your efforts do not meet with success, keep trying. More often than not, success comes just when you are about to believe that you are a failure. So it was with Churchill. So it was with Lincoln. So it was with writers who had their books rejected by publisher after publisher, only to go on to high acclaim. If achievement were easy, we would take no pride in it. Greatness demands persistence. The great leaders never give up. They keep going, inspired by a vision they refuse to lose.

Looking back on his life, Moses must surely have asked if he had really achieved anything at all. He had led the people for forty years only to be denied the chance of reaching the destination, the Promised Land itself. He gave them laws they often broke. He performed miracles, yet they continued to complain.

We sense his pent-up emotions as he says: "You have been rebellious against the Lord from the day that I knew you" (Deut. 9:24), and "For I know how rebellious and stiff-necked you are. If you have been rebellious against the Lord while I am still alive and with you, how much more will you rebel after I die!" (31:27). Yet Moses never gave up or compromised on his ideals. That is why, though he died, his words did not die. Physically old, he remained spiritually young.

Cynics are lapsed idealists. They begin with great expectations. Then they discover that life is not easy, that things do not go as they had hoped they would. Our efforts hit obstacles. Our plans are derailed. We do not receive the recognition or honour we think we deserve. So we retreat into ourselves. We blame others for our failures, and we focus on the failings of others. We tell ourselves we could have done better.

Perhaps we could have. Why, then, did we not? Because we gave up. Because, at a certain point in time, we stopped growing. We consoled ourselves for not being great by treating others as small, deriding their efforts and mocking their ideals. That is no way to live. That is a kind of death.

As Chief Rabbi, I often visited old-age homes, and it was in one of these that I met Florence. She was 103, going on 104, yet she had about her the air of a young woman. She was bright, eager, full of life. Her eyes shone with a delight in being alive. I asked her for the secret of eternal youth. With a smile she said, "Never be afraid to learn something new." That was when I discovered that if you are prepared to learn something new, you can be 103 and still young.[1] If you are not prepared to learn something new, you can be twenty-three and already old.

Moses never stopped learning, growing, teaching, leading. In the book of Deuteronomy, delivered at the very end of his life, he rose to an eloquence, a vision, a passion that exceeded anything he had said before. This was a man who never gave up the fight.

Psalm 92, the Song of Shabbat, ends with the words, "Planted in the house of the Lord, [the righteous] flourish in the courts of our God. They still bear fruit in old age, they stay fresh and green, proclaiming, 'The Lord is upright; He is my Rock, and there is no wickedness in Him'" (92:14–16). What is the connection between the righteous bearing fruit in old age and their belief that "the Lord is upright"? The righteous do not blame God for the evils and suffering of the world. They know that God has planted us as physical beings in a physical universe, with all the pain that involves. They know it is up to us to do the good we can and encourage others to do more. They accept responsibility, knowing that for all the trials and torments of human existence, it is still the greatest privilege there is. That is why they bear fruit in old age. They keep the ideals of their youth.

Never compromise your ideals. Never give in to defeat or despair. Never stop journeying merely because the way is long and hard. It always is. Moses' eyes were undimmed. He did not lose the vision that made him, as a young man, a fighter for justice. He did not become a cynic. He did not become embittered or sad, though he had sufficient reason to be. He knew there were things he would not live to achieve, so he taught the next generation how to achieve them. The result was that his natural energy was unabated. His body was old but his mind and soul stayed young. Moses, mortal, achieved immortality, and so, by following in his footsteps, can we. The good we do lives on. The blessings we bring into the lives of others never die.

1. The Talmud (Shabbat 30b) says something similar about King David. So long as he kept learning, the Angel of Death had no power over him.

Afterword

Seven Principles of
Jewish Leadership

What then is Jewish about Jewish leadership? Clearly, not everything is. The Torah candidly acknowledges our indebtedness to other sources of wisdom. It was Moses' father-in-law, Yitro, a Midianite priest, who taught him a fundamental lesson in leadership – how to delegate. Jews were not the first people to have priests or kings. The first priests we encounter in the Torah were not members of the covenantal family: Abraham's contemporary, Melchizedek, described as "a priest of the most high God" (Gen. 14:18), Potiphera, Joseph's Egyptian father-in-law, a "priest of On" (Gen. 41:45), and Yitro himself. As for kings, the Torah foresaw that the Israelites would one day say, "Let us set a king over us *like all the nations around us*" (Deut. 17:14).

In general, leadership is associated in Judaism with *ḥokhma,* "wisdom," which is the universal heritage of humankind in the image and likeness of God. The rabbis said, "If they tell you there is wisdom among the nations, believe it."[1] We can learn much from the great classics on

---

1. Lamentations Rabba 2:13.

303

leadership, from the West and the East, the Greeks and Romans, alongside Confucius and Lao-Tzu.[2] Nonetheless, there are features of Jewish leadership that seem to me important and distinctive.

1. Leadership is service

The highest accolade given to Moses is that he was "a servant of the Lord." He is called by this description eighteen times in Tanakh. "Do you think that I am offering you authority [*serara*]?" said Rabban Gamliel to two of his colleagues who declined invitations to take on leadership roles, "I am offering you the chance to serve [*avdut*]."[3]

Robert Greenleaf, in his classic *Servant Leadership*,[4] derives the principle from a Buddhist story by Herman Hesse. Yet the idea of leadership as service is fundamental to the Judaeo-Christian tradition, and explains the otherwise inexplicable, that *humility* is the highest virtue of a leader (Moses, we are told, was "very humble, more so than anyone else on earth," Num. 12:3). The idea that humility is a virtue would have sounded paradoxical to the ancient Greeks, for whom the *megalopsychos*, the great-souled man, was a figure of effortless superiority with a strong sense of his own importance.[5]

Judaism entered the world as an inversion of the highly hierarchical societies of the ancient world symbolised by the ziggurats of Mesopotamia (the Tower of Babel) and the pyramids of Egypt, visible symbols of an order narrow at the top, broad at the base. The Jewish symbol, the menora, was the opposite: broad at the top, narrow at the base, as if to say that the leader must hold the honour of the people higher than his own.

---

2. Lao-Tzu is the source of one of the great truths about leadership: "If the leader is good, the people say, 'The leader did it.' If the leader is great, they say, 'We did it ourselves.'"
3. Horayot 10a–b.
4. Robert K. Greenleaf, *Servant Leadership: A Journey into the Nature of Legitimate Power and Greatness* (New York: Paulist Press, 1977).
5. See Alasdair MacIntyre, *Dependent Rational Animals: Why Human Beings Need the Virtues* (Chicago: Open Court, 1999).

Martin Luther King put it well: "Everybody can be great because anybody can serve." It is the cause we dedicate ourselves to and the people we serve that lift us, not our own high estimate of ourselves.

2. Leadership begins by taking responsibility

When we see something wrong, we can complain or we can act. Complaining does not change the world. Acting does. Judaism is God's call to action, summoning us to become His partners in the work of creation.

The opening chapters of Genesis are about failures of responsibility. Confronted by God with their sin, Adam blames Eve; Eve blames the serpent. Cain says, "Am I my brother's keeper?" Even Noah, "righteous, perfect in his generations," has no effect on his contemporaries.

By contrast, at the beginning of Exodus, Moses takes responsibility. When he sees an Egyptian beating an Israelite, he intervenes. When he sees two Israelites fighting, he intervenes. In Midian, when he sees shepherds abusing the daughters of Yitro, he intervenes. As an Israelite brought up as an Egyptian, he could have avoided each of these confrontations, yet he did not. He is the model of one who says: if no one else is prepared to act, I will.

Leading is about being active, not passive, choosing a direction, not simply following the person in front of us. Leaders do not complain, they do not blame others, nor do they wait for someone else to put it right. They act. They take responsibility. And they join with others, knowing that there are limits to what any individual can do. They engage and enlist those who feel, as they do, that there is something wrong that needs to be put right.

Leaders work with others. Only twice in the Torah does the phrase *lo tov*, "not good," appear. The first is when God says, "It is not good for man to be alone" (Gen. 2:18). The second is when Yitro sees Moses leading alone and says, "What you are doing is not good" (Ex. 18:17). We cannot live alone. We cannot lead alone. Leadership is teamsmanship.

As a result, there is no one leadership style in Judaism. During the wilderness years there were three leaders: Moses, Miriam, and Aaron.

Moses was close to God. Aaron was close to the people. Miriam led the women and sustained her two brothers. During the biblical era there were three different leadership roles: kings, priests, and prophets. The king was a political leader. The priest was a religious leader. The prophet was a visionary. So in Judaism, leadership is an emergent property of multiple roles and perspectives. Leaders work with people who are strong where they are weak. They do not feel threatened by people who are better at some things than they are. To the contrary, they feel enlarged by them. No one person can lead the Jewish people. Only together can we change the world.

3. Leadership is vision-driven

Before Moses could lead, he experienced a vision at the burning bush. There he was told his task: to lead the people from slavery to freedom. He had a destination: the land flowing with milk and honey. He had a double challenge: to persuade the Egyptians to let the Israelites go, and to persuade the Israelites to take the risk of going. The latter turned out to be as difficult as the former.

The book of Proverbs says, "Without a vision, the people perish" (29:18). The prophets were the world's master visionaries, and their words inspire us still. In a lovely prophecy, Joel speaks about a time when "your old men will dream dreams, and your young men will see visions" (2:28).

Somehow Jews have always had visionaries to lift the people from catastrophe to hope: poets, philosophers, mystics – even the secular Zionists of the nineteenth century had something spiritual about their utopias. Joseph dreamed dreams. Jacob, alone at night, dreamed of a ladder stretching from earth to heaven. We are the people who were never cured of our dreams.

Vision gives dignity to our aspirations. Throughout Tanakh, only the bad people seek power for the sake of power. The good seek to avoid it. Moses insisted on his inadequacy. So did Isaiah and Jeremiah. Jonah tried to run away. Gideon, offered the chance to become Israel's first king, said, "I will not rule over you nor will my son rule over you. God will rule over you" (Judges 8:23). It is the vision that matters, not the office, the power, the status, or the authority. Leaders are led by their vision of the future, and it is this that inspires others.

4. The highest form of leadership is teaching

If the supreme challenge of leadership is adaptive – getting people to embrace the need for change – then leading means educating: getting people to think and see in new ways. All three leadership roles in biblical Israel – king, priest, and prophet – had a teaching dimension. Every seven years, the king read the Torah to the people at a national gathering (Deut. 31:12). Malachi said about the priesthood, "The lips of a priest guard knowledge and men seek instruction from his mouth" (Mal. 2:7). The prophets were teachers to the people, guiding them through the wilderness of time.

The greatest moment in Moses' career came in the last month of his life, when having led the people for forty years, he assembled them on the bank of the Jordan and delivered the speeches that constitute the book of Deuteronomy. There he rose to the greatest heights, telling the next generation of the challenges they would face in the Promised Land, setting forth his vision of the good society. That was when he became *Moshe Rabbenu*, "Moses our teacher." The great leaders are educators, teaching people to understand the meaning of their time.

It follows that they themselves must learn. Of the king, the Torah says that he must write his own *sefer Torah* which "must always be with him, and he shall read from it all the days of his life" (Deut. 17:19). Joshua, Moses' successor, was commanded: "Keep this Book of the Law always on your lips; meditate on it day and night" (Josh. 1:8). Without constant study, leadership lacks direction and depth.

This is so even in secular leadership. Gladstone had a library of more than thirty thousand books. He read more than twenty thousand of them. Gladstone and Disraeli were both prolific writers. Winston Churchill wrote some fifty books and won the Nobel Prize for Literature. Visit David Ben-Gurion's house in Tel Aviv and you will see that it is less a home than a library with twenty thousand books. Study makes the difference between the statesman and the politician, between the transformative leader and the manager.

5. A leader must have faith in the people he or she leads

The rabbis gave a remarkable interpretation of the passage where Moses says about the Israelites, "They will not believe in me" (Ex. 4:1). They said that God reprimanded Moses for those words, saying: "They are believers the children of believers, but in the end you will not believe" (Shabbat 97a). A leader must have faith in the people he or she leads.

Authoritarian leadership is contrary to the basic principles of Judaism. When Solomon's son Rehoboam tried to lead high-handedly, the kingdom split in two (1 Kings 12). When Rabban Gamliel asserted his authority over his colleague R. Yehoshua in a way that slighted his dignity, the disciples removed him from office (Berakhot 27b). A leader who institutes a reign of fear is deemed to have no share in the World to Come.[6] Leaders need not believe in themselves, but they do need to believe in those they lead.

6. Leaders need a sense of timing and pace

When Moses asks God to choose his successor, he says: "May the Lord, God of the spirits of all flesh, choose a man over the congregation who will go out before them and come in before them, who will lead them out and bring them in" (Num. 27:16-17). Why the apparent repetition?

Moses is saying two things about leadership. A leader must lead from the front: he or she must "go out before them." But a leader must not be so far out in front that, when he turns around, he finds no one following. He must "lead them out," meaning, he must carry people with him. He must go at a pace that people can bear.

One of Moses' deepest frustrations was the sheer time it takes for people to change. In the end, it would take a new generation and a new leader to lead the people across the Jordan and into the Promised

---

6. *Mishneh Torah, Hilkhot Teshuva* 3:13.

Land. Hence R. Tarfon's great saying: "It is not for you to complete the task, but neither are you free to desist from it" (Mishna Avot 2:16). Leadership involves a delicate balance between impatience and patience. Go too fast and people resist. Go too slow and they become complacent. Transformation takes time, often more than a single generation.

7. We are all summoned to the task

This is probably the deepest Jewish truth of all. The mission statement of the Jewish people – "a kingdom of priests and a holy nation" (Ex. 19:6) – surely means just this: a kingdom every one of whose members is in some sense a priest, and a nation every one of whose members is called on to be holy. We are called on to be a people of leaders.

At the heart of Jewish life is the principle formulated by the rabbis as *kol Yisrael arevim zeh bazeh,* which means, in effect, "All Jews are responsible for one another" (Shevuot 39a). As R. Shimon bar Yoḥai put it: "When one Jew is injured, all Jews feel the pain."[7] This means that when there is a problem within the Jewish world, none of us can sit back and say, "It's not my responsibility."[8]

It is this more than anything else, I believe, that has led Jews to make a contribution to humanity out of all proportion to our numbers. We are a nation of activists. It also creates problems. It makes leadership within the Jewish community notoriously difficult. Chaim Weizmann, Israel's first president, famously said that he was head of a nation of a million presidents. We say in Psalm 23, "The Lord is my shepherd," but no Jew is a sheep.

The good news about the Jewish people is that we have many leaders. The bad news is that we have few followers. The first recorded words of a fellow Israelite to Moses were, "Who made you a ruler and judge over us?" (Ex. 2:14). Moses had not even dreamed of becoming a leader and already his leadership was being criticised. This means that leading within the Jewish community is never less than challenging.

---

7. *Mekhilta DeRabbi Shimon bar Yoḥai* to Exodus 19:6.
8. See Maimonides, *Sefer HaMitzvot,* positive command 205.

But that is how it is: according to the effort, said the sages, is the reward (Mishna Avot 5:23).

These are high ideals, so high that they can sound intimidating. But they should not be. We fall short. We stumble. But David Brooks gets it right when he says that "we are all stumblers, and the beauty and meaning of life are in the stumbling."[9] We will never reach the stars but we can still be guided by them.

I began this book by explaining that I never thought of becoming a leader. It was a life-changing encounter with a great leader that persuaded me otherwise. I learned over the years that we make mistakes, but it is from our mistakes that we learn. You cannot get it right without first getting it wrong. If you lack the courage to fail, you will lack the courage to succeed.

It is from our worst mistakes that we grow. We learn humility. We discover that you cannot please everyone. We encounter resistances, and as with the body so with the soul: it is resistance training that gives us strength. What matters is not that we succeed, but that we enter the arena, are forced to fight with the weaknesses of our nature, that we put ourselves on the line, commit ourselves to high ideals, and refuse the easy options of cynicism, disillusion, or blaming others. The mere fact that we tried, and kept trying, and had faith in what we were striving to achieve, and never, despite the setbacks, lost that faith, in the end brings a surprising joy. Brooks again: "Joy comes as a gift when you least expect it. At those fleeting moments you know why you were put here and what truth you serve."[10]

Ronald Heifetz and Marty Linsky end *Leadership on the Line* with a not dissimilar thought. Finding meaning in life comes from discovering ways "to contribute to the worldly enterprise, to enhance the quality of life for people around you.... Any form of service to others is an expression, essentially, of love."[11]

---

9. David Brooks, *The Road to Character* (New York: Allen Lane, 2015), 268.
10. Ibid., 270.
11. Ronald Heifetz and Marty Linsky, *Leadership on the Line*, 220.

Somehow out of a life of struggle, the heroes and heroines of faith discovered how small we are, yet how great is the task to which we are called, and their example can light a flame in each of us, leading us to strive for something larger than the self, so that whether we succeed or fail, we know at least that our life was lit by its exposure to those great ideals of love and truth and service, that we made our contribution to our people's story and helped heal some of the fractures of a still injured and imperfect world. "Don't wait for Me," whispered God to Abraham. "Go on ahead."[12] That is what He whispers to all of us, and in the going is the blessing that confers moral beauty on a life.

12. See Rashi to Genesis 6:9.

About the Author

Aglobal religious leader, philosopher, author and moral voice for our time, Rabbi Lord Jonathan Sacks served as chief rabbi of the United Hebrew Congregations of the Commonwealth between September 1991 and September 2013.

Described by HRH The Prince of Wales as "a light unto this nation" and by former British Prime Minister Tony Blair as "an intellectual giant," Rabbi Sacks is a frequent academic lecturer and contributor to radio, television, and the press in Britain and around the world. He holds sixteen honorary degrees, including a Doctor of Divinity conferred to mark his first ten years in office as chief rabbi, by the then Archbishop of Canterbury, Lord Carey.

In recognition of his work, Rabbi Sacks has won several international awards, including the Jerusalem Prize in 1995 for his contribution to Diaspora Jewish life, the Ladislaus Laszt Ecumenical and Social Concern Award from Ben-Gurion University in Israel in 2011, the Guardian of Zion Award from the Ingeborg Rennert Center for Jerusalem Studies at Bar-Ilan University, and the Katz Award in recognition of his contribution to the practical analysis and application of halakha in modern life in

Israel in 2014. He was knighted by Her Majesty The Queen in 2005 and made a Life Peer, taking his seat in the House of Lords in October 2009.

The author of twenty-five books, Rabbi Sacks has published a new English translation and commentary for the *Koren Sacks Siddur,* the first new Orthodox siddur in a generation, as well as powerful commentaries for the *Rosh HaShana, Yom Kippur,* and *Pesaḥ Maḥzorim.* A number of his books have won literary awards, including the Grawemeyer Prize for Religion in 2004 for *The Dignity of Difference,* and National Jewish Book Awards for *A Letter in the Scroll* in 2000, *Covenant & Conversation: Genesis* in 2009, and the *Koren Sacks Pesaḥ Maḥzor* in 2013. His Covenant & Conversation commentaries on the weekly Torah portion are read in Jewish communities around the world.

After achieving first-class honours in philosophy at Gonville and Caius College, Cambridge, he pursued post-graduate studies in Oxford and London, gaining his doctorate in 1981, and receiving rabbinic ordination from Jews' College and Yeshivat Etz Chaim. He served as the rabbi for Golders Green Synagogue and Marble Arch Synagogue in London, before becoming principal of Jews' College.

Born in 1948 in London, he has been married to Elaine since 1970. They have three children and several grandchildren.

www.rabbisacks.org / @RabbiSacks

The fonts used in this book are from the Arno family

The Covenant & Conversation Series:

Genesis: The Book of Beginnings

Exodus: The Book of Redemption

Leviticus: The Book of Holiness

Numbers: The Wilderness Years

Deuteronomy: The Book of the Covenant

Essays on Ethics

Ceremony and Celebration

Maggid Books
The best of contemporary Jewish thought from
Koren Publishers Jerusalem Ltd.